Robin Neillands is a travel writer and journalist, a Fellow of the Royal Geographical Society and a man who likes going for a walk...preferably a long walk. He has traversed France, 600 miles from the Channel coast to the Carmargue, and walked right across Spain, a hard 700 miles from Santander to the Rock of Gibraltar. In 1992 he walked across Ireland. He wrote books about those adventures before setting out to walk through Scotland.

Apart from walking and travel writing, Robin Neillands is a well-known popular historian, who has written books about the Hundred Years War, the Wars of the Roses, Napoleon and Wellington, the D-Day Landings of 1944 and his old regiment, the Royal Marines Commandos and a history of Germany in the last five months of the Second World War.

Walking through Scotland

From the Border to Cape Wrath

ROBIN NEILLANDS

WARNER BOOKS

A *Warner* Book

First published in Great Britain in 1995
by Little, Brown and Company
This edition published in 1996 by Warner Books

Copyright © Robin Neillands 1995

Maps drawn by Terry Brown
Photography by Geoff Cowen, Robin Neillands,
Judith Greeven and Keith Howell

A CIP catalogue record for this book is available
from the British Library.

ISBN 0 7515 1055 6

Typeset by Solidus (Bristol) Ltd
Printed and bound in Great Britain by Clays Ltd, St Ives plc

Warner Books
A Division of
Little, Brown and Company (UK)
Brettenham House
Lancaster Place
London WC2E 7EN

This one is for Keith Howell,
especially in waking hours.

Contents

Acknowledgements

A great many people helped me with this book, but a lot of thanks are due to Peter Chambers, late of the *Daily Express*, who first suggested the finish at Cape Wrath. For help in the planning stage and on the trip, many thanks to Judith Greeven and Geoff Cowen. Thanks also to Keith Howell of the Brittany Ferrets and Derek 'Ginger' Wilkins for their ever-enjoyable company in Scotland. For help with accommodation *en route* my thanks to Elisabeth Holt of GCI PR and Mount Charlotte Thistle Hotels, Julia Record of Mount Charlotte Thistle Hotels, Sue Mecrate-Butcher of Best Western, Michael Yeo of Pride of Britain, Erika Schule-Grosso of Relais-Chateaux and Katrin Holtkott of Small Luxury Hotels. Thanks to Motorail and Scotrail for help in getting to Scotland and very special thanks to David Elliot for putting up with us all at Cape Wrath.

For help in Scotland my thanks go to the staff of the Scottish Tourist Board in Edinburgh, David Webster and George Mack of Sunlaws House, Kelso. Further north thanks go to Ken Chernoff and his saxophone at Johnstounburn House, Humbie, Peter Ratcliffe of the King James Thistle Hotel, Edinburgh – with special thanks here to Bill Torrancé – and Giles and Ros Weaver of Greywalls, Gullane. Pressing on into the Highlands, thanks to Stephen Owen and Mark Simkins of the Keavil House Hotel, Dunfermline, and Ian and Brenda Milward of Knockie Lodge, Whitebridge, not forgetting Tigger, the in-house Labrador. The badgers on the terrace of the Buchanan-

Smiths' Isle of Eriska Hotel are unforgettable, as was the hospitality of the Sinclairs at Arisaig House. Moving further north, Anne Bettany of the Mercury Hotel, Inverness, and Ian MacKenzie of Culloden House were kindness itself; I will not easily forget Ian's lessons in dowsing and haggis-hunting.

Robin Neillands
London 1995

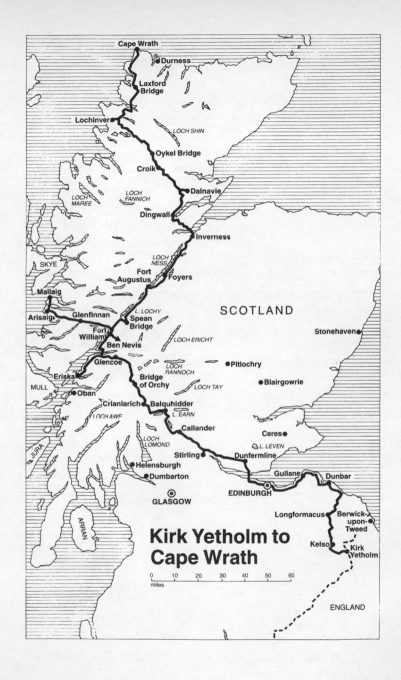

Cape Wrath
Durness
Laxford
Bridge
Lochinver
LOCH SHIN
Oykel Bridge
Croik
LOCH FANNICH
Dalnavie
LOCH MAREE
Dingwall
Inverness
SKYE
LOCH NESS
Fort
Augustus
Foyers
Mallaig
L. LOCHY
Glenfinnan
SCOTLAND
Arisaig
Spean
Bridge
Fort
William
LOCH ERICHT
Stonehaven
Ben Nevis
Glencoe
LOCH RANNOCH
Pitlochry
Eriska
Bridge
of Orchy
LOCH TAY
Blairgowrie
MULL
Oban
Crianlarich
Balquhidder
L. EARN
LOCH AWE
Callander
Ceres
LOCH LOMOND
L. LEVEN
Stirling
Dunfermline
Helensburgh
Gullane
Dunbar
Dumbarton
EDINBURGH
GLASGOW
Longformacus
Berwick-
upon-
Tweed
JURA
Kelso
Kirk
Yetholm
ARRAN

Kirk Yetholm to
Cape Wrath

0   10   20   30   40   50   60
miles

ENGLAND

1

Preparations

> Be there a man, with soul so dead,
> Who never to himself has said,
> 'This is my own, my native land,',
> Whose heart has ne'er within him burn'd,
> As home his footsteps he has turne'd
> From wandering on a foreign strand.
>
> Sir Walter Scott,
> *The Lay of the Last Minstrel*

One hates to argue with a national poet, but the answer to that splendidly phrased question is 'Yes, Sir Walter, there are plenty of such men, and I am one of them.' I have been wandering in foreign strands for years, so I know that when it comes to a happy conjunction of person and place, birth and heredity has nothing to do with it. Nationalistic fervour is not an asset acquired in the cradle, and the world is full of people seeking a place that holds them by the heart. A lucky few have even found it.

And yet, all that being said, wherever they live and however happy they might be there, few people are ever quite free of their homeland, the place of their birth. Some people never even try to be, but it still strikes them as curious. Writing to J.M. Barrie from his new home in

1

Samoa, Robert Louis Stevenson said, 'It is a singular thing that I should live here in the South Seas, under conditions so new and striking, and yet my imagination so continually inhabits that cold, old huddle of grey hills from which we come.'

Many people will share that thought. Even if we are indifferent to our native land, we may also feel that we have missed out on an emotion or a bond that is rightfully ours. A feeling for home is a kind of birthright.

Now, to get to the point, by ancestry and birth I am a Scot. I was born in Glasgow of Scottish parents and brought up by my Scots grandmother who was as Highland as the heather, and as far as I have been able to establish I have not a drop of other blood in my body.

My grandmother will appear often in this book, and with good reason. She brought me up from birth until she died when I was 18, and she gave me a daily dose of her beloved Scotland. She sang Scots songs, loved Harry Lauder, endured McGonigal, knew the pages of Robert Burns and fed me Scots porridge, fine milled stuff that set in the plate, could be whirled around in the milk with a spoon, and was made with salt as it should be. She forced me to like kippers and finny-haddock and potato soup – I still love soups – and oatmeal cakes and tattie-scones.

Outside it might be the bomb-scarred streets of London or the soft fields of Wiltshire, but indoors it was Bonnie Scotland, and the copper stick was on hand to enforce my obedience to her Scottish standards.

From the age of three, though, I have lived in England or abroad, and, though I went back to Scotland from time to time, it was never from choice. It is not that I disliked the place, far from it, simply that it is a big world with a lot to see and I never felt the slightest particular impulse towards, or interest in, the land of my birth.

And yet again, by inclination, I am a soldier, as my

ancestors were, and they were Scottish soldiers. When the Highland battalions swept past behind the pipes, I would rush to the edge of the parade ground. I was able to keep my fingers from my ears, but I consoled myself that I was not alone in this. You do not have to be a Scot to share a soldier's reaction to that wild war music. Gurkhas and Sikhs and many other soldiers share it, and some years ago, when I wrote a book about the 7th Armoured Division, the famous Desert Rats, one of my correspondents told me about watching the Eighth Army parade past Winston Churchill through the streets of Tripoli:

> I do not remember exactly when it took place, but marching straight from the desert came the infantry of the 51st Highland Division, those marvellous fighting Jocks, with 50 pipers leading the parade. The sound of the pipes was quite wonderful and certainly moved me greatly.

He had tears in his eyes, remembering that day, and his account moved me, which is why I remember it. It came as a little tug on the heartstrings, a reminder that I, too, was a Scot and had reason, if I so wished, to be proud of it. The snag is that I am not a dissembler and I find it pointless as well as difficult to support an emotion I don't actually feel; indeed, as a galvanized Englishman I sometimes find it difficult to express an emotion I *do* actually feel.

On the other hand, when my time came I joined the Royal Marines and not a Highland regiment. Here again, this was a move towards something rather than a step away from Scotland. I wanted to be a Commando and crawl about at night with a black face and a knife between my teeth. That sort of behaviour had gone out of fashion by the time I joined – curses! – but we did a lot of our training in Scotland and, as this book will reveal, we had a lot of fun there. Many of the happy memories I have about Scotland date back to that time, and since they came back on this walk I have recorded them here.

This business of national feeling is something I shall return to, but there is also this business of walking as a means of getting to know a country. At this point it is not too early to explain that this is not a book about walking. This is a book about Scotland, about how one self-exiled Scot rediscovered his native land, but walking was the way I did it and I should say why.

About ten years ago I walked across France. France is a country for which I have a long-standing affection, a feeling expressed so often that the French Government recently gave me a medal for it. I walked across France from the Channel Coast to the Camargue delta, and enjoyed every step of it. That done, I wrote a book about it, threw the maps away and hung up my boots ... for ever. Three years later I got the walking itch again, and since I had done France I decided to walk across Spain.

I do not recommend walking across Spain. Spain is hot and hard and dry and dusty and not infrequently mountainous. On the way south from Santander to Gibraltar I nearly died twice, was mugged once, lost a great deal of weight, and just after I wrote the book the publishing company went bust. My advice to anyone contemplating a walk across Spain is to lie down in a dark room until the feeling passes off.

By now, however, a small tradition had been established: every two or three years, Rob goes for a walk. Not a long walk by serious walker standards, at about 700 miles, but then I am not a serious walker. This can actually be an advantage, for on my next walk I elected to walk across Ireland, a country where being serious is a solecism. I chose Ireland because, after Spain, I wanted a country with an abundance of water.

It is therefore worth recording that for the first two weeks of my walk, across Northern Ireland, on the way from the Antrim coast to Valencia Island in County Kerry far to the south-west, the sun shone down each day from a cloudless sky and I got very thirsty indeed.

Now there is no reason to go walking. Most people avoid walking across entire countries under a heavy pack, and, as far as I can see, this abstinence does them no particular harm. Anyway, I am not here to urge anyone to take up the trail. Walking is the way I get to grips with my subject, nothing more, and as a method of travel it has both advantages and drawbacks.

I walk because I have a need for physical effort. I walk because after a few days on the trail life slows to a bearable and understandable pace and the usual pressures ease off. We are not really built to live the way we do, and a walk takes me back to that reality. I walk because it gives me time to look around and get my thoughts together and I walk for no reason at all except that I enjoy it.

On the other hand, walking has snags, not least for the writer. There is a limit to how far you can travel in a day and what you can see along the way. Something three miles off the route is not five minutes in the car, but two hours there and back, and you may not be able to fit it in. Walking is not an escape from decision-making; indeed you have to be making decisions all the time, on the weather and time and distance, on whether to press on or turn back.

Time is not unlimited and if you see or visit one place, somewhere else must be left out. Walking can be exhausting and is usually tiring, so it helps to be fit, or at least fitter, before you start, or you will pay a heavy price in the first week or so. On the credit side, though, and in spite of the snags, if you keep on putting one foot in front of another, you will get where you are going in the end. First-class travel on Concorde can do no more and will show you less.

Three walks completed, three countries covered, so where to go next? Certain criteria have to apply and the first of these is time and distance. Six weeks is as long as I can afford to spend on the hoof and at an average of 15 miles a day, allowing for the odd day off or delay, that works out at a total distance of about 600 miles. In practice, I rarely take a day out of my boots and I usually walk about 20 miles a day, but 600 miles at my age is a long enough stroll for anyone. That puts the Trans-Sahara and most of the New World walks well out of court on the time and distance factor alone.

Then I need something to write about. There are those who find that just writing about the walk is enough: the hills, the dales, the blisters, those fascinating conversations with erudite countryfolk I never seem to meet. God, the sheer romance of it all ... how lucky some walkers are! Huddled in my raingear, with wet socks bunched up under my feet and rain trickling down my neck, the romance of walking is the last thing I can think about.

Even so, I would be the first to admit that any walk, indeed any journey, is all the better for a theme, and in my case the best theme is history. In my other life, I am a military historian, and if a land has history I will enjoy going there. A walk, then, becomes a line to hang the history on, and, as I hope to demonstrate, the history becomes more relevant and more fun if you discover it on the ground while walking. Spiced with tales from other visits, the history of Scotland is the theme of this walk, and if I can add my personal opinion to some of that, so much the better, though I start with an open mind.

The final little point that brought me to Scotland is language. I need to walk through a country where I can chat to the local people as I go along. I managed in France and I managed in Spain and I managed a word in edgeways in Ireland, but as the years go by I am running out of countries. I know that everyone in Holland speaks English, but that alone would not make me want to go there, and there are a lot of countries where I have no desire to go at all.

I am told that Sweden is a splendid country with wonderful walking and beautiful women, but then I remember a ghastly fishing trip to Finland, where I was eaten alive by mosquitoes, bored to death by my companions and, even worse, failed to catch anything. The point is that I then learned that the bulk of holiday visitors to Finland come from Sweden; if Finland is a desirable destination for the Swedes, then a walk through Sweden didn't bear thinking about.

Readers should also know that I do this for a living. After the walk comes the book, and it does not follow that the publisher will wish to publish a book about where I want to walk. There is the proposal and the synopsis and the arguments and the committees and the perhaps-not, and the what-about, and then the back-to-the-drawing-board, or in this case the map.

Scotland came upon me gradually. It seemed to flit about in the corners of my mind for a long time until the day came when I got out the map and took a good look at it. There is no point in doing anything which you cannot at least do differently or better, and an awful lot of people have written about and walked around Scotland. Many years ago John Hillaby walked across Scotland in the course of his *Journey Through Britain*, and since his book is the one that started this long-distance walking business, for me at least, I could hardly compete with it. Hillaby, however, was not the first, or indeed the latest, and when all is said and done I have a right to my own walk and my own story ... and there are precedents galore for that, for Scotland is a marvellous country for writers who walk.

Samuel Johnson and James Boswell both wrote about their journeys to the Hebrides and the Western Highlands, and some of my favourite tales, like Stevenson's *Kidnapped* and Buchan's *Thirty-Nine Steps* all contain passages and chapters about long treks and derring-do in the remoter parts of Scotland: a great, wild country for the man on the run.

The shelves of Scottish bookshops groan under the weight of walking books, the car-parks below the bens are jammed at weekends with the cars of the Munro-baggers. The Scots go walking and read about walking and therefore know about walking, and if I was going to write a book about walking through Scotland, I would have to find a fresh theme, or as we hacks call it, an angle. Hmmmm!

I have a bunch of writing and journalist cronies collectively called the 'Brittany Ferrets', and the Senior Ferret, Peter Chambers, began his career with the *Aberdeen Press and Journal* and knows Scotland well, so he gave me my first piece of advice. 'Don't end up at John o' Groats,' he said. 'It's boring. Go west and end up at Cape Wrath.'

It is a well-known fact in travel-writing circles that my boredom and culture thresholds are both low enough to trip over. Ending in the north was a new idea in itself, for when I go on a long walk I usually prefer to walk north to south, because that way seems to be downhill. I know this is daft, and I thought it was purely my own fancy until I met a walker who said that however flat it actually is, the north side of a hill always seems steeper than the south side. However, I preferred Cape Wrath to John o' Groats anyway, partly because of the name, partly because thousands of people do the 'Land's End to John o' Groats' every year on foot or by cycle, and I see no point in doing what everyone else has done. If I was to end at Cape Wrath, though, where was I to start?

I may walk across countries but I do it for a living. This being so, you have to economise on your time and get across in the shortest time and distance possible. That means walking in a straight line, but a straight line south from Cape Wrath did not work and took me to nowhere of consequence. I inched the ruler along the Border and came at last to Kirk Yetholm, and there it stuck. I thought about starting at Kirk Yetholm for quite a while, for Kirk Yetholm is the northern terminus of the Pennine Way and I walked that more than twenty years ago, when the Way and I were a whole lot younger and less trampled on by time and people. I think it was that moment, when the ruler stopped at Kirk Yetholm, that I finally decided to walk across Scotland, to take up where I had left off all those years ago, rediscover my own country in an enjoyable way and find out exactly why my dear grandmother was so taken with the place.

Just before setting out I was hunting along the bookshelves, trying to find a couple of books to take along. I always take a book of poems, not because I like to lie on some grassy bank murmuring verse to myself in a sensitive fashion, but because you get more reading for less weight in a book of poems than in any other kind of anthology. Anyway, I opened one at random, read a few lines and said to myself, 'That's it, that's exactly what I want to do.' The lines were from Eliot's *Four Quartets*, and they go like this:

> We shall not cease from exploration,
> And the end of all our exploring
> Will be to arrive where we started,
> And know the place for the first time.

Don't tell me there is no such thing as fate. That was as plain a hint as I was going to get that this was something I had to do. Maybe, when I had walked across Scotland I would feel at home there. God knows, I have been rootless long enough.

This, then, is the story of a journey on foot through Scotland, from the Border to Cape Wrath. To get between the two I did not travel in a straight line. On the way I roved about a bit, as the map at the start of this book will reveal. I wanted to see a lot of Scotland and learn about it while doing so. I wanted to see Flodden and Culloden, the Great Glen and Glencoe. I wanted to wander where Mary Queen of Scots had dallied with Bothwell and where John Knox had ranted at her for doing so. I wanted to understand the Border Wars and the Anglo-Scots history and the fall of the Highland clans. I wanted to understand the matter of religion and the centuries of tangled politics, but there is more to Scotland than that. The love of a land is made up of little things, of sounds and sights, tastes and smells and, above all, of traditions and history, of food and folklore, of jokes.

I wanted to find out why Scotland is famous for golf and whisky, haggis and bashed neeps, tartans and porridge and all the things for which Scotland is famous. This includes writers and poets like Burns and Scott and Buchan and Stevenson, and my old Highland grannie had given me a good grounding in their work to help me on the way. As I went on through Scotland, much that my grandmother had taught me, including many things I had long forgotten, came back into my mind.

I have long since discovered that the best way to get the hang of a place is to explore it on foot, but that is not easy; before you start a long walk you have to know what you are up against. I therefore began my studies with a look at the scale of the place and at some of the problems I might expect to encounter.

Scotland is a northern land. It covers an area of around 30,000 square miles, which does not seem so large until you try to walk across it, but the distance from Dumfries on the Border to Thurso on the north coast is 367 miles. Starting at Kirk Yetholm and wandering to and fro would put my wandering walk up to around the 500-mile mark.

Scotland is sparsely populated, with just five million inhabitants. Most of these are gathered in the Central Lowlands, around Glasgow and Edinburgh, leaving the rest of the country delightfully empty. The weather promised to be less than delightful, for Central Scotland lies on the same latitude as Moscow but is warmed and watered by the Atlantic Drift. I read a lot of books about walking in Scotland, by Tom Weir and Hamish Brown and Cameron McNeish, and they all give accounts and warnings about how changeable is the Scottish mountain weather and how foul it can get in the hills.

Scotland is by no means all mainland. There are about 700 islands, large and small, of which 130 are inhabited, and one of my first and hardest decisions was that the islands would have to be left out. This was partly because I did not have the time and partly because the islands are a study in themselves, but also because other writers, past and present, have written about them in depth.

Even without islands this journey never strayed far from the sea, and in the course of it I walked west, from the North Sea to the Atlantic. That is easy to do in Scotland, where the coastline is marvellously indented with firths and sea-lochs, which could add immensely to a coastal walk. Should a crow fly down the West Coast it need cover a distance of no more than 260 miles. If it chooses to walk along the shoreline it must cover a distance of more than 2,000 miles. I resolved to walk in a straight line wherever possible and stay away from the coast.

Half my time in Scotland would be spent in the Highlands, which make up about half the Scottish land mass, and although I have seen several definitions of where the

Highlands begin, the official geographic definition puts them north of a line – the Highland Boundary Fault – which runs between Stonehaven in the east and Helensburgh in the west. John Prebble, the best of all the writers on Scotland's tangled history, shows the Highland Line as a great curve which runs from Dumbarton in the south-west, round past Blairgowrie and Pitlochry to a point on the Cromarty Firth, anywhere north or west of that line being in the Highlands.

Politically, the Highlands, the home of the Jacobite clans, was often held to begin either north of the Great Glen or beyond the River Forth and the fortress city of Stirling, which last is the place I prefer, not least because it features as such in Stevenson's *Kidnapped*. 'Ye ken the saying,' says Alan Breck, as he and David Balfour emerged above the Carse of Stirling, 'Forth bridles the wild Heilandman. . . . We passed the Heiland Line in the first hour and if we could but pass yon crooked water we might cast our bonnets in the air.'

Scotland is a land of lochs and rivers and mountains. There are currently around 277 peaks in Scotland over the 3,000 ft (914m) mark, the so-called 'Munros' (of which more anon), and the number varies as survey follows survey, to the frustration or delight of dedicated Munro-baggers. Some of these, especially the 1,344m top of Ben Nevis, Britain's highest mountain, lay on my route and must be climbed. There are lochs without number, but my path lay beside the greatest of them, Loch Ness, along more material wonders like the Caledonian Canal and across the Forth beside the famous Forth Railway Bridge, which is 1.6 miles long normally but expands by no less than 3 feet on a warm summer's day. Billy Connolly says that the Forth Bridge is the most beautiful bridge in the world, and if Billy says it, it must be true, so a diversion over the Forth went down on the list.

One of the problems was the finish. As the planning moved north so the information got more sketchy, and a good plan depends on good information. Then I had a spot of luck. I was explaining the project to friends of mine, Jane and Chris Bramwell, when Jane said that she knew the man who owned Cape Wrath. Jane is like that: she knows people.

'We met him in Derbyshire, and he owns Cape Wrath ... you remember, Chris? Yes, you do. David Elliot, the doctor? He lives in Billericay and he owns Cape Wrath.'

It turned out to be true. I rang David Elliot, who turned out to be a surgeon and we had a long chat. His family owned 40,000 acres on Cape Wrath and more land elsewhere in Scotland. David had a bothy by the Kyle of Durness and would like to join us for part of the walk if the timings matched with the time he would be up at his bothy, cutting peat. Otherwise, he would be happy to offer us a dram or three of whisky and a mattress on the floor. David sounded like a man after my own heart and we swapped telephone numbers.

When to go on a long walk is always a problem. Those who don't do it suggest the summer, which is rarely a good time, too hot, too crowded, and in my case, usually too busy. So I would not be going in summer, or not quite. I took advice on when to go from my Scots friends and their vote was for May or October. In October there is purple heather on the hill, but this is the time for the stalking of the deer, when walkers are not welcome on the braesides. In May the days are getting longer all the time, and from other walks I have learned to use every second of daylight. Besides, in May I might hope to avoid the attention of that savage inhabitant, *culicoides impunctatus*, the notorious Highland midge.

The existence of that hard-biting fly, the Highland

midge, is a fact about which the Scottish Tourist Board is surprisingly reticent. Legends and funny postcards credit the midge with infiltrating under kilts and thereby originating the Highland Fling, but the midge in reality is not funny at all: in high summer on hot, muggy days, it can make life in the Highlands intolerable. However, modern sprays are said to be efficacious and midges detest sunlight, high winds, cold weather, and so many other things that I am surprised they are so troublesome. Fortunately, the midge season does not start until June and is over by the end of August, and in practice I never even saw a midge between the Border and Cape Wrath.

Apart from the midge, most of Scotland's wildlife is interesting, benign, even beautiful: otter, polecat and pine-marten survive here and though I saw none of these I did see red squirrel, golden eagle and the magnificent red deer, drifting like ghosts across the hills of Ross and Sutherland. Scotland's fauna is largely unspoiled by introduced species, but I did hear that the notorious Canadian blackfly had arrived in Scotland, dozing in a shipment of timber from Quebec, and there is said to be a large and thriving colony of wallabies on an island in Loch Ness, the sight of which makes unsuspecting yachtsmen resolve to stay off the whisky.

The months before a walking trip are spent reading up on the history of the place, trying to find out more about access and worrying about the route. In this case I had fewer worries than usual on the two latter problems because the British Ordnance Survey (OS) topograhic maps are the finest in the world, and the Scots are remarkably relaxed about access outside the shooting season, from August to October, when the grouse-shooting and deer-stalking are in progress. My route wandered about for reasons I have already given, but I did intend to follow at least two of Scotland's long-distance footpaths, the Southern Upland Way and the West Highland Way. Otherwise I would make my way wherever my fancy took me, avoiding main roads wherever possible, but making no great effort to encounter famous sights or follow classic routes.

My main resolve before departure was to get fit and lose some weight. I did not intend to backpack but, being an old and canny soul, I still had to carry a tent and a sleeping bag and a fair range of hard-hitting gear just in case the weather clamped in and caught me on the mountain. I hate the weight, but as I always intone while stuffing more kit I will never use into my rucksack, 'Better to have it and not need it, than need it and not have it.'

It is the writing kit rather than the walking kit that weighs heavily upon me: the guides, the notebooks, the cameras and film, the maps. A full kit list is shown in the appendix, but the one item every walker will need in Scotland is a full set of windproof clothing. Halfway up Ben Nevis I met a man who told me that in Scotland it was the wind that made the difficulty, a fact I had already discovered and was to discover again and again. Even on sunny days the Highland wind, straight from Norway or the Arctic Ocean, can practically cut you in half.

By laying off the booze and going for bracing walks at weekends I lost 20lb and got my daily average up to 17 miles without too much difficulty. There remained the matter of companions, for I wanted some company for the last stage of the walk, across Ross and Sutherland from Inverness to Cape Wrath.

To do that stretch in a reasonable amount of time I would have to push on hard, and I only hoped my companions could do the same. The problem with companions on any trip is that if the trip is my idea and there is a purpose to it and a book at the end of it, I feel responsible for the health, safety and wellbeing of anyone who opts to join me. Frankly, I would rather not be: it is all

I can do to look after myself. The other, far more pertinent, problem is that few people can come for the whole trip and by the time they do arrive I have been walking for several weeks, am fit and able to do 20 miles over the hills each day, while they are fresh from the office and need building up a bit.

My usual walking cronies are the Brittany Ferrets, a small, agreeable group of freelance hacks and PR consultants with whom I have been wandering in France and Spain for the best part of twenty years. The main force of Ferrets were not available for this expedition but I was lucky: the first volunteer for the hard part of the trans-Scotland bash was Keith Howell, one of the Brittany Ferrets. Apart from looking irritatingly dapper at all times, even in howling winds and pouring rain, and not, in the best tradition of British walkers, usually looking like an unmade bed, Keith is as tough as old boots and able to cover any kind of country if there is a drink and a bed at the end of it.

The next companion was my old friend and former business partner, Geoff Cowen, who plans my routes, gives me advice, points out things he thinks I ought to write about and does the worrying. To give credit where it is due, Geoff planned the route from Inverness to Cape Wrath, and the fact that we got there intact and on time is largely his doing. My only worry was if Geoff would actually turn up on time in Inverness ready for the last great bash, for Geoff has an addiction: rugby.

Now I am aware that many people, the Welsh, the Wallabies, and Geoff, will not hear a word against rugby players. I know of otherwise sensible fathers, those whose youth has been spent rolling about in the mud, who dream of the day when their daughter will bring home one of those clean-cut young men who are horribly fit and full of patriotism and spend their Saturdays in rather brief shorts, playing a Real Man's Game. If it were so, I could understand it.

The snag is that Geoff's rugby is not like that, at least to my world-weary eyes. His rugby seems to be played by hulks with dented foreheads, alarming scars and gnawed ears, each a kind of biped tomcat, the Old Neander-thalians. Frightening as they look, Geoff loves them all dearly; they bring out the Mother Hen in him. Whatever the reason, it is hell to get him away from the club house any time during the rugby season, which seems to get longer every year.

Geoff is simply very, very keen on rugby – even his daughter Sara plays it – and his rendezvous-keeping over the years has been gravely affected by the sudden intrusion of the Old Neanderthal First Fifteen who are either (*a*) winning, (*b*) losing or (*c*) in trouble with the police, and requiring Geoff's help at once. Why fifteen hulking great youths cannot win matches and keep out of trouble without the presence of my ageing crony is a mystery to me, but, having planned the route and marked the maps and given me a lot of lectures, Geoff announced that he wanted to see Cape Wrath and would *definitely* be in Inverness outside the station at 11 a.m., with Ginger.

I smelt a rat.

'Who is Ginger?' I asked suspiciously. I have known Geoff for over thirty years and I had never heard of Ginger.

'He's a friend of mine,' said Geoff.

I smelt another rat. Apart from me, his wife Eileen, his daughters, half the people at the pub and Eric the currency smuggler, Geoff has no friends ... apart from Pickle the Border terrier and Kizzy the Border collie. Unless. . . .

'He's not one of those bloody rugby people is he? You are not going to bring along a rugger-bugger, so you can sit up half the night and talk about the time the First Fifteen

trashed a hotel in Bratislava, are you? Not day, after day,
after day . . . Oh my God, you are. . . .'

'I might,' said Geoff. 'It will give me my daily sanity fix
while you are droning on about history or literature or
something else you know bugger-all about, not to mention
your feet, or some other bloody thing. Ginger's all right,
you'll like him.'

Ginger was, and I did, so that was all right. In fact,
Ginger turned out to be a gem, a good member of the team.
Then Geoff came up with another reason.

'We have to go to Cape Wrath, because Reggie went
there . . . or so he says.'

Reggie is Geoff's father-in-law, and since Geoff, like me,
is in his late fifties, it will be seen that Reggie cannot be in
the first flush of youth. Anyway, Geoff and I went to see
Reggie; if Reggie had been to Cape Wrath he could give us
some up-to-date, practical details of the ground, the
weather, the facilities, hints and tips, all sorts of good
things. Reggie was a contact – how useful.

'So, when did you walk to Cape Wrath, Reggie?'

'I didn't walk. I went there on my bicycle,' said Reggie.
Well, a bicycle would do. A bicycle ride was tough and
rugged; we could relate to a bicycle.

'And when was this?'

'1929,' said Reggie.

I still don't know how I kept my hands off him.

Information that is 65 years old is not all that useful, and
some of Reggie's advice struck us as distinctly dated, but I
restrained myself.

'Don't forget to ask the lighthouse keeper for tea,' said
Reggie. 'They do a lovely tea, the lighthouse keepers . . .
three sorts of jam, clotted cream, scones, ginger cake, all
for one-and-ninepence.'

I had a dim idea what the lighthouse keeper would do if
four Sassenach yobbos turned up at the foot of the tower

asking for cream teas, but I let it go. The four of us arranged to meet in Inverness – outside the railway station – a month from now, and not later than noon, ready to set out from there on the last wild lap to Cape Wrath. With that much settled, I packed the rucksack for the last time and set out for Euston Station.

There is one final thought before this journey begins. Some years ago I read a review which commented that the book – not one of mine – said as much about the author as it did about the subject. This may well be an advantage but I have my doubts about it. My heart is with the little girl who was asked to review a book on penguins and wrote, 'This book has told me more about penguins than I really want to know.'

My intention is to tell the story of a journey, but journeys are not made in one direction. This walk through Scotland will go forward through space but backward in time, for I was born in that far-off country and brought up in a very Scots household. Over the past few weeks a lot of memories have come back to me and some of this I will surely pass on.

I am writing this before the journey begins, with the rucksack in the corner and the cab at the door, and I know that, try as I might, and I might not try very hard, I will appear in this story more often than I intend to. Those who know all about penguins need come no further.

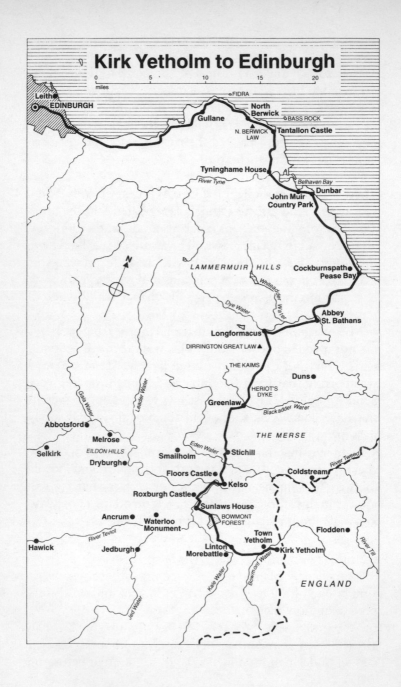

Kirk Yetholm to Edinburgh

0   5   10   15   20
miles

Leith
EDINBURGH
FIDRA
Gullane
North Berwick
BASS ROCK
N. BERWICK LAW
Tantallon Castle
Tyninghame House
River Tyne
Belhaven Bay
Dunbar
John Muir Country Park
LAMMERMUIR HILLS
Cockburnspath
Pease Bay
Whiteadder Water
Dye Water
Abbey St. Bathans
Longformacus
DIRRINGTON GREAT LAW
THE KAIMS
Duns
Gala Water
Leader Water
HERIOT'S DYKE
Greenlaw
Blackadder Water
THE MERSE
Abbotsford
Melrose
EILDON HILLS
Selkirk
Dryburgh
Smailholm
Eden Water
Stichill
River Tweed
Coldstream
Floors Castle
Kelso
Roxburgh Castle
Sunlaws House
Ancrum
Waterloo Monument
BOWMONT FOREST
Town Yetholm
Flodden
Hawick
River Teviot
Jedburgh
Linton
Morebattle
Kirk Yetholm
River Till
Kale Water
Bowmont Water
Jed Water
ENGLAND

2

Setting Forth

> I had desired to visit the Hebrides, or Western
> Islands of Scotland, so long, that I scarcely
> remember how the wish was excited.
>
> Dr Samuel Johnson, *A Journey to the*
> *Western Islands*, 1773

Anticipation is sometimes the best part of travel, but, as
Robert Louis Stevenson was to remark, 'The great affair is
to move.' I began the journey in my second favourite form
of transport, roaring through the night by train to the
Scottish Border, remembering many other such journeys
years ago when my unit of the Royal Marines would go
and play at winter warfare in the hills around Aviemore.
One of the Marines was Peter Davey who would get on the
train in London speaking the King's English and alight at
Speyside speaking unintelligible Scots. This he would
continue to do until we got back south again.

I can hardly blame him; lapsing into the vernacular is
simply one of the hazards of a trip to Scotland. We had a
plan to fine anyone 10p for saying 'Hoots!' or 'Awa' wi' ye'
or 'Y'know ye ken', or calling anyone 'Jimmy', but this had
already been abandoned after Keith ran up a tab of over
£15 in under half an hour at the pub. As often before on

this train ride, I slept most of the night, and soon after
nine in the morning I was eating breakfast inside the ramparts of Berwick-on-Tweed, marvelling at the wonders of
present-day travel.

When Dr Johnson and Boswell set out on their journeys
around Scotland at the end of the eighteenth century, the
journey by coach from London took at least 18 days. The
train now speeds from London to Edinburgh in a little
under four hours. Travelling by stagecoach may sound
romantic, but I suspect it was actually hellish, jerking along
on unmade roads, in all weathers, with fleas in the bed, rats
behind the wainscot and highwaymen lurking around the
corner.

Even at the time, stagecoach travel was far from popular.
Those who could afford it took passage to Newcastle on
returning colliers and then boarded the stage north from
there. There was a brisk trade in coal between London and
the Tyneside coalfields – hence those smoke-induced London fogs, and the old saying about 'carrying coals to
Newcastle'. The grimy, shallow draught colliers were the
fast and easy route to Scotland long before the railway
arrived.

But I digress; here I am on the Border, and a few miles
to the west lies the hamlet of Kirk Yetholm and the start of
my walk. It is a Saturday morning but the good people of
Berwick seem in no great hurry to get about, for the place
is almost empty, bathed in a chill spring sunshine, but
warm enough if you stay out of the wind and in the shelter
of the ramparts.

Berwick, which lies just in England but seems very Scots,
is a Border town, surrounded by intricate ramparts. It was
the last town in Britain to be endowed with new town
walls. This refurbishment of the fortifications was carried
out on the orders of Elizabeth I, who instructed her masons
to build fortifications that would 'keep Our Kingdom safe

against the Scots'. Since the work cost a pretty penny and Elizabeth was notoriously tightfisted – as careful with money as the Scots are supposed to be – she must have turned in her grave when the accession of her heir, James I of England and VI of Scotland, united the two kingdoms in 1603 and made those defences unnecessary.

Anyway, the ramparts look superb and they are still in splendid condition, giving good views south along the coast to the castles at Lindisfarne and Bamburgh and the smooth hilltops of the Cheviots, all of them standing out clearly this morning in the sharp North Sea light. I could have spent more time here, mooching about Berwick or ambling south to visit the Holy Island, but it lay off my route. I had to get on to the start of my walk at Kirk Yetholm.

However, this Border country has to be explored. I had no intention of leaving here before taking a good look round, not least because the Borders have played a significant part in Scotland's story. This is the interface between Scot and Sassenach, the place where their long enmity found free and frequent expression. Battlefields abound on the Border and, though I like walking battlefields, here I was spoiled for choice and had to be selective.

Close to Berwick lies one battlefield I had visited before, the site of Homildon Hill. In 1332 the young Edward III led an army to the Border to aid his vassal King of Scots, John Balliol and laid siege to Berwick which the Scots then held. In the summer of 1333, Archibald, Earl of Douglas, Regent to the heirs of Robert the Bruce, led an army out of Scotland to raise the siege. On the morning of 19 July Archibald found the English Army drawn up here, on the slopes of Homildon Hill.

Homildon Hill is the battle where the English archers first displayed that murderous talent they were to employ with such fatal effect later on at Crécy, Poitiers and

Agincourt and a long series of Anglo-French and Anglo-Scots battles, running down the years to Flodden Field, Pinkie and Solway Moss, all well inside the sixteenth century. The tactics established at Homildon Hill scarcely changed in the next 250 years, which is why this battle is significant in Anglo-Scots affairs.

The Earl of Douglas dismounted his knights and formed them up with the common spearmen into large phalanxes known as *schiltrons*. Clutching their 12 ft-long spears, the Scots advanced to the foot of the hill and were within 200 yards of the English line when the archers bent their bows and sent an arrowstorm into their ranks. It was said afterwards that 'Every English archer carries in his quiver 20 Scottish lives', but this cannot have been a surprise. Earl Douglas was well aware of what the English archers could do long before he came to the field.

Indeed, Douglas had promised to cut the right hand off any archer he captured, but it never came to that. The carnage which followed the initial blast of arrows was quite terrible. In the next three hours the gallant Scots lost about 10,000 men in this hopeless affray, while the English losses were negligible. The Earl of Douglas was among the first to die, and, with his army destroyed, Berwick-on-Tweed surrendered to the English King on the following day.

You can wallow in history along the Border and I decided to do just that by taking the bus towards Kirk Yetholm and hopping off at one or two of the towns along the way. The first town I came to was Coldstream, a place which advertises its long connection with the Coldstream Guards by having little model Guardsmen mounted on the shopfronts. This link makes a nice story which dates back more than three centuries to the winter of 1659–60, when Colonel George Monck, a Parliamentary soldier, was in garrison here with his regiment.

After the death of Lord Protector Cromwell, and the fall of his son Richard Cromwell – or 'Tumbledown Dick' – Monck supported the return of Charles II. To enforce the King's claim he marched his regiment to London, where their presence was sufficient to overawe the more republican-minded of the citizens. By way of reward Monck then became the Duke of Albermarle and his regiment became the Coldstream Guards, the only regiment of the British Army that can trace its history back in an unbroken line to Oliver Cromwell's New Model Army. The regiment still retains the original Crown-less brass buttons of the New Model Army to commemorate this connection – but their Commander-in-Chief today is HM The Queen.

All this I learned from the small regimental museum in Coldstream before another bus took me on to Kelso. I was sorely tempted to travel on through Kelso and look at some of the other Border towns, but lugging a rucksack around on a sightseeing trip is not a lot of fun. So, instead, I turned south for Town Yetholm. Kirk Yetholm, the end of the Pennine Way and the start of my journey, lies just across the valley, set under the loom of the Cheviots, the hilly home of those great Cheviot sheep that flooded the Highlands in the late eighteenth and early nineteenth centuries and did more damage to the clans than Cumberland's dragoons.

Kirk Yetholm used to be a gathering place for the Scottish gipsies, or tinkers, who would flee for refuge to the wilds of Cheviot when the King's officers made a foray against them. The main visitors to Kirk Yetholm today are the muddy survivors of the 250-mile Pennine Way walk from Edale in Derbyshire, who can obtain their Pennine Way certificate for 50p, and a free pint on the late Mr Wainwright, at the Border Inn pub in Kirk Yetholm. Either of these should be an adequate lure, but the walking trade is not what it was.

'We don't get as many Pennine walkers as we used to,'

said the publican, Mr Russell. 'It has come down to about 800 a year from 2,000 or more ten years ago. I used to give them their pint and send Mr Wainwright a bill about once a year, and back would come his cheque. There are more long-distance footpaths today, so I suppose they are busy walking those.'

To get in the mood for my walk and to see a little of the Pennine Way, I left my pack here and went south for a mile or two, until the road got too steep for comfort and the round slopes of the Cheviots were in plain sight, with what I took to be the Pennine Way curving down the green hill into the valley ahead. That seen, I turned back to Kirk Yetholm where, apart from myself, there were only two other walkers about: a man and his son returning from a few days camping in the Cheviots, both footsore and weary. Otherwise Kirk Yetholm dozed in the afternoon sun as I sat outside the pub with a pint.

Then, as I was brooding over my map, working out an easy route west to my first nightstop at Sunlaws House, a gaggle of motorbikes came roaring up to the pub, the riders plastered with mud after a morning trail-riding in the hills. The bikers were friendly enough, but all that revving of engines and stomping of boots was too much of a distraction on a peaceful afternoon. It was time to go, so I heaved on the pack and set out for Sunlaws: on my journey at last, and glad of it.

As a rule I am against walking along roads. The hedges obstruct the view, the motorists will try to kill you and the tarmac plays havoc with your feet. Neither is it much good walking on the grassy verges. Smooth as they might appear, they will have been rutted and compacted by heavy lorries and make uncomfortable walking. However, from time to time, needs must. After crossing the bridge over Bowmont Water and walking for a while beside the river, I came onto the lane near the cemetery below the green hill of Yetholm Law. There was then no choice but to follow the road from there towards Morebattle and Linton, strolling along, swishing at dandelion heads with my stick, taking short peeks at my map and wondering how the Border came to be up here; after all, this is a fair way north of Hadrian's Wall. The answer is complicated.

When the British islands entered history with the invasion of Julius Caesar in 55 BC, the north of these islands was inhabited by an intransigent race known as the Picts, from *pictii*, the 'painted ones'. These Picts were probably Celts from north-west Europe, driven out of the Continent by wilder tribes around 500 BC and forced to emigrate across the North Sea. The Romans referred to the land of the Picts beyond the Firths of Forth and Clyde as 'Caledonia'. At the end of the first century AD, General Agricola invaded Caledonia but, having failed to conquer it or advance further north than the Tay, the Romans fell back across what is now the Lowlands and the Border.

In AD 122 the Emperor Hadrian decided to build a 73-mile wall from the North Sea to the Solway Firth to mark out the northern limit of the Roman Empire. This wall, 16 feet high and equipped with towers and mile-castles, took five years to complete. Later on, around AD 140, after another campaign in the north, the Romans built another wall, the Antonine Wall, between the Clyde and Forth, but again they could not hold it. They fell back to Hadrian's line and stayed there. Beyond that Roman Wall the Picts were left to live as they pleased and the Wall remained a boundary until the legions left Britain in AD 411.

Meanwhile, the Picts were in trouble. Another invader, the *Scotti*, a Celtic tribe from Ireland, came across the narrow water between Antrim and Kintyre early in the fourth century and soon overran much of the country of the Picts. These *Scotti* spoke Gaelic, and established a kingdom in what is now Argyll. By the middle years of the ninth century, when Alfred was uniting the English kingdoms of Mercia, Wessex, Northumbria and the rest, the Picts and Scots had fused together and established a kingdom in Strathclyde.

The first 'King of Scots' that we know about was Kenneth MacAlpine, who lived in the middle years of the ninth century. Like his contemporary, the English King Alfred, Kenneth spent his energies fighting the invading Danes and Northmen who eventually settled in what is now Sutherland, Orkney and Shetland. Kenneth became King of Scots in AD 843, defeated the Picts, united the tribes, fought off the Vikings and is now buried on Iona: a good man, King Kenneth.

It was not until the next century that the Scots had time to war with the Saxons, but from then on the warfare was fierce and continuous. Finally, after decades of conflict, in 1018 the Border was finally fixed along the Tweed, where it still remains, and Scotland became much the shape it is today. Soon after the Border was fixed, Macbeth killed Duncan at a battle near Elgin in 1040, and ruled until 1057 when he was killed by Malcolm Canmore. I had thought that Macbeth did not exist outside Shakespeare's 'Scottish play', but we shall pick up his trail again in Dunfermline.

The Border, though fixed, was not settled when the Normans killed Harold on Senlac Hill and made their way to the north. Lying north and south of the territorial frontier, the Border became home to a hardy and truculent race of warriors, the reivers, the 'Steel Bonnets'. These violent men 'who feared God little and Man not at all', kept the Border in uproar for centuries. All the kings of England and Scotland tried to suppress, or at least control their Border lords, the English relying on the powerful Percies and Nevilles, the Scots on the Earls of Douglas, but the Border lords, the 'reiving families' – the Kerrs, Elliots,

Bothwells, Homes, Charltons and the rest – paid no heed to any authority.

They rode across the Border, north and south, to raid, loot, burn and kill, forging alliances with old enemies today, falling on former friends tomorrow to steal their cattle and burn their farms. They continued to do so until the two kingdoms were united under James I and VI in the early seventeenth century. Relics of those wild times dot the Border to this day in the shape of small castles or 'peel towers'. There is a good example of these at Smailholm, a tower set on a rocky hill to the west of Kelso, a grim keep which now contains a collection of costumed figures relating to the tales of Sir Walter Scott. The Border towns – Jedburgh, Kelso, Selkirk, Hawick and the rest – are still very proud of their reiving past and celebrate it every year at the 'Common Ridings', when the descendants of the 'Steel Bonnets' ride out to mark the boundaries of their land.

Thinking about all this took me a good distance on my way towards Sunlaws, the passage of miles and the weight of the pack almost unnoticed. That is one advantage of thought and you must try it. When there is nothing much to see, a good daydream, John Hillaby's 'Skull Cinema', certainly helps to pass the time. If no history presents itself I can usually get along by imagining myself winning the VC, and ever since the time when these books started to sell in the United States, the Congressional Medal of Honor as well. Why be modest? When that palls and after the parade, when I have collected the gongs from our grateful rulers, I imagine what I would do if I won £5,000,000 on the football pools; it used to be only £1,000,000 but on recent walks I have had to take account of inflation. Since I don't actually do the pools and have no great interest in money or possessions, in my daydream I give most of it away. It is surprisingly hard to give away £5,000,000 in the course of an afternoon's walk.

Thoughts apart, I could still notice that this Border is splendid walking country, a rippling place of smooth hills and ridges, the valley filled with open fields, spattered with green woods and copses. I saw hares, plenty of them, each one starting up at my approach, to race away jinking across the fields, long ears flapping in the wind. Lapwings soared up gently from ruts in the plough only to settle back again when they saw no danger, skylarks spiralled somewhere overhead, lost against the blue. Today, for the first time this year, I heard a cuckoo. I was to hear the cuckoo every day of this walk and we went north together with the spring.

So the time passed pleasantly enough, the sun setting brightly ahead, the road climbing steadily but not too steeply. Eventually I turned off onto a track past the farm at Old Caverton and up into Bowmont Forest, with the Kale Water below me to the south, soon linking up with the River Teviot, itself a tributary of the River Tweed which it reaches a few miles further on at Kelso.

From the top of the hill I could see a couple of distinctive landmarks and paused to pick them out on the map. That needle shape must be the Waterloo Monument near Ancrum, a place where the Scots beat the English during the 'Rough Wooing' of the 1540s, and those black triple tops would be the Eildon Hills which rise to about 420 metres and dominate this part of the Border. These triple tops have their own walk and their own legend. The walk is the Eildon Way, a short, steep haul up from Melrose; the legend has it that King Arthur and his knights sleep in a cave beneath the Eildon Hills, ready to ride out when needed and save England once again.

Below those hills lay Melrose Abbey, another place destroyed in the Rough Wooing, a Cistercian abbey founded in 1136 by King David I, and one I had to see before

I set out towards the north. Beyond Bowmont Forest, which is no great wood, came another road, and beyond that yet another hill or 'law' as they call them hereabouts. I had done about nine miles from Kirk Yetholm when I came out above the Teviot valley and made my way downhill past Whitehillfoot Farm, with the turrets of Floors Castle now in sight to my right. Then I ran into the farmer's wife, out for a walk on the hill.

I was on a footpath, but whether I was entitled to be there was another matter. Having suffered regular abuse over the years from English farmers, who by and large *hate* walkers, I was a trifle apprehensive, but my first meeting with a Scots farmer was a blueprint for all the rest I was to meet on this journey. She could not have been more friendly. She told me to cut across their 'set aside' down to the 'policy', the fields and grounds around Sunlaws House, and as a bonus, she gave me some good advice.

'I like to come up here at the end of the day and just take a look at it,' she said. 'To see what we have done and what still needs to be done. If you are just working, working, all the time, and don't stop to look at it and think, you never know if you are doing the right thing, do you?'

I had not thought about that before. If I don't work, I worry; on balance I would rather work, but I think the lady is right. Resolving to spend more time thinking about things and less time worrying over them, I went down the hill, crossed the fields and came out onto the drive leading up to Sunlaws. Ten miles into my walk in one afternoon was quite enough for my first day on the trail.

A day off at Sunlaws House was one of my travel-writing perks on this journey, but a useful one. Sunlaws is a rather splendid sporting hotel, owned by the Duke of Roxboroughe, who lives in the family home at Floors Castle by Kelso, in the centre of his vast estates. As is the case everywhere these days, a lot of the money necessary to maintain the estate comes from letting out the shooting across the fields and the fishing in the rivers, but anyone a-sporting on the Roxboroughe estates has to stay at Sunlaws House.

This can be no hardship. Sunlaws is a very, very comfortable hotel with books and a bar and very good food, and is just the sort of place where a gentleman of a certain age can set himself up for a few weeks' walking. Sunlaws is also a sporting hotel, so at least half the guests were in tweeds and breeches or had just climbed out of their waist-high rubber waders. However, given this mission to recover my roots, Sunlaws offered another benefit: one of the hotel's cultural activities is their 'How to be a Scot' course. This offers lessons in kilt deportment, wild haggis hunting, bagpipe-playing, Highland dancing, porridge-eating and whisky-swilling – I reckoned on getting high marks for that one – as well as fly-fishing and caber-tossing.

I might as well admit that I did not do too well at the caber-tossing: not only could I not toss it, I could not even lift it. They say it's a knack, like fly-fishing. I was not very good at that either. Try as I would, I could not catch a single fly, and the ghillie found it safer to lie flat on the ground when my hook went whistling about the bank.

What I did excel at was kilt deportment, which went some way towards solving the Great Scots Mystery: what does a Scotsman wear under his kilt? I do not ask this question in jest or to mock; the kilt is a splendid and practical garment and one of the after-effects of the deportment lesson was a resolve to buy one as quickly as possible. Even so, what to wear under it, if anything, is a matter that deserves consideration.

Traditionally, the Highlander wore nothing under his kilt, and we have evidence for this. Writing about the

Highlanders while helping General Wade build this road across the north in the first half of the eighteenth century, Edward Burt wrote:

> The common habit of the Highlander is far from being acceptable to the eye. A small part of the plaid is brought down and set in folds about the waist to make a short petticoat that reaches about halfway down the thigh. This dress is called a 'quelt' and for the most part is worn so very short that on a windy day, or going up a hill, the indecency of it is plainly discovered.

Well, not many people wore undergarments in the eighteenth century anyway, so we need not make too much of that. More recently, I can recall entering the 'Gents' at Bisley and finding a Scottish officer at the urinal, kilt held up in both hands and a look of bliss on his face. 'Young man,' he said, 'Transferrrrr at once to a Highland regiment. There is nothing like the kilt for urrrrination ... or forrrnication!'

That evening concluded with the usual drunken attempts to dance a 32nd-some or a 64-some but I have no recollection that bare arses were commonly visible as we reeled about. Perhaps the rule is that nothing is worn under the kilt in the regiments, but since that can be draughty or the kilt abrasive to the naughty bits, underpants are tolerated provided they remain unseen. This would be in line with my own Service experience. I can recall drilling on a wide parade ground in Malta, in the full heat of a Mediterranean summer, and our Commanding Officer deciding that to prevent a mass collapse we could remove our blue serge tunics. We did so, all 600 of us, revealing a ghastly assortment of tee-shirts, grey vests, sweat-drenched civvie shirts and vulgar tattoos. The CO took one look, sighed wearily, and said, 'Put 'em on again.'

The curious thing about the great kilt mystery is that no one has the definitive answer. My grannie, who had me in a kilt at the age of seven, told me that men usually wore short underpants called 'trews' for dancing or hammer-throwing. While I have taken a close interest in hammer-throwing ever since, I have not seen trews or anything else. Besides, trews are usually taken to be tight tartan trousers, of the sort worn by officers of the Highland Light Infantry and Rupert Bear.

I don't want to go on and on about this rather indelicate matter, but I did decide to pursue my researches elsewhere during this journey. The most sensible underwear for the kilt would seem to be a pair of jungle-green or tartan Y-fronts but 'Men's Underwear' at Marks and Spencer in Edinburgh told me there was no demand for such garments.

Moreover, this research was not without risk. Determined to get the definitive answer, I finally accosted the Sergeant of the Guard at Edinburgh Castle and said, 'Excuse me, Sergeant, but I've always wanted to know, exactly WHAT is that sentry wearing under his kilt?' The Sergeant looked me in the eye and said, 'Why don't you fuck off' . . . so I did.

Kilt deportment is a serious matter, not least when sitting down. The trick is to back into the chair, sweep the folds of the kilt flat with one hand and sit down quickly, before they get crushed. Then the sporran and the heavy folds of the kilt between the knees will keep you decent until the time comes to rise again. I guess it's a knack, but blood will tell and I soon got the hang of it.

This 'Learn to be a Scot' course was all great fun but in the days of the clans some of these activities were used by the chiefs to sort out the best men for the chief's personal bodyguard. Others are now an integral part of the Highland Games or that great Highland entertainment, the *ceilidh*. This is pronounced 'caylee' and is an evening devoted to Scottish dancing. I also have some experience of Highland dancing from those military excursions to Aviemore in my youth.

During those long-ago winters in Aviemore, the Marines used to lurk in the hut at Rothiemurchus during the week and descend on the villages of Speyside each weekend in search of entertainment. It was then decided by some of the bright sparks in the troop that it would improve our (never high) standing with the local community, and rather more importantly with the local girls, if we learned a bit of Highland dancing and could lead the ladies out for a reel or two at the Saturday dance.

Some improvement was necessary. The local girls had already discovered that being led out by a Commando Sergeant in boots led to trampled feet or, if we had been told to dance in our socks, a fearful loss of control on the corners. Matters came to a head when one of the troop got out of control twirling his partner round in the 'Gay Gordons' and twirled both of them through a plate-glass door.

Incidentally, my military friends tell me that the men of that gallant, distinguished and recently-disbanded regiment, the Gordon Highlanders, once known as the 'Gay Gordons', prefer to be known as the 'Terribly, Terribly, Happy Gordons' and take offence if anyone says different.

So we resolved to improve our Highland dancing. This was an early example of what is now called 'Hearts and Minds' or how the vulgar soldiery can ingratiate themselves with the locals. We first prevailed upon our officer, Lt. Alan Blackshaw, a noted mountaineer, to replace our morning session of PT with half an hour's-worth of reels and strathspeys. Wearing his well-known, 'I know I will have cause to regret this' expression, Alan agreed, and for the next week we solemnly set to partners every morning.

'Front rank, the lads; rear rank, the lasses, an' a one, two, three, four. . . .'

For music we had a Marine called Jock Connolly who could play the concertina, but there was, as ever, a snag. The only tune Jock could play was the 'Eton Boating Song' and it is not easy to dance an eightsome reel or the 'Dashing White Sergeant' to that dirge-like tune.

However, the Royal Marine Commandos are a resourceful lot who do not let a little snag like that stand in their way. Any damn fool can dance to the proper music, so we kept at it and were pretty confident in our dancing by the weekend, when we were let loose on the community. It was a fine night, the girls were willing and we were eager, but it all ended in tears. The local *ceilidh* band could not play the 'Eton Boating Song' and we couldn't dance reels to anything else.

It would be a crime to leave the Border without a look at some of the Border abbeys and at Abbotsford, the home of Sir Walter Scott, so the next day was devoted to a tour of the local attractions. Besides, on the second morning I was pretty stiff from my first day's walk and not a little hungover after a convivial evening in the bar where my intention of walking to Cape Wrath had met with a gratifying amount of attention. I therefore had to skulk about until the other guests had left for riverbank or covert. Only then could I emerge, climb into a car and take off for a tour around the Border.

The Border towns – Kelso, Hawick, Jedburgh and the rest – are now largely devoted to the wool trade. They have been for the last century and a half, and are still making a profitable trade from the happy conjunction of sheep and tartan. The great Cheviot sheep have been here for centuries and once provided the wealth of the Border abbeys, but the abbeys had gone when the local wool trade really began to flourish at the start of the last century, a success partly due to the writings of Sir Walter Scott.

The wearing of tartan was suppressed in Scotland after the '45 Rebellion. The skills of weaving and dyeing tartan cloth had therefore almost died out in the northern glens when the Acts forbidding the wearing of Highland dress were finally repealed at the end of the eighteenth century. There were, however, plenty of weaving and dyeing skills and a lack of employment on the Border. Hawick and the other Border towns were already centres for the wool and knitting industries and, with Scott's romantic tales of Highland life, like *Rob Roy*, to drive the trade along, the weaving of tartan cloth became a profitable occupation, as it remains to this day.

In the late 1770s, the local dyeing industry had to discover ways to recreate the natural colours of the tartan, using heather for the greens, watercress for the violet, rhubarb for the yellows and so on. These colours were fixed in the cloth by the use of urine, which the weavers would collect in buckets from the neighbouring houses each morning; it sounds disgusting but it created a whole new industry.

The burgeoning trade in tartan cloth got a great boost in 1824 when Sir Walter Scott persuaded George IV not only to visit Scotland but also to get into full Highland rig: kilt, plaid, bonnet, sporran, the lot. The Royal knees had to be concealed beneath pink tights, which may have spoiled the otherwise martial impression, but other lords took the hint, and wearing tartan then became all the rage. The trade got another boost in the 1850s when Queen Victoria and her numerous brood took up residence at Balmoral and went native. It has to be remembered that the Royal Family were then barely out of their Saxe-Coburg and the Electorate of Hanover period, but Prince Albert took to the

tartan in a big way and before long Balmoral was festooned with it. They even developed a Royal Stewart
tartan, one of the many new designs created to satisfy a
demand for a clan tartan. Most of the present clan tartans
did not exist in the years before Culloden and the trade in
tartan cloth has continued to flourish ever since.

The Border towns all have woollen mills and shops
selling every kind of woollen and tartan goods, but I am
not a shopper and let these go by. The great attraction of
the Border towns for me are the ruined abbeys, all built by
the Scots King, David I, in the early years of the eleventh
century and all destroyed by the orders of that arch-vandal,
Henry VIII, in the course of what Scotland's history
describes as 'The Rough Wooing'.

In the middle decades of the sixteenth century, being
anxious to forge an alliance with Scotland, Henry proposed to the then Regent of Scotland, the Earl of Arran,
that the infant Princess Mary, later Mary Queen of Scots,
should marry his heir, Prince Edward, later Edward VI.
The Regent preferred to maintain the 'Auld Alliance' with
France and wanted to marry the infant Mary to the
Dauphin of France. To point out the error of this decision
or change the Regent's mind, in 1544–5 Henry sent
Thomas Seymour, Earl of Hertford, to ravage the Border
and the Scottish Lowlands and Seymour set about this task
with evident enjoyment.

Holyroodhouse, and much of Edinburgh, was sacked
and burned. In the course of two campaigns the wonderful
abbeys at Melrose, Kelso, Jedburgh and Dryburgh were
utterly destroyed, together with 5 towns, more than 200
villages and 16 castles. The burning of Melrose was a
particular sorrow, for Melrose held the heart of Robert the
Bruce, but the destruction of the abbeys was only a part of
it: the whole Border was devastated and the dead lay
thickly in the streets and fields.

The Scots made no great effort to stem this invasion. Their martial confidence had been sapped by the defeats at Flodden in 1513 and Solway Moss in 1542; when a Scots army did finally muster against the English in 1547 it was crushed with heavy loss at Pinkie Field, six miles east of Edinburgh. It was a lack of places left to ravage rather than any Scots response that finally sent the English armies back across the Border.

The abbeys remain. Though in ruins, they are still beautiful and still worth visiting. Kelso Abbey lies in the centre of the present market town, Jedburgh's Abbey church became the town kirk after the Reformation and is very well preserved, Melrose is a dream in rose-red stone, set beneath the black bracken tops of the Eildon Hills, and Dryburgh contains the graves of Earl Haig, that scion of the whisky family who commanded the British Armies in France during the Great War, and Sir Walter Scott, one of my personal heroes. Scott loved this wild Border country and lived and died here in his fine house at Abbotsford.

My admiration for Scott is not entirely due to his books and poetry. The main reason for my regard is that when he lost all his money he refused to borrow or go into bankruptcy, but elected to work off his debts by writing. Refusing offers of help from his many friends, he declared, 'I will involve no friend, rich or poor. My own right hand shall pay for all.' In the end it did, but the effort killed him.

Scott was born in Edinburgh in 1771 and like his great successor, Robert Louis Stevenson, he was a sickly child, lamed by polio. He trained as a lawyer and eventually became Sheriff of Selkirk, but started writing at an early age and had his first great success with his poem, *Lay of the Last Minstrel*, published in 1802. Other books and poems followed, with three of the most famous books, *Ivanhoe*, *Heart of Midlothian* and *Guy Mannering* coming out between 1815 and 1820. More books and a great deal of lyrical poetry were published every year thereafter, and Scott became famous throughout the kingdom.

Scott was now making a fortune from his writing and put part of the proceeds towards the purchase of the house at Abbotsford on the Border. He lived here from 1812 to 1832, writing his books and assembling an eclectic collection of treasures: paintings, books, armour and relics of famous folk.

Study the glass cases at Abbotsford and you can see a lock of Mary Queen of Scots' hair, Rob Roy's sword, the *quaich*, or drinking cup, of Bonnie Prince Charlie, and Flora Macdonald's diary ... or you could until May 1994 when the burglars arrived. The house itself is somewhat peculiar, with turrets and crenellations, and Scott himself described it as 'A kind of conundrum castle, which pleases a fantastic person with its style and manner,' as indeed it does.

Scott was happy at Abbotsford and all was going well until the late 1820s, when disaster struck. Scott had gone into partnership with both his printer and his publisher and, when they went broke, Scott found himself liable for debts of around £120,000, a colossal sum at the time. His efforts to repay the money eventually ruined his health. He died from a stroke in 1832, but the royalties from *Ivanhoe* and all his other books and poetry eventually paid the debt in full. His descendants still live at Abbotsford and the desk he slaved away at is set as if he had just got up and gone for a stroll in the garden.

I had been to Abbotsford before and would have gone there again to brood over the relics and browse around the grounds, but there were burglars about on the Border during my stay. On one night they struck at Floors Castle and made off with some of the Duke's treasures, and on another they raided Abbotsford, rifled some of the display cabinets and stole Prince Charlie's *quaich* and many other historic items. Abbotsford was therefore being turned over by the police and out of bounds to visitors. Instead I went to 'Scott's View' on a hillside high above Dryburgh, and walked from there down to the abbey.

Scott used to ride up to this viewpoint almost every day. It is said that when the carriage was taking his coffin over the hill to Dryburgh, the horses stopped here automatically, as they had done so often when he was alive. One can see why he loved this spot. From the viewpoint there are splendid vistas over the Border country, the River Tweed far below, the hills and woods curving away in a great, green, rippling wave, off towards the misty horizon.

Off the road, a few hundred yards below Scott's View, a path leads into the woods towards a memorial erected to the memory of the fourteenth-century Scots patriot, William Wallace. This takes the form of a statue, clearly erected in Victorian times and now in sore need of restoration, with Wallace clad in a blend of Roman and Highland dress. It is not exactly pretty but a path leads down the hill from there to Dryburgh Abbey, a most splendid spot for strolling about on a quiet afternoon.

With Dryburgh seen, there was time for just one more sight before dinner. There is enough to see and do along the Border to keep one busy for weeks, but when forced to choose just one place to end the day, I chose to see the battlefield at Flodden.

Flodden bulks large in Scottish history. The English remember Cullodon rather better, but Cullodon was the graveyard of the clans and many Lowland men – and not a few Highlanders – fought for Cumberland against the Jacobites on Drummossie Moor. Flodden was a pure Scots disaster inflicted on the entire nation by the English. It was the greatest defeat Scotland ever suffered at the hands of the Sassenach and one that will never be forgotten as long as pipers play 'The Flowers of the Forest', that sad lament composed to commemorate the dead of that bloody fray, and played to this day at Scottish military funerals.

As so often before, the French entangled the Scots in that great catastrophe. Henry VIII of England had invaded France in support of the Pope's Holy League against Louis XII. The French therefore invoked the terms of the 'Auld Alliance', that ancient compact by which the French and Scots had promised to aid each other if either were invaded by the English.

King James had plenty of reasons to stay aloof from this quarrel. James IV of Scotland was married to Margaret Tudor, King Henry VIII's sister and by fighting against the Pope's ally, he risked excommunication. However, James was a romantic soul, a poet and a lawgiver, and unfortunately he was no soldier. Pedro de Alaya, the Spanish ambassador to Scotland at the time, wrote, 'He is courageous, even more than a King should be. He begins the fight before he has given his orders and he does not think it right to begin any fight without himself being the first in danger.' Such qualities may be admirable in a knight-errant or fighting man but they are fatal in an army commander.

Loyal to the 'Auld Alliance', when the French called for assistance, James IV stood by his nation's word and led a splendid army, 20,000 strong, into England. As men had feared, the Pope promptly excommunicated the King and placed Scotland under interdict. This was less of a problem than the large English Army under Thomas Howard, Earl of Surrey, the King's Lieutenant of the North, which mustered below the Border and came north against him, supported by the English Fleet. The advancing English and Scots armies somehow missed each other in the Border hills, but when the Scots turned back they found Surrey's well-equipped army, also of about 20,000 men, waiting to bar their passage home below Branxton Hill.

The two armies met on the slopes of Branxton Hill on 9 September 1513. There is a cross and a memorial there today, just a few hundred yards from the church at Branxton where so many of those Scots killed in the battle lie buried. There is a display board by the cross and with that, a little imagination, and the battlefield lying in front of you virtually unchanged, the events of Flodden Field can easily be recalled.

It was another of those dreary, rainy Border days, of low cloud and wind. The battle began late in the afternoon with an artillery duel, where the larger, more numerous and better handled English guns did eerie work among the ranks of the Scottish spearmen. After a short while the Scottish Borderers, mustered under the Earl of Home, broke rank and charged the English line, only to fall in swathes under the arrows and bills of the English infantry. Having done that much and achieved nothing, the Earl of Home took his men away.

Then the Scottish spearmen in the centre came forward, their feet slipping on the muddy grass as they came down the slope to lock ranks with the English and die where they stood. The Highlanders from Argyll and Lennox, who had come south on the orders of their chiefs, stayed on the ridge and watched the battle below, until they were suddenly attacked from the flank by English horse and the archers of Sir Edward Stanley's rearguard.

The Battle of Flodden went on into the dusk, Scottish spear against the more effective English bill, arrow and artillery against stubborn courage. Having disposed of the Highlanders, Stanley brought his men down the hill onto the Scots' rear. With no quarter offered or asked for, surrounded by their enemies and cut off from retreat, the Scots fought to the last man.

Those stubborn spearmen still made good,
That dark impenetrable wood,
Each stepping where his comrades stood,
The instant that he fell....

as Scott wrote, accurately, in *Marmion*. James IV died at
Flodden and all the earls with him and a good 10,000
fighting men their country could ill spare. The House of
Stewart – or Stuart – never really recovered from the events
of that fatal day.

I prowled about the muddy slopes of Branxton Hill and
went in the little church, but evening was coming on and
the rain with it, just as it did on the day of the battle. I had
had a good look round this splendid Border country,
enough to make me vow to go back again, but I now had
to get on. The sun was tumbling down behind the rain
clouds to the west as I went back to Sunlaws and there I
prepared to set out on my journey of discovery through this
land of Scotland and its gallant, oft-defeated but quite
unconquerable people.

3

Across the Southern Uplands

Come fill up my cup, come fill up my can,
Come saddle your horses, and call up your men,
Come open the West Port, and let me gang free,
And it's room for the bonnets of Bonnie Dundee.
Sir Walter Scott, *Bonnie Dundee*, 1830

When I came out of Sunlaws next morning it was raining hard so I went back in and put on the complete range of hard-hitting gear, my gaiters, wind- and waterproofs. This day saw the start of a considerable walk, a couple of days at least, north and east to the North Sea coast, along at least part of the Southern Upland Way, and poor weather is much better than hot weather when you have a long way to go. That's what I told the guests who assembled in the hall to see me off, but I don't think they believed me.

Poor weather, with lowering skies and teeming rain, was in more than adequate supply that morning. I went off jauntily enough, twirling my walking stick, but by the time I got to the end of the drive and turned across the fields for the banks of the Teviot my garments were already streaming with water; but who cares? The real walk had begun and for the next few weeks my time and my life were my own. That is one of the rare joys of this type of walking, the

45

gleeful thought on some windswept heath that 'They can't get at me here.'

The rain looked set to last the day and I had a long walk ahead of me, 20 miles at least to the start of the Southern Upland Way, Scotland's 212-mile-long coast-to-coast footpath, and one I wanted to have a look at. The rain itself was no problem, but my first task was to get beyond Kelso and off the main road. I dislike walking on roads at any time, but walking on roads in the rain means a regular drenching with muddy spray thrown up by passing cars and lorries. Kelso lay about three miles to the north, or rather more by the riverbank path, but at least there was a path, so I turned down towards it.

In fact the map gave me a choice of routes, evidence of which I could see ahead in the shape of a railway bridge. Scotland seems to be full of abandoned railway lines, and when the sleepers have been removed these are excellent for walking. One such railway line lay ahead of me here, on the right bank of the Teviot heading straight for Kelso and I should have taken it. Being daft, I crossed the river on the footbridge that lies under the viaduct and struck out along the towpath. This was a mistake.

The towpath by the Teviot, and indeed those by most of the salmon rivers in Scotland, is not a towpath at all but simply a way for salmon fishermen to get to their beats. This being so, the path peters out from time to time, usually at the most inconvenient spot, leaving the walker with no choice but to turn back, climb up the bank or hack a way on through bramble and bog.

This path finally led me to a place where I had the choice of turning back, wading around a small headland or climbing up a sheer grassy bank in the hope of finding a footpath at the top. I opted for the latter choice and floundered up the slope, grasping wet tufts of grass and thorny branches, to arrive at the top nicely muddy, quite out of humour, and thoroughly wet. Meanwhile, the salmon fishermen stayed waist- or armpit-deep in the river far below and thrashed the water in a fruitless search for fish.

As walks go I don't recommend it. I passed the ruins of the medieval Roxburgh Castle built by David I, and came out onto the main road where the Teviot runs into the Tweed; it had taken me two hours to walk down into Kelso and I was not pleased. The rain had taken on that persistent tone that tells you it is in for the day, so on arriving in the town I slunk into a café to dry off a little and consult the map. My route today lay almost due north to Greenlaw, after which I must press on across the heather moors to find the Southern Upland Way and, with a bit of luck, a few stories. First, however, I had to work out the way to go.

I like maps and often read them like books, for pleasure. Like many walkers, I can happily spend hours brooding over an OS map comparing routes, estimating times and difficulties, trying to get a feel of the land before I actually go out and walk it. One of the advantages of walking in Scotland is that the land is liberally supplied with forestry plantations, which may do little for the wildlife but have distinctive irregular shapes that are very useful landmarks for the walker. From the map I could see that on a dreary grey day like today some of these would be useful pointers on the more exposed parts of the country, especially in the open country north of Greenlaw, a small village about nine miles to the north of Kelso.

From the map, it looked as though my way there would lie mostly along roads and lanes, but north of Greenlaw lay moorland and the chance to do what I really enjoy, groping my way across country, off roads, using map and compass. This is easier done if you can see where you are going, but the mist was on the rooftops, the rain was still lashing down and it seemed best to get up and get on with it, whatever the weather. First, though, I had to have a look around Kelso.

Kelso grew up around the abbey established in 1128 by King David I, who gave the Cistercians a grant of land opposite his burgh and castle of Roxburgh, on the far side of the Tweed. Under the King's eye the abbey flourished, especially in sheep, with a flock that once contained 7,000 animals, and prospered until the Earl of Hereford ravaged the Border and destroyed the abbey in 1545, putting everyone inside to the sword, including 100 monks.

The town, however, continued to flourish. Kelso Square is said to be the largest town square in Scotland and the streets which surround it – Horsemarket, Cornmarket and Woolmarket – are evidence that this was, and to a degree still is, a thriving market town.

Given better weather, I would have lingered on in Kelso, not least for a look at Floors Castle, the largest inhabited castle in Scotland, but the weather I did not mind in the least in the countryside was sorely depressing in the town. At least Floors Castle looked good, even in the rain, a sprawling building designed by William Adam in the 1720s but glorified a century later with a wealth of pepperpot towers and windows, so that the castle now has 365 windows, one for every day of the year. None of that interested the lady in the Tourist Office who was far more anxious to tell me that Floors Castle had been used as the location for Tarzan's ancestral home in the recent film *Greystoke*, and that the local gardens were famous for the Kelso onion, the world's largest, which can weigh up to 11lb.

In the end I trudged out of town on the streaming tarmac and made the best of a bad job by putting my feet down fast along the minor road, over the Eden Water at Stichill, going as hard as I could for Greenlaw. Had a bus come along I would certainly have stopped it, for there was nothing to be gained by this, but there was no bus and no one seemed keen to offer a lift to a dripping fool with a great big pack.

So on I went, swept by drifts of spray from passing lorries, all the way up to Greenlaw, and I arrived there in the early afternoon with a decision to make. Should I pack it in for one day and hope for better weather tomorrow, or should I press on towards Longformacus and the junction with the Southern Upland Way which comes in here from the east? Decisions, decisions, is there no escape from them? If I went for the first option, I would soon be under cover, over a teapot and dry, while if I went for the latter, the day might not be a total loss.

I also had one of those route choices and, since it may appeal to some other walker, the alternative is worth listing. One of those abandoned, dismantled railway lines runs through Greenlaw and off to the east beside the Blackadder Water before turning north towards Duns, a place that I have visited before and would like to see again.

Duns lies on the edge of the Lammermuir Hills and is a good day-walking centre for that splendid country but it is a fine little town as well, boasting at least two famous sons. The most recent is the World Motor Racing Champion, Jim Clark, who was born near Duns, and won 25 Grand Prix and the World Championship twice and was buried here after his death in a crash on the Hockenheim Circuit in 1968. There is a Jim Clark Room in the town, full of his trophies, and Jim lies buried in the churchyard at Chirnside, on the old railway line, a few miles further to the east.

The second famous son is the medieval scholar, John Duns Scotus, who was born here in 1266 and became a famous lecturer at the Sorbonne in Paris. Unfortunately, he then began to advance views on religion which were considered so extreme by both Church and laity that he came to be regarded as a fool. His name became a byword for stupidity and the origin of the word 'dunce'.

If the weather had been better, or if I had had the time, I might have diverted through Duns, but as it was I decided to press on to Longformacus, partly because it was too early to stop, partly because while walking along the road I had seen plenty of B&Bs and had no reason to worry about finding accommodation, and partly – mostly – because road-walking is no fun at all and I wanted to walk on some moorland before the day was over.

As is often the way of it, the rest of that afternoon's walk was delightful. The sky stayed grey and the rain spattered in from time to time but the moors were springy, my gaiters kept the wet out and there were plenty of natural land-marks to make the miles slip away. I can tell that this was the wettest day of my walk, for the No. 74 OS map is soiled and crumpled from the rain while all the other maps are still in fairly good condition.

Between Kelso and Longformacus I was walking across the western edge of the Merse, the great, flat, river-threaded flood-plain of the Tweed, with the Lammermuir Hills looming up ahead in the mist. I had already left the smooth ridges of the Border behind, but great walking country lay ahead in the Lammermuirs. Unfortunately, my route skirted the heart of these hills as I headed east for Dunbar and the coast, but I would at least get a touch of them on the path from Longformacus to the Whiteadder Water. All this is splendid walking country and if the map is anything to go by, well provided with tracks, footpaths and open moors, seemingly devoid of people.

Certainly I didn't see another soul after I turned off the road towards Duns and into the Moss plantation. I was soon out on the open moor, heading for the crease of Heriot's Dyke, with the grey waters of the circular Hule

Moss pond seen just away to my right as the mist lifted for a moment.

Mist or not, you cannot get lost here, for some distance to the north a road runs across these moors. The only trick required from me was to stay on track. I came past the low banks of a feature called 'The Kaims' which looked like some medieval or Dark Age earthwork, of which there are plenty hereabouts, picked up a track and came out onto the road, on track and just by a spot on a fence where a large owl was drying out its feathers, looking balefully at the sky through great yellow eyes.

The owl and I exchanged shrugs; then it flapped away heavily on round wings and I crossed the road and followed the track due north towards the dim bulk of Dirrington Great Law and the hamlet of Longformacus.

The rain gave up as the evening arrived and the clouds lifted to reveal a rolling hilly country barring my path to the north, all looking delightful, but I had done enough for one day. My boots were sodden and my clothes damp and I wanted a good Scots tea. I arrived at Longformacus just after six and, having passed a finger-post that told me I had reached the Southern Upland Way, I decided to call it a day.

If you discount the route from the Border to John o' Groats, which is not an official trail, the Southern Upland Way is Scotland's longest long-distance footpath, which is why I wanted to walk it – or at least a bit of it. The distance from Longformacus to the end of the Way at Cockburnspath on the North Sea coast is 20 miles, which is just about right for a long day's walk, with the small snag that the weather next day was still grey and there was not much to write about on the way.

The rugged parts of the Southern Upland Way lie to the east or centre of the country around Moffat. From Longformacus it was downhill, over fields and through copses, pleasant enough but not dramatic. That, on the other hand, gave me time for some thinking. I had only been three days in Scotland but I had already learned a lot and needed to sort it out.

It was already apparent that this land of Scotland contained at least three separate countries or communities – or had done for much of its history. There was the Highlands, the land of the Gael, the Scotland of romance and legend, and the Lowlands, which sounded more Presbyterian, more stern and dour, and at this stage of the journey, more dull. There was also the distant North Scotland of the Highlands and Islands, where the Vikings had ruled, but that could come later. From my reading of history so far, the Lowlanders hated the Highlanders as much or more than they hated the English, perhaps because many of the Lowlanders, and certainly many of the Lowland lords, had English lands and English or Norman roots. I had not realised that.

Finally, between the Lowlanders and the Sassenach stood the rolling land I was now leaving, the home of the fierce Border people who had every man's hand against them, and from what I could read of them, rightly so.

Those shattered Border abbeys, at Kelso, Dryburgh, Jedburgh and Melrose, can help to link these fragments together and carry the story forward, with a little help from William Shakespeare.

When Scotland assumed its present shape, the King of Scots was Kenneth II, (AD 971–95) who, like his three successors, was much engaged fighting the Danes and Norsemen who raided the Scottish coast as they did those of Ireland and England, and had already begun to settle in the remoter parts of the north and north-west. Then came Malcolm II (1005–34), whose son was Duncan, the man murdered by Macbeth in Shakespeare's play.

Macbeth may or may not have had a murderously

inclined spouse, but having killed Duncan he ruled Scotland for 17 years at the time when Edward the Confessor sat on the throne of England. Edward supported Duncan's son, Malcolm, who invaded Scotland in 1057 and killed Macbeth near the town of Aberdeen, with no help at all from witches or the woods of Dunsinane, and this Malcolm, Malcolm III, or Canmore – the Great Chief – is the first really significant Scots monarch after Kenneth Mac-Alpine.

During Malcolm Canmore's reign (1057–93), the land of Alba became the Kingdom of the Scots, but the fatal influence of the English began to seep across the frontier, a seepage that turned into a flood when William the Bastard, Duke of Normandy, came across the Channel and killed Harold the Saxon on Senlac Hill.

Malcolm Canmore had a Saxon wife, Margaret, sister of the Saxon pretender to the English throne, Edgar Atheling. It has to be remembered that the court of Edward the Confessor was basically a Norman court in a Saxon kingdom. Edward had spent most of his life in Normandy, liked Normans and had chosen Duke William as his successor; it was Earl Harold's refusal to accept the late King's choice that led to the invasion and Conquest of 1066.

Margaret, though Saxon, and like her brother a fugitive from Duke William, was equally enamoured of Norman ways. She married Malcolm in 1068, two years after the Conquest, and many Saxon chiefs and thanes came north to shelter at her court; the word 'Sassenach' or Southerner is derived from the word Saxon, though the Highland Scots apply it to Lowlanders as well as the English. These 'Sassenachs' were soon followed by Norman lords who found life under the great King William either oppressive or downright dangerous.

Given that the Normans were notorious land-grabbers

and violent to boot, their welcome in the north is more than surprising, but the Normans were the wave of the future. Their knights fought on horseback and were irresistible in the charge. They spoke French and had access to the culture and learning of France. They were accustomed to feudal duties and, if uneasy vassals, were always looking for a lord to hold their fealty. Having a strong Norman element at court was common in Christian lands from the Roman Wall to the frontiers of Syria, and the Court of Scotland was no exception. Having a few Normans about the place gave a Court a bit of style, a touch of Gallic 'ton'. The problem in Scotland in 1070 was not the presence of Norman knights but the wishes of the Conqueror, William I of England.

William the Conqueror did not like having his vassals setting up shop in another king's court. Moreover, in the closing days of the eleventh century, the Border between England and Scotland was still a matter of dispute. In 1072 King William came across the Tweed and rolled up to the Tay, slaughtering everyone who got in his path, laying claim to much of the Lowlands and putting the fear of God into Malcolm Canmore.

Malcolm sought a peace and to get it offered William his fealty, though it was not – and still is not – clear whether this oath of fealty was as the King of Scots or in return for possessing the disputed Border territories of Lothian and Cumbria. William and his successors chose to believe that the Kings of Scots were henceforward vassals of the Kings of England and centuries of strife and woe followed that act of homage by Malcolm Canmore, an act confirmed by the marriage of Malcolm's sister to the Conqueror's third son, Henry Beauclerc, who in time became Henry I of England.

Malcolm's submission to the Conqueror was a political act with far-reaching consequences, but Margaret, his

Queen, trod a path which was no less harmful to the Scots for being far more insidious. Malcolm doted on his saintly wife and indulged her fancy in filling his Court with Saxon fugitives and Norman knights who, as is often the case, got on well enough in another man's country, probably because they were at least united in grabbing what they could get and despising the natives. Before long the Court of Scotland seemed much like that of England or France and hardly Scots at all.

Queen Margaret invited French clergy in to reform the Scots clergy and make them drop their Irish ways. She moved the Court from Dunfermline to the castle rock in Edinburgh and built the abbey-church at Dunfermline as the mausoleum of the Scots kings, who had previously been buried on Iona. Scots nobles spoke English or French, drank wine, enjoyed the joust and the hunt and had little in common with the Lowland people who tilled their lands, and nothing at all in common with the wild Highlanders to the north.

This did not mean that the Scots and Normans were now living amiably together; far from it. The Border Wars flourished and in 1093, a few weeks before Margaret died, King Malcolm was killed outside the gates of Alnwick. He was succeeded by his brother, Donald Bane, and then in rapid succession by Duncan II, Edgar I and Alexander I. Then came David I, who built the great Border abbeys.

David I ruled Scotland from 1124 to 1153 and it is fair to say that the Scottish love of learning and the importance the Scots still place on a good education dates back to his time. David, however, was only half a Scot and his Court, like those of his predecessors, had a strong English tinge to it. During his reign the gap between Lowlander and Highlander grew and became unbridgeable.

By David's time, the King of Scotland had his seat in Edinburgh, in the castle on the rock above the town, looking out to the northern hills across the grey and glinting waters of the Forth, but David was the most English – or Norman – of all the early Scots monarchs. He had many English – or Norman – friends, and it was in his reign that the English really began to infiltrate the old Kingdom of the Scots. David invited them in and gave them lands and titles, and among the first to arrive were three men whose descendants became contenders for the Scottish throne.

Bernard de Ballieul or Balliol was a knight from Picardy. He was followed by young Robert de Brus – or Bruce – whose family had barely survived on a single manor at Brix in Normandy. On the heels of the Bruce came a younger son of a Breton knight, Walter Fitzalan, who became the King's Steward – or Stewart.

Nor were these Anglo-Norman emigrés confined to the Lowlands: the chiefs of some great Highland clans were part of this migration, like the Frazers, who came from La Frèzeliers and still bear the strawberry – or *fraise* – on the family arms. The Sinclairs, or St Clairs, the Chisholms, the Hays, or de la Haye, all came from France and took root in Scotland. They were given Highland lands provided they controlled the local populace, and were eventually absorbed into the Highland culture.

David had need of these warlike, armoured lords because he had wars at home against the wild tribes in that recalcitrant third of his kingdom who lived in the west and beyond the Great Glen. His mailed Franco-Scot or Anglo-Scot cavalry gave him a great advantage in his campaigns in the north where land once conquered was nailed down with castles.

Normans liked the shelter of strong walls, and many of the great castles of Scotland date back to these early lords, but David's Norman cavalry were of less use in the wars against the English. He was defeated by the Prince Bishop of Durham at the Battle of the Standard in 1138, and only the outbreak of war in England between Stephen and the Empress Matilda saved his kingdom from invasion. Peace then came to Scotland, at least for a while, and the King turned his mind to peaceful, local matters, but still with that English tinge.

Monks fled north from the civil wars in England during that time, 'when Christ and his saints slept' and were offered rich lands and abbeys in return for developing a thriving trade in wool. To encourage some healthy competition, the Cistercians had Melrose and Kelso, the Benedictines Dunfermline and the Augustinians had Jedburgh and Holyrood, just a mile from the King's castle in Edinburgh. While England festered during a decade of civil war, Scotland enjoyed an early Renaissance, but while it flourished Scotland changed, at least south of the Highland Line.

The old Celtic 'bréhon' law was based on the wishes and needs of the community and family, not on the will of the lord. The 'bréhon' law had provisions covering the settling of disputes by arbitration and sanctions against the fostering or encouragement of civil disorder. Bréhon edicts had ruled Celt and Gael in Ireland and the north for generations, but they were now replaced with feudal custom, statute and writ, privy chamber and council.

During David's reign the Scottish Parliament began to emerge, well ahead of its English counterpart. All this was for the good, but it was not all good. A division grew up between Lowlander and Highlander that remained unbridged for centuries until the final clash between the two cultures came on Drummossie Moor on a chill April day in 1746.

History should be served in small, digestible doses. We have moved the history of Scotland forward a few centuries, seen how the English and English ways got a foothold in Scotland and made the – to me at least – surprising discovery that many Scottish patriots came from Anglo-Norman stock. What came out of all that will come later, but working this out and fitting it into the scheme of things had carried me gently into Longformacus, where I spent an evening drying my clothes, writing my notes and wondering how I could reduce the contents and weight of my rucksack.

I was still brooding about Balliol and the Bruce when I set off, a trifle stiffly, next morning for my swing up the Southern Upland Way towards the North Sea. The day was dry if chilly, the primroses were lying in swathes beside the path, and once the muscles had warmed up a bit I made good time on an enjoyable and well-marked route. This was a day of easy walking over rolling rather than hilly country, where open moor had given way to fields and copses.

For a while I followed a road and then the Upland path swung off across the fields before descending to another road by the Whiteadder Water. There I walked off the map that had brought me north from the Border, a part of Scotland that any walker will enjoy and one I will return to. There was pleasure in putting that crumpled map away, for the first map covered is a small mark of progress on any journey.

The Southern Upland Way, which runs from Portpatrick in the south-west right across the country to Cockburns-path would be a good two-week walk and at one time I had considered starting in Portpatrick and making this path the first *tranche* of my walk. This would have meant abandoning my usual direct route across a country and replacing the Border with the country that features in one of my favourite books, John Buchan's *The Thirty-Nine Steps*.

Whenever they film *The Thirty-Nine Steps*, Richard Hannay is always shown sprinting for dear life across the

Highlands, while in fact, or at least in the book, he was on the run across the hills of Galloway. There can be no argument about this. At the end of Chapter 2 he is buying a ticket for Newton Stewart and early on in Chapter 3 he is getting off the train in Dumfries. Far be it from me to spoil a good screenplay with a few facts, but Hannay's exploits were set well south of the Highland Line.

It is therefore unlikely that Hannay's hurriedly acquired Hielan' accent –

> 'There's waur jobs and there's better,' I said
> sententiously. 'I wad rather hae yours, sittin' a'
> the day on your hinderlands on thae cushions.
> It's you and your muckle cawrs that wreck my
> roads! An' we a' had oor richts, ye sud be made
> to mend what ye break'

would have convinced the villains of The Black Stone, when they came upon him disguised as a road repair man – and after a lifetime in South Africa would not there be a touch of the Afrikaans in his speech? At least he didn't say 'Ye noo ye ken.'

Well, let us not haggle, for I owe Buchan a lot. After my Spanish walk, when an effort to save weight left me with no option but watching Spanish television night after night, I had vowed never again to go walking without a few good books and to hell with the extra weight. Evenings spent watching *The Jewel in the Crown* in Spanish – 'El es maricon. Merrick?' 'No es possible!' 'Donde estan los Gurhkas, por favor?' – hour after hour of it, can do that to you.

I therefore had *The Thirty-Nine Steps* and various other Scottish-themed books in my pack. I like to stop every so often for a breather and a quick read, and I stopped now to look up some of my favourite Buchan gems. One of the best comes early on in *The Thirty-Nine Steps* when Scudder, explaining how he had managed to disappear by faking his death and planting a corpse in his flat, declares airily, 'You can always get a body in London if you know where to go for it.' I have been sorely tempted to ask Harrods about that one, for their telegraphic address is 'Everything London' and they used to offer everything on demand, from a pea to an elephant.

Another gem comes later on, when Hannay, wishing to impress the young Sir Harry with his bona-fides 'took down a hunting knife from a stand on the walls and did the old Mashona trick of tossing it into the air and catching it between my lips; that wants a steady heart.' It also takes a raving lunatic, but it did the trick and established Hannay as a good egg.

John Buchan – later Lord Tweedsmuir and Governor-General of Canada – came from Perth, another place I would have to leave for another time but *The Thirty-Nine Steps* came with me on my journey and was one of the motivators for the trip, spelling out a side of Scotland that I now hoped to see – wild, remote, maybe dangerous. Hannay and I went on together to Abbey St Bathans, covering 10 miles from Longformacus, and all that before noon.

Abbey St Bathans is a pretty place with a youth hostel and a hotel or two and the remains of the Cistercian abbey that was set up in King David's time; St Bathan was a Celtic monk who followed Columba at Iona. I stopped there for an hour out of the boots, a bit of Buchan and a pot of tea, before crossing the river, and zig-zagging my way up to Whiteburn and then along the way to Blackburn, then across the A1(M) road and down beside the railway line to the coast at Pease Bay.

I have ended three cross-country walks on a beach, but I am glad that this one was only a short stop on the journey because the beach at Pease Bay is backed by a large caravan site and not all that romantic; in fact it was downright depressing and I was not all that encouraged by the fact that the Southern Upland Way seemed to vanish, reappear and finally peter out in a carpark. I had come a long way across a fair country in the last couple of days and this was not what I had hoped for; in quite a huff, I got on a bus and took myself off to Dunbar.

4

Dunbar to Gullane

As long as ye are learning the lads Latin and Greek
it is easy work, but when ye come to play golf,
ye maun hae a heid.
        C.B. Macdonald, *Scotland's Gift: Golf*, 1928

From Dunbar my route lay north and west, along the
North Sea coast and the south shore of the Firth of Forth,
to Gullane and Edinburgh. From there I would cross the
Forth by the road bridge and make my way into Dunfermline and the Kingdom of Fife. I reckoned on allowing three
days for this stage of the journey, which would allow for a
gentle stroll along the coast, with plenty of time to see the
sights and explore the origins of Scotland's great contribu-
tion to the world of leisure: golf.

Maybe, since I do not actually play golf, I could also
throw in a look at the world of whisky, but between them
these two subjects should provide a little more insight to
my native land, I thought as I ambled towards Edinburgh.
In the event, I got rather more than an insight, for this
south coast of the Firth of Forth is full of interest and
history, quite beautiful country set against the backdrop of
the Lammermuir Hills and well worth exploring. On the

other hand the weather was not good and I was freezing even as I walked along.

It had stopped raining, but the soft weather of the previous three days had been replaced with clear skies and a biting north wind straight from the Arctic, a wind that blew, on and off, for the rest of my journey and was to prove a sore trial in the weeks and miles ahead. As I emerged from my B&B in Dunbar next morning, the wind cut into me like a knife and nearly tugged the map from my hand as I tried to get oriented and work out a route down to the John Muir Country Park. Before I went there, though, there was some more of that Anglo-Scots history to get through, though it meant a leap forward from the days of David I to the middle of the seventeenth century.

I was always told that the three things a gentleman never discussed in the Mess were women, politics and religion. This would make for pretty dreary conversation, especially for an historian. Politics and religion brought the English to Dunbar in 1650, and it came about like this.

After the English had chopped off the head of Charles I, they fell out with their Scots allies, for the Scots were still anxious for a monarch, provided the monarch agreed to abide by parliamentary rule. The Scots therefore invited the heir to the throne, later Charles II, to sign the Covenant that spelt out this agreement and come to Scotland for his Coronation. Oliver Cromwell, on the other hand, wanted no truck whatsoever with any king, let alone a Stuart, and when the Scots invited the young Charles over for his Coronation, Cromwell invaded Scotland with an army of 20,000 men, sending a message to the General Assembly of the Kirk beseeching them, 'in the bowels of Christ, to think it possible that you might be mistaken'.

To ask any politician to change his mind, let alone one who was also a Puritan divine, was a vain plea. It eventually came to blows on that often fatal day, the third of September, in the year 1650. When the Scots Army, under the old warrior David Leslie, met the Ironsides at Dunbar, it looked likely that Cromwell would suffer his first defeat, for the English were heavily outnumbered and very far from home.

However, there have been few armies in the history of the world like the New Model Army, a stout-hearted body of soldiers, strong in discipline and fearing the Lord. Cromwell flayed the Scots with artillery, broke their front with cavalry, and sent in his infantry to finish the fight with sword, pike and musket. Three thousand Scots fell in the battle and three times that number were wounded or made prisoner.

Cromwell then ravaged the Lowlands and laid siege to Edinburgh Castle, but the Scots still crowned Charles at Scone and made him agree to the Covenant. They also hanged his stoutest supporter, the Marquis of Montrose, but Charles was not unduly worried about that or indeed about the terms of the Covenant which he totally ignored after the Restoration. For the moment, though, Cromwell had the best of it, as was his habit. In 1651 Charles led a Scots Army into England and on the following 3 September, Cromwell broke it utterly at Worcester. It would be another nine years before Charles II regained his father's throne in England, and after Worcester all the remaining Royalist strongholds in Scotland, save one, fell to Cromwell's army. The one that held out was the Bass Rock, off the coast here at Dunbar.

I had read up on the Battle of Dunbar the night before, and finding out that John Muir had been born in Dunbar was something of a bonus, for Dunbar alone is not much to write home about. It has the remains of an old castle on the point, a pair of harbours, the Old and the Victoria, each wave-whipped and littered with rocks, and a wide main street where the houses on either side are threaded with narrow alleyways or wynds. I ducked into a café to brood over the map, and found myself sharing a table and some talk with a man who had recently arrived to live in Scotland after emigrating from South Africa.

'I like it here,' he told me, 'and the weather is not half bad; in the summer it can get very warm, the golf is wonderful and the people have made me very welcome. In fact,' he went on, 'they are probably nicer to me than they are to you. There is a notice in my office that says "We support Scotland first; and then anyone who is against England." A lot of Scots people can't abide the English ... have you met any hostility on your travels?'

I had not, but then, to be honest, I had not met a great many Scots. There seem to be a great number of Sassenachs living and working in Scotland, especially in the travel and hotel industry, and as the days went by I began to notice that a Scots accent in Scotland was quite hard to hear. That said, those Scots I had met were perfectly friendly and made me welcome in a quiet, unassuming way.

This shortage of Scots on my travels did begin to bother me, but then Scotland is a large and comparatively empty country. Most of my meetings took place in the evenings, and if the Scots are not over-abundant in the countryside they are positively rare in hotels. Perhaps one of the reasons for this is that they are not very good at hotel-keeping. With certain exceptions – the Scots'-run Isle of Eriska Hotel is one which springs to mind – the Scots leave the business of running hotels to others: the English, the Americans, even the Swiss.

This could be wise. On our way back from Cape Wrath, we came across a hotel by the shores of Loch Lomond and elected to stop for the night. This was partly because our drivers, Geoff and Ginger, were tired but also because a notice on a blackboard set beside the road offered dinner, bed, breakfast and entertainment for just £20 a night; once that information had been absorbed, brakes started to squeal. This visit turned into an experience.

The hotel was one of those Scots baronial places and catered for coach parties; there was a great slew of coaches in the carpark and the dining room was full of white-haired ladies and gentlemen tucking into dinner; this was at ten past seven in the evening. If we wanted dinner, they told us at reception, we had better hurry. I then asked the porter where the bedrooms were.

'Weel, you go uppa stairs an' through the first door and then there's a wee flight o' steps an' anither door and past a mirror, througha nither door an upput —'

'Hold on,' I said. 'Why don't you pick up that case and show us where the bedrooms are?'

'Oh no,' he said, smiling. 'I don't carry cases.'

Well, someone has to prop up the reception desk or the receptionist might get bored . . . and so to dinner.

For the price, dinner was very good, and our waitress, Nora, was charming. Not very efficient but charming. She was wearing a mini-skirt and very large boots which made the floor creak as she thundered across it, and her favourite phrase was, 'Here ye are then.' Nora's big aim that night was to get to the Saturday dance and do some jigging . . . and then came Irving.

Irving, grey-haired, fifty-ish and American, wandered into the room like someone enjoying a near-death experience. He took the table next to ours and looked so stunned that we offered him a drink. Irving was from Simi Valley, California, and on a car tour of Britain. He and his lady wife had spent the previous night at Sunlaws House, 'owned by the Lord Roxbrough, you know', and were to spend the next night at Sharrow Bay, a very smart watering hole in the Lake District. Irving did not know how he had been booked into this £20 a night joint but heads would roll when he got back to Simi Valley. At this stage he had not met Nora and we waited for the encounter with anticipation.

Irving was the kind of man who was used to being greeted in restaurants by slim-hipped resting actors of uncertain gender who spoke thus:

'Good *evening*, good people. I am Mark, your table-service person for this evening and I would like to share our menu with you. For your eating pleasure our talented chef, Pierre, has first prepared a delicious *mélange* of tropical island squid and kiwi fruit, coddled in Jersey cream and lightly toasted. . . .'

You get the picture? Now enter Nora, clumping.

'Here ye are then . . . can you hurry up and order for chef's awfu' busy and I have my boyfriend inna bar . . . and the beef's aw' gone. It wasna verra good anyway.'

Irving reeled.

'Miss, miss . . . excuse me please . . . this bayzil and tomayto salad, does it have dairy products in it?'

'No, don't be daft . . . what an idea . . . it's got green bits and tommyatoes . . . it's verra good.'

Irving ordered the basil and tomato salad and it duly arrived.

'Here ye are then. . . .'

'Miss . . . this salad, what is this white stuff . . . bayzil is green and tomaytoes are red . . . what is this? Is it a dairy product?'

'I'll awa' ask chef,' said Nora.

Nora was back in a flash to say that chef said it was very good. The origins of the sauce were not revealed and Irving was still brooding over this when the dining-room door opened and Shirleen, his wife, swept in. She had been waiting in the foyer in the vain hope that the porter would carry her mound of Vuitton luggage to the Bonnie Prince Charlie suite, and was now in a very bad mood.

'Irving . . . what kinda dump is this . . . and *my God* . . .

what are you *eating*? Young lady, my husband cannot eat dairy products.'

'It's a salad,' said Nora stoutly, 'an chef says it's verra good ... or there is a wee bit of soup left. ...'

We slunk off to the bar where we were joined after ten fraught minutes by Irving and Shirleen. Irving did not drink, at least not with Shirleen around, but she asked for 'A vodka martini, straight up with a coupla' olives and a twist.' They don't do things like that on the shores of Loch Lomond and the barman said so, adding, 'Is she daft or what?'

Shirleen was in the middle of telling us that she only stayed in five-star hotels or, were they available, ten-star hotels, when the door opened and Nora came in, boots thundering on the parquet.

'Hello, Nora,' we said. 'Have a drink.'

'I'll take a pint o' cider,' said Nora. 'Are youse guys coming to the dance?'

Now I have to say that the food was eatable and the rooms perfectly adequate and you don't expect the Ritz Carlton Splendide for £20 a night, but I did form the impression that the staff at this hotel were a little vague about their duties.

All that lay in the future, but I already liked the country and felt quite at home here. All I really wanted was for the wind to drop and the weather to warm up as I went west out of Dunbar and down the hill to Belhaven Bay, the golf course and the John Muir Country Park.

John Muir is a famous man in the United States of America, one of the 'Fathers of Conservation' and the originator of the American National Park system. He was born on 21 April 1838 in a house in Dunbar High Street which has now been turned into a museum, but in 1849 the family emigrated to the United States and settled in Wisconsin where Muir grew up to be a lover of the outdoors. In 1867 he set out in an epic, 1,000-mile walk from Louisville, Kentucky, to the Gulf of Mexico, a route that might still be well worth following.

As long walks will do, that trip turned Muir into a wanderer. In the following years he walked in the Canadian Rockies, in the foothills of the Californian Sierras and, most significantly, in the Yosemite area of northern California. These were not insignificant expeditions, for this was at the time when wild Indians still roamed the mountains and the western plains. The Sioux defeated Custer at Little Big Horn in Montana in 1876 and the Apache were still making Arizona uncomfortable in the 1880s, years after the opening of America's first National Park at Yellowstone.

During Muir's lifetime America began to change from a wilderness into the great industrial nation it is today, and by 1889 Muir had joined forces with a journalist, Robert Underwood, in a campaign to save some of the California wilderness before it was all gone.

This campaign did not make these men over-popular with the local ranchers, sheepmen and lumberjacks, but they persevered in spite of local hostility, and in 1890 three National Parks were created in California: the Yosemite, the General Grant and the Sequoia. Muir did more than affect local conservation issues: in 1892 he founded the Sierra Club, which still flourishes in the vanguard of the American conservation movement. In 1903 he went and lobbied politicians in Washington, enlisting the help of Presidents Theodore Roosevelt and Taft in his campaign. By the time he died in 1914, there were National Parks in every State of the Union.

In Great Britain Muir is hardly remembered outside Dunbar and the tight circle of outdoor activists, but in America monuments and memorials to his work abound. In the United States, 21 April, his birthday, is now John

Muir Day. There is a Muir glacier in Alaska, a John Muir Trail down the Sierra Nevada in California, a Mount Muir in Wisconsin and dozens of John Muir country parks right across the land, from New York State to Oregon. In Britain there is just this one, on the outskirts of Dunbar.

The John Muir Park in Dunbar occupies eight miles of coast and about 1,700 acres of beach and marshland, which might have been teeming with birds had the tide been out or the wind a little less violent. As it was there were some oyster-catchers zooming above on their beautiful black and white wings, uttering shrill 'peet-peet' cries of protest as the wind tossed them about, and some sturdy ducks and waders strutting about at the edge of the sand. That apart, the birds, sensible creatures, were lying low and awaiting gentler weather.

Beyond Belhaven Bay the coastal path was not all that easy to follow, for the wind had piled up the tide and put most of the beach under water. However, with the help of some scrambling over rocks and a short cut through the gardens of Tyninghame House, I did well enough, being blown along fields and lanes until I reached Tantallon Castle, with the great bulk of the Bass Rock looming up offshore.

Tantallon Castle is a great, soft-pink coastal keep, the round thirteenth-century drum towers and 50 ft-high curtain walls much eroded by wind and weather. It belonged to the Earls of Douglas, who held it for three centuries until Oliver Cromwell came north to fight the Scots at Dunbar and deployed his cannon against the walls.

The Bass Rock, a mile out to sea, is a great, solid, bulk of an island, 350 feet high, protected by seemingly sheer cliffs, and a nesting place for seabirds, especially gannets, or the 'solan goose' as the locals call it, puffins, guillemots and fulmars. On a soft day it is possible to take a boat out to the Bass Rock, and even go ashore for a spot of birdwatching, but today, with great waves breaking on the foot of the cliffs, this trip was not an option.

The Bass Rock has played a long role in Scottish history, as a fortress and a prison and before that as a hermitage. The hermit was St Baldred, who had a cell on the island where he lived until his death in AD606. The Rock later came into the hands of the Lauder family who held it from about 1316 until 1671 when it became a prison, and a grim one. As I have already related, it had its most significant hour when it was twice the last place in Britain to hold out for the Stuarts, first against Cromwell's ever-victorious army and then against the troops of William of Orange.

It happened like this. After the execution of Charles I in 1649, the Civil War continued in Scotland, where the Marquis of Montrose was still in arms for the King – or for his successor, Charles II. Montrose returned to France from Denmark in 1650, was defeated by a Lowland army, captured by the Macleods in Assynt, a place through which I would be passing, sold to the Government and executed.

After his trouncing at Worcester, Charles fled to France via the oak tree at Boscobel, and Scotland was swiftly overrun by the Parliamentary Army, with only those few Royalist troopers on the Bass Rock holding out until the spring of 1652.

Years passed, Cromwell died, and the King enjoyed his own again, but he had no legitimate heirs. On Charles II's death the Crown passed to his brother, James II, who instantly revealed the old Stuart vices of political intolerance and a denial of democracy. That remark made about the post-Revolutionary Bourbons, that 'they had learned nothing, and forgotten nothing', might have been applied with equal accuracy to the Stuarts. Even worse, King James was a practising Catholic, and the people would not have it.

The 'Glorious Revolution' of 1688 swept James II from

the throne, and the Scots clans and the Irish kerns rose again, on behalf of the Stuarts and the Catholic cause, with the usual lack of success. However, even after the defeat of King James at the Battle of the Boyne in Ireland, the surrender of Scotland and the salutary massacre of the MacDonalds at Glencoe in 1692, four Jacobite troopers continued to hold out on the Bass Rock until they were prevailed upon to capitulate in 1694, emerging from the Rock with their arms and colours and sailing to join the exiled King James in France.

Well, enough history for the moment, and enough of this latest English attempt to coerce the Scots. As always, it is the place that provides the reminder and brings the story to life. This bulky piece of territory is the last evidence we have that it is all true: there stands the Bass Rock, just off shore, grim and imposing, the sort of place that four determined men probably could defend against an army.

Leaving the Bass Rock on my right, I came round the corner of the cape and saw ahead the bulk of the North Berwick Law, another volcanic creation like the Bass Rock, and between me and the town just one of the many golf courses that line this part of the coast which were to stay with me and provide soft walking for the rest of the way into the suburbs of Edinburgh.

Golf is Scotland's national game and most successful export after whisky, but the game did not originate in Scotland. The game is supposed to have originated in Holland, where leading golf historians think it was played on the iced-over canals in winter, as early as the year 1300. Indeed there are contemporary late-medieval paintings which show people playing a game which looks remarkably like golf, using very recognisable clubs, apparently attempting to drive the ball against a stick.

The first clubs were made by bowyers, who found the golf trade a useful and profitable alternative to the declining trade in archery. The early balls were stuffed hard with feathers, and a good drive was no more than 200 yards before the gutta-percha ball was invented about 1850.

There is no mention of golf in Scotland before about 1450. Wherever it originated, though, this is where it took root and began to flourish. Records suggest that the game was well rooted here by the end of the fifteenth century, so much so that all Scots kings from James IV issued edicts against it, preferring that their people should devote any spare time to the more martial exercise of archery. In spite of such official disapproval, golf grew in popularity and not only among men: one of the spiteful charges levelled against Mary Queen of Scots – in the late 1500s – was that she was so indifferent to the murder of her husband Darnley that she played golf on the day after his death.

According to the best current statistics, Scotland can boast some 422 golf courses of which North Berwick has two, and my destination, Gullane, three, including famous Muirfield. In Scotland the game began here, along the coast of Lothian and across the Firth of Forth in the Kingdom of Fife. These are the traditional Scottish 'links' courses, strips of undulating coastal land, where smooth turf greens and fairways are split by clumps of wind-tugged grass and sandy bunkers. Right from the start, golf in Scotland was a classless game and one which appeals to all levels of society and is open to anyone big enough to swing a club.

I was skirting greens and golfers as I walked into North Berwick, looking around for a warm spot and a cup of coffee, wondering whether to make the ascent of North Berwick Law, the breezy, 600 ft volcanic outcrop that overhangs the streets of the town. In order to think this over in the warm I went into a pub and was offered a glass of toddy.

Toddy is a great Scottish drink, my grandmother's

sovereign remedy against any ills or for any celebrations. If you were fine, whisky; if you were sick, whisky. It was believed that I was a sickly child but I sometimes wonder if I simply had a chronic hangover, for a glass of toddy, a stiff half-tumblerful of whisky, hot water and honey was poured down my throat almost nightly. Where the whisky came from in wartime remains a family mystery.

Anyway, the taste of the toddy brought all that back and more. I remember one night in 1941; I cannot have been more than six years old and my grandmother came to get me from where I was sleeping under the stairs. People did that during the London blitz, because it had been noticed that even if a house was bombed and destroyed, the stairs often remained standing. She took me to a window near the top of the house and from there we could see the sky over London. It was a terrible sight, the night sky deep-red with flames, from one end of the horizon to the other. The East End and the London docks had been set ablaze by the German Luftwaffe, and God knows how many people were dying in those fires.

'Take a look at that,' said my grandmother, 'and don't you ever forget it.' Over fifty years later I can still see it, recall the shock and taste the sip of whisky we had with our tea in the kitchen afterwards. Tastes are very evocative and the taste of toddy brought it all back.

On this journey in 1994 I could have celebrated the creation of malt whisky, an elixir created exactly 500 years ago, in 1494, when James IV of Scotland ordered a monk, Friar John Cor, to distil the spirit we now know as whisky; the ingredients of Highland water, barley and yeast have not changed and nor have the oak casks so necessary for the maturing of the Right Stuff. Whisky does not age in the bottle and the Right Stuff might spend 10, 12 or even 15 years in cask before it is bottled and sold. Most whisky sold today is a blend, but I prefer single malts and so do most people with any sense at all.

I could have stayed on in that warm bar and had a few more toddies before getting full enough to climb up Berwick Law, but in the end I decided that if the wind could freeze me in the streets, it would paralyse me on the top of the hill and I would do better to press on to Gullane. Besides, there would be other, mightier mountains to climb as I made my way further north. The Law is not as big as it was, anyway, for the stone of the hill was quarried away to build the town. The Law is crowned by a whale's jaw bone, the latest of several that have stood on the top; the first set went up in 1709, the present set in 1936.

Berwick calls itself the 'Biarritz of the North', which seemed a considerable conceit when I arrived, if only because of the weather. However, having warmed up a bit in the Tourist Office, I began to get the point, for North Berwick, like Biarritz, has been a favourite place with kings. Robert II of Scotland gave the town a charter in 1373, all the other monarchs enjoyed visiting the town, and Charles I of England, who was born in Scotland, lived in Berwick when he was trying to buy the Bass Rock from the Lauder family.

One sight not to be missed in Berwick is the Auld Kirk by the harbour. There is not a lot of it left but what remains has some tales to tell. The church was the resting place of the Lauders, but is noted as the place to which the Earl of Bothwell summoned the witches of Scotland and urged them to conjure up gales to drown James VI on his voyage home from Denmark. The story goes that Bothwell appeared at this coven, disguised as the Devil, and to seal the bargain the witches hurried forward to kiss his buttocks, which he suspended over the pulpit. After all this, however, the spells still failed to work. The King sailed home on smooth seas, but when he heard of this ill-meant event it began his lifelong detestation of witches and witchcraft that saw many a poor old woman condemned to be hanged or burnt.

The fishing and excursion boats were sensibly staying in harbour on this breezy morning, but the lifeboat station was open to view and manned by the secretary, Len Groom, who ushered me in, helped me off with the rucksack, grunted gratifyingly about the weight of it, and gave me a tour of the station.

The North Berwick station has an inshore lifeboat, a large inflatable dinghy, ideal for operating in the shallow, rock-strewn waters of the Firth of Forth. In the previous year the boat had been launched 23 times and saved six people in imminent danger of death, and a good many others who were heading in that direction.

'We can go out in a Force Seven, maybe a Force Eight – that's gale force – if the wind is in the right direction. We don't count the ones that are just daft or getting into trouble', said Len. 'We only count the ones who are in a really bad way by the time we get there and would die if we didn't. It's not stupidity that gets people into trouble but carelessness. Highly intelligent people make the most daft mistakes when they get on the sea. They'll take boats out in poor weather, without checking the hull or the engine, without paddles or lifejackets or flares. We have people who go out and get stuck on a rock because they forget that the tides come in and go out, and youngsters who fool about in rubber dinghies or on airbeds and suddenly they are a mile offshore and heading for Norway. So we launch the boat and bring them back, but I can't tell you how many or who they are. Quite often, we fetch someone back and by the time we have recovered the boat and got organised, they have cleared off. It's not often they even stop to say "thank you". They are probably embarrassed about the trouble they've caused, but they shouldn't be; in a way it's what we are here for and we are happy to do it.

'We don't have many fishermen or seamen in the boat these days. If we had to rely on finding seamen we would never get to sea at all. The present cox'n is a schoolmaster. Among the dozen or so we have on regular standby are a joiner, a plumber, the landlord of the Auld Hoose Hotel, the caddymaster at Gullane Golf Club, a plasterer, and the local manager for the Scottish Widows Insurance Company – it's no trouble manning the boat.'

It never is any trouble manning the boat, and I think that is rather wonderful. The Royal National Lifeboat Institution is one of Britain's most popular charities, and, apart from a mechanic who looks after the boat, all the crew are local volunteers, ordinary men who quite often do the most extraordinary things, not least by going to sea when sensible people are staying indoors and worrying about the roof slates. Nobody forces them to do this; they do it from a sense of duty, because they are pledged to.

I once met a taxi driver in Cornwall, a member of the local lifeboat crew. After he had told me about a few very hairy rescues on that iron-girt coast, I asked him why he did it, what made him dash to the lifeboat slip when the maroon went off? It took him quite a time to think of an answer and the best he could manage was, 'Well, you have to go, don't you; it would be a terrible thing to have someone in trouble and not do anything about it. I don't think about it really – but I think it's a bit of an honour, being in the crew of a lifeboat.'

The lifeboat service, the RNLI, was found in 1824 by Sir William Hillary and has since saved more than 125,000 lives around the British coasts alone, not counting all those who are pulled back from the brink of disaster and are not included in this total.

There were lifeboats before the RNLI was formed: the first lifeboat station was established at Formby Head in Lancashire as early as 1770, and the first proper lifeboat, aptly named *The Original*, a craft specially designed for sea rescue, was stationed at South Shields from 1789. There are now lifeboat stations all round the coast of Britain and Ireland and, without them and these marvellous, modest, local volunteers, life at sea around these islands would be far more hazardous than it is.

There is another advantage for the foot-powered traveller: the chance to meet and talk to local people. Travel by car and you miss a lot, and just by being in a car you erect a barrier between yourself and the people you meet or might meet. Go on foot and you have time to stop, and are far more readily accepted, and barriers that might exist simply don't appear. I had a good chat with Len in the lifeboat station, then heaved on my pack again and set off back through the town, heading for my nightstop at Gullane.

North Berwick today is a holiday resort, and has been since Victorian times, when the golf courses and the beaches first began to attract the good people of Edinburgh. I made my way between these two attractions, towards Gullane, past the island of Fidra, one of a number of islands, skerries and isolated rocks which litter the seas offshore, many of them with curious or romantic names. There is the Dog, and the Lamb Rock, the Law Rocks and, along the coast itself, the Hummel Ridges and the Bubbly Buss, but the largest of the offshore islands is Fidra, a rocky promontory where the eider ducks come to breed. The name is Norse and means 'Feather Island' but according to the local people Fidra is supposed to have given Robert Louis Stevenson his idea for *Treasure Island*.

I think this unlikely. Stevenson certainly knew this part of the Lothian coast for he was born and grew up in Edinburgh, and Gullane sands appear in *Catriona*, his far less successful sequel to *Kidnapped*, but the idea for *Treasure Island* has a less physical origin than the rocks of

Fidra and for this we have the word of Robert Louis Stevenson himself.

Indeed, Stevenson wrote an essay on the subject that any writer would appreciate and enjoy reading, for it begins with the grim fact that although Louis – as he was usually called – had written a good number of works before *Treasure Island*, it was always referred to as his first book.

> By that time, when I was 31, I had written little books and little essays and short stories and been patted on the back and paid for them, though never quite enough to live upon. I had quite a reputation. I was a successful man yet it made my cheeks burn to think that I should spend a man's energy upon this business and yet could not earn a livelihood.

Amen to that.

When Stevenson came to write *Treasure Island*, he was staying with his parents near Pitlochry, a good way from the Firth of Forth. Also in the house was a schoolboy staying for the summer holidays, and Stevenson and the boy would draw together until, says Stevenson, 'one of the rooms was like a picture gallery'. On one of these artistic occasions they drew the map of an island, the shape of which took Stevenson's fancy 'beyond expression', and having coloured it in, he took up his pen and named it 'Treasure Island'.

Then it seemed to him that, as he studied the map, faces began to appear; men with brown skin, brass earrings and tarry pigtails, one-eyed men with bright cutlasses to hand, and a one-legged seadog with a parrot on his shoulder. He saw a ship in the sound and waves on the reef and as his imagination soared he heard the seaman's parrot screeching 'Pieces of Eight!' and a capstan chorus singing:

Fifteen men on the dead man's chest,
Yo, ho, HO and a bottle of rum,
Drink and the devil have done for the rest
Yo, ho, HO and a bottle of rum!

as they pushed and pulled on the capstan bars . . . and so a great classic was born.

Stevenson sat down to write 'The Sea Cook' as the book was first called, one dreary morning in September, and records that he never before or afterwards sat down to write with such complacency. He wrote fast, 15 chapters in 15 days with hardly a pause for thought . . . and then he ran right out of steam.

The proofs of the first chapters were already awaiting correction and his mind was a blank. It took a week or two and a trip to Davos, where he went often to repair the ravages of tuberculosis in his lungs, before he felt the story flowing back. Then, and at the same pace of a chapter a day, he finished it.

There remained the problem of the map. Stevenson had written the story around the map, which plays a major role in the plot, and the map was vital. However, when the time came for the book to appear he sent the manuscript and map to Cassell, his publisher, and the publisher lost it . . . or never received it.

Disaster. 'It is one thing,' says Stevenson, 'to draw a map at random, to set a scale in one corner and write up a story to those measurements. It is quite another to re-read the whole book and redraw a map with every allusion in the story duly replicated in the map.' It took Stevenson and his father a week or more to redraw the map. They inserted all manner of little additions, like spouting dolphins and sailing ships and the forged signatures of Billy Bones and Captain Flint, 'But somehow,' says Stevenson sadly, 'it was never "Treasure Island" to me.'

Well, that is how *Treasure Island* came to be written. I do not know what part these tales or my musings have in this story, but thinking about things like this got me over the hills and through the day. I never intended to write a book full of walking directions, which is one way of filling up a page, and the maps in this book will be an outline of the journey, no more.

To a large extent I don't plan the route on any detailed basis: I simply set out from 'A' and aim to arrive at 'B' by that evening or in a few days' time, but if I end up somewhere completely different I don't really give a damn. It is the wind and the hills and the pleasures of getting there that make it all worth while; otherwise there is no real point in it. I do know that if I keep going, and keep one eye on the map, then in a few weeks' time I shall arrive at Cape Wrath.

Anyway, by the time I had thought all that through, for I know the *Treasure Island* Story well, Fidra was hard on my starboard arm and I was running with the wind on my stern for Gullane and the considerable luxury of Greywalls Hotel, where I proposed to rest up and warm up before pressing on into Edinburgh for a day in the city.

Greywalls has three claims to fame; maybe four. The house was built by Sir Edwin Lutyens, the garden is attributed to his oft-time collaborator, Gertrude Jekyll, and the hotel backs onto the links of Muirfield. The fourth element is that the hotel is very good and very tolerant of walkers. This is more kindly than you might suppose, for walkers, by and large, are an untidy, muddy, impoverished breed, while golfers, and especially the golfers who come to Greywalls, are generally elegant, very dedicated to their sport and not short of a dollar or two.

All the golfing greats have stayed at Greywalls in their day and the greats still do: Ballesteros, Faldo, Langer and the rest all put up in this elegant watering hole during the various championship matches that take place on the nearby links, and the less proficient golfing guests make up for any excess of handicap by being very, very keen.

In fact, they can be rather too keen. I was fast asleep when the sound of golfing chat came through my window at just after seven next morning. My window looked out onto the tenth tee, so God alone knows what time these players had got up to start their round. Playing at Muirfield is not even easy, for this is one of Scotland's private courses and to play there requires special permission.

Muirfield belongs to the Honourable Company of Edinburgh Golfers, a body which is slightly more exclusive than the Vatican Council, though it has a similar attitude towards women. They are simply not recognised; women cannot be members of Muirfield, are only allowed in a small part of the clubhouse and can only play a round if accompanied by their menfolk. How the members get away with it in this day and age beats me, but this is Scotland after all, where the old ways hang on and even flourish.

The Honourable Company of Edinburgh Golfers – there's a splendid title for you – was founded in 1744, about 300 years after golf arrived in Scotland, but it is not the oldest golf club in the world. That honour – curses – belongs to a Sassenach institution, the Royal Blackheath, founded as early as 1608, but then the English were always very clubable. On the other hand, the Royal Blackheath did little to advance the game, and it was left to the Honourable Company of Edinburgh Golfers to lay down the first Rules of Golf, a set of 13 instructions which are still more or less in place throughout the world today.

Take Rule 5, for example: 'If your ball carries among watters or wattery filth, you are at liberty to take your ball, allowing your adversary one stroke'. Rule 12 states: 'He whose ball lies furthest from the hole is obliged to play first' – a rule which answers one question that has faintly puzzled me for years while watching championship golf from my comfortable seat on the sofa.

Rule 13, on the other hand, seems to apply to the hazards that awaited golfers at Muirfield: 'Neither trench nor dyke nor soldiers' hides nor soldiers' lines shall be accounted a hazard.'

One way to avoid such hazards is to consult the caddy, which the golfers outside my window were now doing at some length. Caddies, who carry the clubs and are full of sound advice on club and direction and, of course, hazards, were another Scottish invention and have been around for a long time, but there are arguments about the origin of the name and how they came to the golf courses.

The polite version says that it comes from the French word 'cadet'. Another version gives it a low-life origin as the eighteenth-century name for the men who hung about the Mercat Cross in Edinburgh where, said a contemporary guide, if you need 'a pimp, a valet, a thief-catcher or a bully-boy, your last resort is to the fraternity of caddies' – hence also the origin of the word 'cad'.

Well, all that has changed as well. Caddies are no longer gnarled old curmudgeonly men, humping clubs for the gentry in hope of a tip. A caddy is an essential element in the champion golfer's team; many top-class caddies are women, and a good caddie today can easily earn £100,000 a year.

I listened to the golfing advice outside my window until I was fully awake. Then I got up and went in to breakfast well before eight in the morning to find the dining room empty and all the golfers gone to the links. My grandmother used to call the time after dawn the 'best time o' the day', but, as I get older, 'I hae me doots.' At least it gave me an early start on the road to Edinburgh.

5

Around Auld Reekie

Coming to the top of a hill, I saw the country fall
away before me down to the sea; and in the midst
of this, the city of Edinburgh, smoking like a
kiln.

Robert Louis Stevenson, *Kidnapped*, 1886

Over the last ten years I have had my fill of walking
through the industrial suburbs of our major cities. I have
trailed for many weary miles through the secondhand car
lots and supermarkets that surround the provincial towns
of France and flogged for hours past factories and carparks
towards the Centro Cuidads of Spain. Whatever the every-
step-of-the-way purists say, I am not going to do it any
more. When the countryside gives out, I give up and take
a bus to the far side of town, and any sensible walker will
do the same.

I used to feel very guilty about this. When I walked
across France I walked every metre of the way, flogging on
in the rain through Tours and Le Mans. Two years later,
trudging past a chemical works near Valladolid, I suddenly
thought, 'This is crazy. No one in their right mind would
devote half a day to walking through an industrial waste-

land.' After that I became more sensible and felt much better.

When I plan a route, by laying out a line on the map which I hope to follow, it invariably leads me through a major town or two. This is often a bonus, for towns have things I can write about, and in the case of Edinburgh a visit was not solely dictated by my route. To get the hang of Scotland's history without a visit to Edinburgh is virtually impossible, for much of Scotland's past and bustling present is concentrated within the boundaries of that fine city.

Besides, after a week on the trail, I was beginning to need a day off. This was because my legs and feet were telling me that they had endured enough punishment for the moment and also because I have never really had the chance to look around Edinburgh, although I must have been there half a dozen times. I therefore put on my comfortable trainers, said an early farewell to Gullane and walked down into the village, where the golf courses astride the main road were already full of players. From there I caught the bus for the half-hour ride along the Firth of Forth to the top of Princes Street in Edinburgh. Once there, I decanted my rucksack into the helpful arms of a porter at the King James Hotel and set out to see the city, 'Auld Reekie', Scotland's capital and a very fine city indeed.

Stevenson explains that the origins of the name 'Auld Reekie' refer to the coal smoke that poured from the chimneys, but that is now a worn-out nickname for this once-grimy capital. Edinburgh has been scraped free from centuries of soot, and stood glittering in the sunshine on this bright, cold, spring morning. Princes Street is a boulevard to rank with the Champs-Elysées, and the man who decided to leave one side of Princes Street free from shops and buildings was a genius. That decision leaves open a wonderful view to the castle across the Nor' Loch, that great ditch between the old town and the new city, which was once a swamp but is now filled with Waverley Station and the railway line as well as many memorials and the public gardens. Seen from the pavements of Princes Street the castle stood out against the blue sky, the grassy slopes below the fortress covered with a golden carpet of daffodils. The capital of my native land was looking its splendid best.

Edinburgh is quite a small city in terms of population, containing just over half a million people, but it does not seem small. Edinburgh can be divided into two parts, the Old Town between the castle and Holyroodhouse and the late-eighteenth-century New Town behind Princes Street, designed by James Craig, a place of wide streets and elegant squares, a great gulp of architectural fresh air after the confines and stinks of the cramped medieval city across the Nor' Loch. There is a lot to see and do in Edinburgh and I could only hope to see some of it in the course of one day but if I could get a grip on this city and learn a little of its past, I would have achieved something.

Fortunately, the historic centre of Edinburgh in the streets below the castle can easily be covered on foot in the space of a few hours, and I began by taking a good look at it from the North Bridge by Waverley Station. This spans the Nor' Loch valley, now drained but once a fetid marsh which acted as the barrier to hostile forces attacking the old town and castle. It also received the contents of the town sewers and was used as a depository for the unwise or the ungodly. Witches were tied up and cast into this noisome bog, as was a young lady foolish enough to marry a man without admitting she had false teeth; they took such things seriously at the end of the eighteenth century.

My first question was why had Edinburgh become Scotland's capital city? This question still exercises the good people of Glasgow and a glance at the map does not help. Edinburgh does not lie in the centre of the Kingdom and there have been plenty of other contenders for the title. Some, like Dunfermline, even held that title for centuries until Queen Margaret prevailed on Malcolm Canmore to shift across the Forth. Scottish kings were crowned at Scone, near Perth, and other candidates, like Stirling, were far more strategically important.

Edinburgh gained the title from a combination of circumstances. It has a useful port in the nearby town of Leith, and, if it was a fair way from the Highlands that was all to the good, for the Highlanders were often feckless and violent. The kings of Scotland and the people of Edinburgh always looked south to the Lowlands and the Border; that was the place they had to keep an eye on.

From the North Bridge it is easy to see why Edinburgh grew up where it did. Edinburgh Castle stands on a volcanic base, and the ridge on which the old city and the castle stands is a natural fortress, protected on two sides by deep valleys. The castle on its volcanic plug was the bastion at the top, the old town developing along the ridge below, right down the Royal Mile to Canongate and the Palace of Holyroodhouse.

The castle draws the eye, and I kept my eye on it as I crossed over the North Bridge and turned into Canongate and up the Royal Mile. The distance between the castle and Holyroodhouse is exactly a mile, but to the casual eye today the Royal Mile is, not to put too fine a point on it, a tourist trap. This narrow, slanting, medieval street is lined with shops selling postcards and tartan cloth and shortbread and various brands of whisky, all set in a great blaze of tartans of no particular taste. This commercial blitz tends to conceal the fact that the Royal Mile is also full of fine houses and a great deal of historic interest. A look at all that would have to wait for a moment, for the time had come to buy a kilt.

I had last worn a kilt when I was seven. My grandmother invested a great deal of money and most of the family clothing coupons – 'points' as they were called – in this treasured acquisition, but when it finally arrived from the tailor's I would not wear it. I think my grandmother and I had a serious falling out over this matter, but a market town in Wiltshire is not the best place for a young lad to sport the kilt.

On the other hand, the full Highland regalia is a splendid thing if you have the knees for it, and I pride myself that my knees are a glory to behold. If the knees are suitable, the kilt is the thing and if the price was right I intended to have one. I was soon to learn, however, that buying a kilt is a serious business and kilts do not come cheap. I chose a kilt shop in the Canongate that seemed to be more serious than most, put myself into the hands of the manager and we began to discuss the tricky business of sett, cloth and tartan before getting on to the sordid subject of price.

The first snag was that, strictly speaking, I wasn't entitled to wear the kilt at all. The Scots have the clan affinities and all that sort of thing on the record and the manager looked me up in his Kith and Kin Reference Guide and gave a gloomy verdict:

'Neillands ... aye, here ye are ... related to Newlands, a Lowland family, not a clan.'

Curses! What is this? Not a clan, forsooth? Had I spent the best years of my youth eating oatmeal, swilling whisky and learning Burns, only to be spurned at the kilt counter ... how could this be? I had nursed a vision of myself in full Highland rig, all tricked out as a Monarch of the Glen, and were this dream to be denied there would be tears.

Fortunately, this is Scotland, and, more than that, the city of Edinburgh, and even more the Royal Mile, where such a little technicality cannot stand in the way of commerce. I was promptly offered a choice of some 2,000 tartans and when further investigation into my antecedents revealed a Murray grandmother and perhaps even a McNeil connection, then my personal tartan was a possibility. The staff soon decided that the choice was wide and my bona fides were both legitimate and acceptable.

If that search had failed I could have fallen back on the general Lowland tartan or, had I been Hank H. Neillands, the Coast-to-Coast American tartan. Warming to his task, the manager showed me the Canadian tartans, one for each of the nine Canadian provinces in that Scot-infested land. There is probably a tartan for the Japanese, for the shop was full of visitors from Tokyo. The tartan has a world-wide appeal and one of my wilder memories of Uganda is seeing a pipe band, all in Stewart tartan and each soldier as black as the ace of spades, swaying past the saluting base before President Idi Amin. There are no bounds to the spread of tartan, and before long we had half a dozen brilliant bolts of cloth on the counter and I was getting really excited about the purchase.

Sanity returned over the matter of cost. According to my adviser, the kilt consumes eight yards of tartan material, and the kilt is but a part of it. Full Highland dress also requires ghillie brogues, stockings, a skean-dhu – the 'black knife' – to stick in the stocking-top for warding off the ungodly, a leather sporran and chain, a few jackets for day and evening wear, and a frilly lace jabot, plus dress shirts and assorted knick-knacks. It all sounded rather pricey, so I edged the talk round to the sordid subject of money.

'Well ... with a good cloth and decent trimmings, and bearing in mind that it's a once-in-a-lifetime purchase, for a gentleman like yourself, something over £700.'

I reeled. For a freelance writer and a Lowlander to boot, £700 is serious money.

'Mind you,' said the manager hastily, seeing a sale slipping away, 'you can pass it on to your son. ...'

Well, that settled the matter. I love my children dearly and hope they will be Scots, but both of them are girls. I settled for two tartan scarves in the Murray tartan, and slunk out of the shop, my reputation in tatters but my wallet intact.

Highland dress, as we know it today, is largely an eighteenth- and nineteenth-century confection. The kilt is derived from the *philibeg*, a long piece of woven cloth that could be wrapped around the body rather like a short toga, to form a kilt and plaid. For life in the Highlands the kilt was and is very practical: the kilt is more suited to heather-clad hills than trousers are, for there are no trouser bottoms to get wet or snag on the heather, the swing of the kilt kept clegs and biting beasties at bay and the hardy Highlander, wrapped in his plaid, could sleep anywhere and in all weathers. The first mention of tartan in Scotland came in 1538 when the Court of James V ordered a bale of 'Heland tartane' to make 'hoises for the King's Grace', which were probably 'trews' or trousers.

That said, 'modern' Highland dress certainly existed in the great days of the clans. There are paintings and portraits of the chiefs dressed in Highland finery that looks very similar to the present-day apparel, but the bulk of the Highland people wore the simpler plaid and *philibeg*, at least until it was proscribed after the 1745 rebellion, when edicts went out against the wearing of Highland dress, weapons or clan insignia. The order that 'no man shall wear the philibeg' was one rule strictly enforced by the English Redcoats who would hang anyone they caught wearing the kilt from the nearest tree. Many Highlanders transformed their kilts into short trousers or 'trews' by the simple process of cutting them in half and sewing the halves into trouser legs but the proscription against their native dress was bitterly resented by the Highlanders.

Tartan is not a Scots word – the Gaelic word for such

striped cloth is *breacan*, and there is no evidence that the Highland clans wore different and identifying tartans before the last century. Highland women dyed the cloth with natural dyes from whatever flowers and plants were available and as the fancy took them, and the clan traditions had nothing to do with it. When the proscription against tartan was lifted, many of the old dye recipes had been forgotten, and modern tartan dyes are usually produced from chemicals.

The edicts against Highland dress were eventually repealed in 1782, not least to honour the gallant soldiers in the Highland regiments who fought in the Seven Years War. It was the later Georgians and the Victorians, and in particular Sir Walter Scott, who romanticised the Highlands and the Highlander and created that Highland dress and tartan industry that flourishes today along the Royal Mile. The 2,000 assorted tartans now attributed to the 'clans' are yet another of these latter-day inventions, for in former times and up to Culloden most clans identified themselves with a sprig of wild flower, gorse or heather, worn in their bonnets, or by cockades – white for Prince Charlie, red or yellow for the Campbells who supported the Hanoverians.

Giving up the idea of a kilt, I went back to the sightseeing, turning down the Royal Mile towards Canongate and John Knox's house. Although it is unlikely that Knox ever lived there, let alone owned it, this fine late-medieval building at least serves as a reminder of that curious, influential and implacable divine who made such a mark on Scottish history.

Knox was born at Haddington in Lothian, some time in the early years of the sixteenth century, and grew up during the heady days of the Reformation. He first trained as a priest, but then fell under the influence of the reformers, and in particular under that of Scotland's great Puritan teacher, George Wishart. When Wishart was burned at the stake for heresy in 1546, Knox put together a group that retaliated by murdering the Scottish Cardinal, David Beaton, and occupying the Cardinal's castle at St Andrews. It took a force of Catholic soldiers imported from France to drive Knox and his followers out again, and Knox spent the next two years of his life as a prisoner, labouring at the oars of a French galley.

The English got Knox free again. King Henry VIII's Reformation was now in full flood and the English were interested in spreading the Anglican religion across the north, where Catholicism remained strong. Knox duly preached the new religion along the Border, from pulpits at Berwick and Newcastle, and his mission was a great success. He refused elevation to the see of Rochester, partly because he did not hold with episcopy, partly because the King's heir, Princess Mary, was a Catholic. This was a wise decision. When Mary succeeded Edward VI in 1553, many lapsed Catholics were caught and burned and Knox only evaded the fires of Smithfield by fleeing to Geneva. There he met Calvin, embraced his Puritan doctrines with fanatical fervour and brought them back to Scotland when he returned home in 1555.

Authority, other than divine authority, did not sit well with John Knox, and earthly authority was even less welcome when it was wielded by a woman. The sight of powerful women like Catherine de Medici, Mary Tudor and Mary of Guise ruling the roost in Europe produced Knox's most furious polemic, *The First Blast of the Trumpet Against the Monstrous Regiment of Women*, a tract which failed to attract much favour from two other, later, rulers, Mary, Queen of Scots and Elizabeth I of England.

Knox returned to Edinburgh and became Minister of St Giles where his pulpit became the centre for the spread of

Reformation, Puritan and Calvinistic views. Protestantism was now sweeping through Scotland below the Highland Line, and beginning to take on a uniquely Scottish form, but to secure the new religion, Knox and his colleagues needed the support of the Protestant champion, Elizabeth I of England. This was easily obtained when Mary, Queen of Scots returned to Scotland, a wilful Catholic beauty and the heir to Elizabeth's throne.

Knox's disputes with Mary, Queen of Scots, and their shouting matches between pew and pulpit, became famous in the north, and history presents Knox as a hectoring, intolerant bigot, reducing a lovely Queen to tears. The true picture of the man is rather less one-sided. Those who stood for either the Old or New religion in the latter decades of the sixteenth century were playing for high stakes with their lives and souls. In the life to come lay Heaven or Hell, but the road to that destination was barred by the axe and block or led through the martyr's fire. Mary Queen of Scots wished to restore the Catholic religion in Scotland and assert the Stuart doctrine of absolute rule, but the Scots, lay or religious, would have none of it and Knox was their spokesman.

In the end it was Mary who over-reached herself, by misjudging the temper and the wishes of her people. From the moment she returned to Scotland in 1561, she was set on the path that led her inexorably to the block at Fotheringhay Castle.

Mary was born at a difficult time. Religious wars were already tearing Europe apart, with England backing the Protestant cause and France supporting the Catholics, but religion was only a part of it. This was also a political dispute, and Scotland, as so often before, was drawn into an Ango-French quarrel.

Mary's mother, Mary of Guise, was a French princess. Her father, James V, died a week before Mary was born at

Linlithgow Palace in 1542, so the baby princess was a valuable political prize. Henry VIII wanted Mary for his son Edward VI – hence the 'Rough Wooing' of 1545 – while the French expected the Scots to support their cause and give the child Mary to a French prince. As happened all too often, the French had their way. At the age of six, but already Queen of Scots, having been crowned at Stirling when she was just nine months old, Mary went to France and duly married the Dauphin. Had he not died of syphilis in 1560 it might all have been very different.

A new king ruled in France but Mary, now 18, was still Queen of Scots and with nowhere else to go she came home to her kingdom. She had the support of the Catholic Highlands but Knox and his supporters had no time at all for this Catholic, French-educated, female monarch with her fancy train of fops and priests. In 1564, showing remarkably poor judgement, Mary married a grandchild of Henry VII of England, Henry, Lord Darnley, and by him had a son, later James I of England and VI of Scotland.

The marriage did not prosper. Darnley did not enjoy his subordinate position as the Queen's consort, and his arrogance upset the Scots lords. It was not curbed even when his wife reminded him that he had 'come to rule me, my Lord, not Scotland'. Among Darnley's many bad traits was an uncontrollable jealousy. This led to him co-operating with the Scots lords in the murder of Mary's secretary and confidant, David Riccio, who was stabbed to death in the Queen's sight in 1566. Riccio's murderers were later forgiven by Mary, at least to outward appearances, but in 1567 Mary found a new and dangerous protector in a Border lord, the Earl of Bothwell.

In 1567, Bothwell had Darnley murdered at Kirk o' Fields by the Royal Mile here in Edinburgh. Bothwell then kidnapped Mary and took her to Dunbar Castle where he first raped and then married her. The marriage, following the murder of Darnley, shocked the Scots, who swiftly put an army in the field to hunt Bothwell down. Bothwell was soon defeated and fled to Denmark where he remained in prison until his death, while the Scots imprisoned Mary in Loch Leven Castle. The lords then took away her son, Prince James, who was brought up to detest his mother.

After a year in Loch Leven Mary escaped, raised another army which was swiftly defeated and then fled for her life to the protection of her cousin, Elizabeth I of England. Elizabeth refused to meet her, and Mary stayed in captivity for another 19 years until she was involved in a conspiracy against the English Queen's life and sent to the block at Fotheringhay. She was by any standards a most unlucky lady.

Before his death in 1572, Knox had the satisfaction of knowing that the Scottish Church – the Kirk – would be established much as he had planned, without bishops, with a role for the laity in Church affairs, and a doctrine based on Scripture. He was not a nice man, but unlike Queen Mary he knew exactly what he wanted.

The old south side of Edinburgh is full of quiet, quaint corners, and in spite of an abundance of drunks is an agreeable place to wander about in, up the cobbled streets and through the wynds and closes, stopping for a look at the various historic sights and attractions. After John Knox's house, the next place to see is the great Church of St Giles, but on the way there I came across another more modern gem at Mrs Casey's sweetshop.

My grandmother would have said that Mrs Casey sold 'sweeties', but Mrs Casey does rather more than that. Everything in the Casey shop is made on the premises and nothing is bought in. There are boiled sweets and chocolates and a great range of fudge, and some of the sweeties have wonderful names. There are acid drops, of course, but also rhubarb rock, mixed boilings and toffee doodles – more than 100 different kinds in all, and sold as they should be sold, by weight, in a small paper bag called a poke. I bought a wide selection of sweeties here and they saw me a long way on my road across the Highlands.

Just a short step off the Royal Mile lies Greyfriars Church, a historic spot for several reasons. In the grave-yard lies John Gray, a man who came to fame only after his death because of his dog 'Greyfriars Bobby'. The story of 'Greyfriars Bobby', a Skye terrier, is enough to make any hardened sinner dash away the manly tear, and if the truth hardly lives up to the legend, the truth is still worth telling.

John Gray was a policeman who patrolled the wynds of the old town in the 1860s when it was the practice for all policemen to be accompanied by a dog. I would have opted for something large and ferocious like a Rottweiler but, for reasons still unknown, Gray chose a Skye terrier called Bobby and took Bobby out on his beat, where the pair soon became very popular. Sadly, though, after only two years, John Gray died and was buried in Greyfriars Churchyard. The legend began when Bobby refused to leave the grave-side after the interment.

Bobby stayed by his master's grave for the next 12 years, until he died in 1872. The faithful hound, mourning for years on his master's grave, is a wonderful tale of dog-like devotion, but it wasn't exactly like that. Greyfriars Bobby roamed all over the city and shot off for a good meal every lunchtime at a local pub, but he did indeed make his way back to the graveside every evening, and this lifelong loyalty to his dead master won the hearts of the citizens. They bought a collar to prevent Bobby being impounded as a stray; they gave him food and drink and plenty of pats and spread his fame across the world. The first sight that meets the eye in Greyfriars Churchyard today is a mem-orial erected by 'The American Lovers of Bobby'.

Greyfriars Kirk has rather more claims to fame than the legend of Greyfriars Bobby, and no history-lover can miss it. The 'National Covenant' was drawn up here in 1638 and among a number of prominent people buried in the grounds is James Douglas, Earl of Morton and Regent of Scotland, who was buried here in 1581. There is a Martyrs' Memorial to the Covenanters shot here in 1679 and a well preserved section of the Flodden Wall, a fortification erected to defend the city after the great disaster of 1513. All these are worth inspection if you are keen on such things, but the 'National Covenant' has effects which endure in Scotland to this day.

To explain that we have to go back to that tragic and irritating figure, King Charles I. Charles I believed in the Divine Right of Kings, that he was in effect God's Deputy on Earth; the details on what subsequently arose from this conviction are very complicated, but that is the gist of it. Regarding Scotland, the King wished to impose his will and changes in religious practice – in particular the use of bishops – on the Kirk and people of Scotland. Bishops had been banished from the Kirk under the Reformed religion but quietly reintroduced by James I and VI in 1610. Had King Charles been more discreet, all might have been well, but discretion was not among this King's few virtues. The last straw came when he introduced a new Service Book, banning any other Bible from the Church. The new book was used for the first time in St Giles Kirk in Edinburgh on 23 July 1637 – and all hell broke loose.

The service was conducted by the Bishop of Edinburgh, in itself a mistake, and the Bishop's first words were greeted with abuse, cries of 'No Popery' and a volley of stools from the women in the congregation. The subsequent riot had to be suppressed by the City Sheriff and the King was most displeased. Given a little common sense, King Charles would have paid more heed to the Scots' finer feelings, but the Stuart kings were never any good at compromise.

The Scots' answer to the King's decrees was the 'National Covenant', a statement of political intentions and religious convictions, dealing specifically with the new service book but then going on to restrict the King's power to impose any constitutional change in Scotland without the consent of Parliament. The Kirk was to be restored to full autonomy, the bishops sent packing, and the King must abide by that Covenant as much as anyone else. The terms of the Covenant affected Church and state and the Covenant which was signed here, in Greyfriars Church, in February 1638, had the support of the majority of the Scots population and led to a break with their Stuart monarchy. The immediate result was that most of the bishops gave up their Sees and retired to England, and the King prepared for war with his Scottish subjects – the Covenanters.

This was the 'Bishop's War' of 1639 which the King lost without a fight. Nothing was settled at the peace talks, for both King and Covenant were determined not to give an inch. The second 'Bishop's War' began in 1640, and after a few brief skirmishes again ended in victory for the Covenant. The King agreed to the abolition of the Episcopate and to the establishment of a free Scots Parliament, an act which encouraged the English 'Long Parliament' to begin its own campaign against the absolutism of the King.

Curiously enough, the terms of the National Covenant also urged the signatories 'to stand to the defence of the King's Majesty'. This the Scots might have done, even against their fellow Parliamentarians and co-worshippers in England throughout the Civil War which soon followed, but for the fact that Charles I had no intention of keeping any agreement with the common people for a second longer than he had to.

This fact being common knowledge, few people would

trust him and those who did, like the gallant Marquis of Montrose, he soon betrayed. The story of the Stuarts is complicated and I will come back to it again, but it can be said that the downfall of the House of Stuart began here, within the walls of Greyfriars Kirk in Edinburgh.

By the early afternoon I had walked a good few miles around the city and was flagging fast, but there were still some places I had to see; the Castle, and Holyroodhouse, and something of the New Town. I also had to see the Writers' Museum which contains a small but excellent exhibition covering three of Scotland's most famous sons, Sir Walter Scott, Robbie Burns and Robert Louis Stevenson.

Scott and Stevenson were born in this city of scribes, as was another of my favourites, Arthur Conan Doyle, the creator of Sherlock Holmes. Conan Doyle seems to be greatly overlooked in his birthplace, perhaps because he chose to base his fictional hero in London, though there is a bronze statue to his memory by the side of the road out to Leith.

Scott we have already met in the Borders and Stevenson we have met before and will meet again in the Highlands, but Robbie Burns must be mentioned here, for this is the only point on my journey at which he appears. Burns was born in Alloa, Ayrshire, in 1759 and spent most of his life there, dying in Dumfries of rheumatic fever in 1796, aged just 37, but he often came to Edinburgh to meet his peers and read his work to an appreciative public, and seems to have enjoyed his visits.

My grandmother was a great Burns fan, and not only on Burns' Night, that evening in January when Scots folk gather all over the world to toast 'The Immortal Memory'. She actually liked Burns' poetry, would read it aloud to anyone who would listen and taught a lot of it to me, though since it is often written in vernacular Scots and sounds best when delivered in a good Scots accent, my recitations of 'The Cottar's Saturday Night' and 'Tam o'Shanter' must have caused her some pain.

An interesting place, this museum in Edinburgh, though, having browsed around the exhibition, I began to wonder if my grandmother knew the man as well as his work. My grandmother was a strict and proper woman while Burns was very fond of the bottle and the ladies. He fathered at least two illegitimate children, and could never afford to be more than a part-time poet after he was foolishly persuaded to sign his most profitable copyrights over to his publisher, William Creech.

Byron once remarked, 'Now Barabbas ... was a publisher,' and so it was again here. Burns' expanding earnings from poetry completely disappeared into Creech's purse, and Burns was eventually forced to join the Customs Service and support his family by working as an Exciseman. He died poor but at least adequately famous, for his obituary in the *London Herald* refers to Robert Burns as 'the celebrated poet'.

If Edinburgh had little influence on Burns' work, it certainly provided Robert Louis Stevenson with the idea for one of his most enduring and horrific characters. When I walked the Robert Louis Stevenson Trail through the Cévennes in 1978, a long-distance footpath opened to commemorate the 100th anniversary of Stevenson's *Travels With a Donkey in the Cevennes*, I was surprised to discover that while the British remember Stevenson for *Treasure Island* and *Kidnapped*, the French remember him best as the author of *Dr Jekyll and Mr Hyde*.

Stevenson got the idea for this tale of split personality from an eighteenth-century Edinburgh dignitary, Deacon Brodie. By day, Brodie was a cleric, a city councillor and a man of impeccable respectability; by night he was a gambler, a thief and a cut-throat. Brodie got away with his double life for a number of years but was eventually caught and hanged from a gallows of his own design in 1788.

So to St Giles Kirk and then up the hill to the Castle. This splendid Gothic kirk is usually referred to as St Giles' Cathedral, but it has only twice served as such and then only for very short periods, I went inside for just a few moments to inspect the memorials to the Scots regiments, the Chapel of the Order of the Thistle, and that spot in the north aisle from where a woman, Jenny Gedees, hurled her stool at the Bishop of Edinburgh in 1637 and brought the entire country about the King's ears. That done, it was on up the hill to the castle.

A 'Kiltie' stood guard outside the gate, at the end of an esplanade flanked with statues and memorials including one to Earl Haig, that much-maligned Edinburgh-born commander of the British armies in France during the Great War. Edinburgh Castle is a vast, sprawling fortress dominating the city below. The first castle was built by Malcolm Canmore, but the fortress was dismantled, rebuilt, restored and remoulded constantly over the centuries, each change adding a little to the structure that looms up on the hill today, attracting the eye from every corner of the city. I took the Castle tour and then tottered on weary legs down the Castlehill, Canongate and the Royal Mile to my final stop, Holyroodhouse.

Holyroodhouse is less visited than the castle, and comes in two parts, the Palace of Holyroodhouse which is today the Royal Residence in Scotland, and Holyrood Abbey, the original foundation, which is now in ruins but, like the Border abbeys, was first endowed by King David I in the twelfth century.

As a rule I don't like guided tours, but Holyroodhouse is so full of history and interest that a guide came in handy. We went through the State Apartments and the rooms where Bonnie Prince Charlie stayed in 1745 and then went on to the place I really wanted to see, that room in the Historical Apartments where the pregnant Mary Queen of Scots was sitting on the evening of 9 March 1566 when the Scots lords came in, dragged out her secretary, David Riccio, and stabbed him to death. The lords suspected Riccio of being a Papal agent, and Mary's husband, Lord Darnley, thought that Riccio was the Queen's lover, but even by local standards this was a bloody deed. A grim spot in parts is this Palace of Holyroodhouse, but a place well worth inspection.

Mary lived here from her return to Scotland in 1561 until she was taken away by Bothwell in 1567. Bonnie Prince Charlie lived here when Edinburgh town – but not the castle – fell to the Jacobite clans in 1745, and most of the other Scots monarchs before and since have spent some time here. If you come this way, don't miss it.

Abbey and Palace are set in a large park, which contains a surprising variety of terrain, including the volcanic 823ft-high spike of Arthur's Seat. Weary as I now was, I climbed to the top of the Seat for a view of the city and the Firth of Forth, and saw far to the north the snow-capped peaks of the Highlands. That sight made me wonder what I was doing walking here in a city when I could be out there in the hills.

There is a lot to see in Edinburgh, far too much for one brief visit and I had not hoped to see it all. Had I even tried it would have taken more time than I had, or become indigestible, but I had seen enough and learned a lot in one day and now it was time to get on. To the hills I would go, across the Firth of Forth and up through Stirling and across the Highland Line into those snow-tipped peaks I had seen from the castle ramparts. . . . First though, I would have an evening in this fine city for a spot of piping, singing and dancing, spiced with haggis and whisky. Limping a little on my pavement-sore feet, I went back to the King James Hotel in great good humour, though wishing I was wearing the kilt.

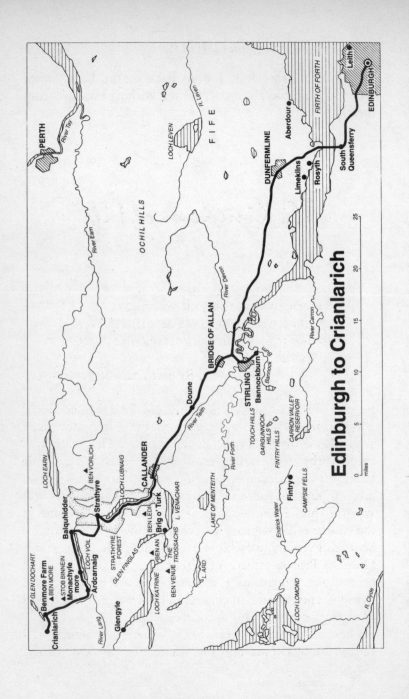

Edinburgh to Crianlarich

PERTH

River Tay

River Earn

LOCH EARN

GLEN DOCHART
Crianlarich
Benmore Farm
BEN MORE ▲
▲STOB BINNEIN
Monachyle more
Balquhidder
Ardcarnaig
LOCH VOIL
GLEN FINGLAS
STRATHYRE FOREST
Strathyre
BEN VORLICH ▲
LOCH LUBNAIG
BEN LEDI ▲
Brig o' Turk
BEN VENUE ▲
BEN AN ▲
THE TROSSACHS
LOCH KATRINE
Glengyle
River Larig
R. Clyde
LOCH LOMOND
CAMPSIE FELLS
Fintry
Endrick Water
L. ARD
LAKE OF MENTEITH
L. VENACHAR
CALLANDER
River Teith
Doune
River Forth
FINTRY HILLS
GARGUNNOCK HILLS
CARRON VALLEY RESERVOIR
TOUCH HILLS
River Carron
Bannockburn
Bannock Burn
STIRLING
BRIDGE OF ALLAN
River Devon
OCHIL HILLS
River Earn
FIFE
LOCH LEVEN
R. Leven
DUNFERMLINE
Limekilns
Rosyth
South Queensferry
Aberdour
FIRTH OF FORTH
Leith
EDINBURGH

0   5   10   15   20   25
miles

6

The Kingdom of Fife

We uncommiserate pass into the night,
From the loud banquet, and departing leave,
A tremor in men's memories, faint and sweet
And frail as music . . .

Robert Louis Stevenson

In spite of that previous statement regarding the benefits of a bus ride from the city centre to the outer suburbs, I walked out of Edinburgh next morning. This walk was inspired by vice rather than virtue. I had a terrible hangover and needed large draughts of fresh, cold air and a bit of physical exercise to persuade me that life was still worth living. These wounds, if self-inflicted, had come in the course of duty during a very enjoyable time at 'Jamie's Scottish Evening', a folklore event held at the King James Hotel by Princes Street. A night at a *ceilidh* is an essential part of any Scottish tour; this one was said to be the best in town, and the man in charge, Bill Torrance, was a friend of mine: the combination was irresistible.

I had met Bill a few years back, when I was a guest at a Burns' Night Dinner and Bill was giving the 'Ode to the Haggis'.

Fair fa' your honest sonsie face, Great Chieftan
o' the puddin race,
Aboon them a' ye tak your plaice, Painch, tripe
or thairm,
Weel are ye wordy o' a grace as long as ma arim.
The groaning trencher there ye fill, your hurdies
like a distant hill',

... and so on, right up to the ringing 'Gie her a Haggis!'

The haggis is known and feared by visitors to Scotland, though I can't think why; haggis is delicious provided you try it before learning the ingredients. Basically, a haggis is assorted entrails ground up and mixed well with herbs and oatmeal, then sewn up in a pig's stomach and boiled until done. Put like that it sounds ... macabre, but the haggis is a good, tasty dish, which comes in a number of forms.

At Mallaig, the port for Skye, I once had haggis and chips, both fried in batter. Derek Lucas, better known as 'Lou', an old Commando friend of mine, eats haggis with whisky poured over it, but then Lew would eat anything with whisky poured over it. The essential thing about the haggis is that it is both a good dish and an important element in Scots folklore. Visitors should not fear the haggis and cannot really ignore it, for how many puddings have been the subject of a full-blown ode? Just try it and I think you will like it.

Anyone like Bill Torrance, who can recite the 'Ode to the Haggis' with verve, panache and a straight face, has to be a man well worth knowing, and, odes apart, Bill is a mine of information on Scottish life, folklore and history. Bill's evenings here at the King James Hotel have been going on for years, attract a full house every night and are an essential part of any visit to Edinburgh. 'When I took this on', said Bill, 'it was on condition that we had the best of everything: the best dancers, the best singers, the best pipers; and that's what we have.'

He does indeed, but he left out the best whisky and hence my condition on the following day. With the evening went dinner and a lot of chat and rather a lot of the wine of the country and the singing of songs written by Harry Lauder, and a joining of hands for 'Olde Lang Syne' which I shared with a tableful of supermarket managers from Copenhagen. What the hell, I enjoyed it.

According to Bill, this evening tour of Scotland's past goes down well with visitors of every nationality, though his exchanges with the audience can be somewhat perilous.

> *Bill*: Mary Cameron will now sing 'Sail Bonnie Boat, like a bird on the wing, Over the Sea to Skye'.... Does anyone in the audience know the name of the gallant lady who helped Bonnie Prince Charlie on Skye?
> *American voice from the audience*: Er ... Sir ... would that be Princess Diana?

In the course of many years spent travelling and travel writing I have become an authority on folk dancing. The most boring folk dancing in the world is either that of Ibiza or the Seychelles, but understanding the message of folk dancing or the words of foreign folk songs is never a problem. The story of all folk songs is the same. They always concern a woodcutter's daughter who is very poor and very beautiful and madly in love with a young man who is also poor, but her father, who is also poor, intends that she should marry the miller who is old and fat but horribly rich. The miller is also far too eager to get his paws on her fair white body.

Anyway (52nd verse), the poor boy goes away and

becomes a gallant soldier and makes a lot of money and comes home on a white horse but arrives too late to save her from a fate worse than death by marrying the rich old man; girls queue up to marry rich old men but why spoil a good story. Otherwise she has just drowned herself to avoid that fate, or her father has changed his mind, and they either all live happily ever after or they all die. Either way, it is terribly, terribly sad. Once you know that story, every folk dance and song in the world becomes instantly understandable.

They are singing that story all over the world, at great length and in unintelligible tongues and sometimes, just so you get the full horror of it all, they tell you the story first. I remember one evening in Dubrovnik when that tale was told – in Serbo-Croat – to an audience of mystified foreigners. When the storyteller was done, after about half an hour, and before the music began, our guide was invited to translate.

He must have been as bored as everyone else because he got up, shambled onto the stage, gestured at the young lady clutching the microphone and said, 'She's going to sing,' and sat down again.

Scots songs, if sometimes sad, are always tuneful, while Scottish dancing is a glory to behold, great fun to dance and very historic in origin. The Romans recorded seeing the Picts or Caledonians dancing round their swords, and this may be the origin of the Sword Dance. The 'Highland Fling' is said to be a hunting dance and displays the antics of the red deer. Those dancing the 'Fling' stay on the same spot, apparently because the men used to dance it standing on their shields. Bill Torrance told us of one dance, the *Sean Triubhas*, which includes a kicking step said to recall the kicking off of the hated trews after the ending of the proscription against wearing the kilt. Scottish dancing and the Highland Games were also banned after the '45 and only permitted again in the 1800s.

At least Highland dancing and singing is lively and tuneful, but I have never really understood why travellers, or at least travel writers, get sniffy about folklore events and folk dancing. Provided I am not dragged from the crowd and forced to join in, I will clap my hands and cheer and join in the chorus and admit at the end of the evening that I have actually had a very good time. One tip I will pass on is to get a table at the back of the room, unless you want to be embarrassed. As I get older I have learned the wisdom of this choice for, as one of my other friends recently remarked, 'A sure sign that you are getting old is when the stripper comes off the stage and you are the one she chooses to unhook her bra.' I would not know about that, but 'Jamie's Scottish Evening' gives the guest a rapid, two-hour tour of Scotland's history and culture as well as a lot of fun and I thoroughly enjoyed it.

I also enjoyed the Scottish food, but then I was brought up to it. My grandmother was what we used to call a 'good plain cook', and while I suppose all men remember home cooking with affection, coming to Scotland had already brought my grandmother's memory back into my mouth. Her porridge was made with salt, and so smooth that when it was poured into a plate and set you could put a spoon into it and whirl it round; with a little milk and sugar it was delicious. She was a great maker of soups, but she also had a grid-iron, a flat plate of black metal on which she would bake 'tattie scones' – potato cakes – and drop scones, which were quite wonderful. I ambled along in the rain that morning, my head throbbing, and thought fondly of my grandmother.

A day in the city of Edinburgh and a night on the town was all very well, but this revelry was getting me no nearer to the Highlands and Cape Wrath. My way now lay north across the Firth of Forth to Dunfermline and the Kingdom of Fife.

To get there I had to cross the Forth Road Bridge, one of two vast structures which now span that wide estuary, and if the railway bridge is more impressive the road bridge is not to be despised either. It also gives a wonderful view of the other, older, bridge. Tottering slightly under the weight of my pack, I made my way down to the Forth, blown along at some speed by a stiff breeze and refreshed by occasional capfuls of rain.

The wind seemed to blow even stronger as I made my way out along the pavement that runs across the road bridge, and blew so hard in the centre that I did not hear the sound of the maintenance vehicle coming up behind. This forced it to stop, but the driver was very nice about it, very proud of the bridges and, once we were into a chat, full of information about these splendid structures.

The road bridge is fairly new, opening in 1964, but the rail bridge is more than 100 years old; the first train crossed the Forth Bridge in 1890. The Forth Bridge is a wonder of Victorian engineering, and, having been put up in an age when utility was no barrier to beauty, it is also very attractive, a massive steel structure that looks like a cobweb in the sky.

The rail bridge is 1 mile and 972 yards long, except on a very hot day when the metal expands and the bridge grows up to three feet longer. On the other hand, a shower of rain adds about 100 tons to the weight; my new adviser was full of such fascinating statistics, so I asked for more and got them.

The cantilever arches span an area of 145 acres. A London Underground train could run through some of the 12ft-wide main columns, and the whole bridge is held together with over six and a half million rivets. It takes a team of painters four years to paint the Forth Bridge and the minute they have finished they start again, using 17 tons of special rust-preventing paint every time.

'We canna' paint everywhere now,' said the maintenance man. 'It's the new Health and Safety rules; They say it's too dangerous to get everywhere on the Bridge ... or so They say.' And so 'They' will go on saying until something rusts through and the Bridge falls down and then what will 'They' say?

Painting the bridge certainly looks dangerous. My friend took me out to where a party were working on the span, and hoisted high on the columns in a nylon rope cradle they were being blown about considerably by the wind. I did not really like being on the structure at all and made good speed to get off it and over to solid ground.

The road bridge is almost as imposing as its older Victorian neighbour but not quite as long, though at over one and a half miles it is almost as long as Edinburgh's Princes Street. I battled my way over against the wind and thought of stopping off at Limekilns just west of the bridge, where David Balfour and Alan Breck made their way across the Forth in *Kidnapped*. Instead I made my way directly to Dunfermline, walking past the Naval base at Rosyth. Somewhere on the way I walked off my hangover and was almost myself again when I arrived later that afternoon in the good town of Dunfermline.

Dunfermline is my sort of town, a place with a past. Dunfermline was the capital of Scotland for many centuries, being elevated to that position when Malcolm III, the one called Canmore, moved his seat to the town in the middle years of the eleventh century. It remained a principal home of Scotland's kings for the next five centuries, and the Town Council does not intend to let you forget that fact. Malcolm Canmore's wife, Margaret, a lady who died in 1093 and became a saint in 1250, has left the most abiding impression on the town, and memorials to her life and work are found everywhere.

Dunfermline contains a St Margaret's Home, a St Margaret's Well – now vanished, but the town's main water supply until the 1960s – a St Margaret's Shrine outside the East Gate to the Abbey, and a whole lot more including, beside the nearby Firth of Forth, the little port of Queensferry. This marks the spot where the Queen established a ferry so that pilgrims coming from the south could cross the river and visit the shrine of Scotland's patron saint at St Andrew's in Fife.

One of the curious things about the Kingdom of Fife is that, although it lies – just – in the Lowlands, it claims to have hosted the first-ever Highland Games which were held at Ceres in north-west Fife in 1314 to celebrate the return of the local men after the victory at Bannockburn. Whether this is true or not there have been Highland Games in Ceres every year from that time to this. Malcolm Canmore was also a devotee of the Highland Games and is credited with holding the first Games at Braemar, an event still held every year and often attended by the Royal Family.

One of the popular events is the dancing, and one of the great things about Scottish dancing is that it is often done by men and very popular in the Highland regiments; indeed, the officers are expected to take lessons and set the tone at the annual Highland balls. Hearing this recalled another of those Bisley evenings in my service days, a night which got seriously out of hand after Terry Brown and I had met a couple of Seaforth Highlander sergeants in the pub at lunchtime and invited them back to our lodge that evening.

By midnight they had not arrived, but the party was going full swing when we heard the sound of the bagpipes. The front door then burst open and a curious procession entered. It was led by the piper, followed by the two

Seaforth NCOs, a large young man clad in a string vest and kilt, and a few kilted hangers-on, all far gone in drink.

This party progressed around the room for a while, making a terrible din; then one of the Seaforth sergeants called for silence, jerked his thumb at the hulk in the string vest and kilt now occupying the centre of the floor and said: 'This is Young Rory, and he will dance with any man in this room.'

Since Young Rory looked like Goliath there was no great rush to take up this challenge. Indeed, some of us began looking around for the exit. However, the honour of the regiment demanded that someone must be sacrificed and we eventually decided that since Terry was the closest thing we had to a judo expert, he should take Young Rory on. Terry duly advanced on Rory, hooked his fingers into the string vest, planted the toe of his boot on Young Rory's stocking-tops and began to climb.

Terry had got to about Camp 2 when Young Rory stirred, plucked him loose and bowled Terry underarm the length of the room. Those of us standing at the bar just had time to leap aside as Terry slid past with a bow-wave of spilled beer and came to a shattering halt against the counter. Terry got to his feet and walked around in circles for a while until we could get him pointed in the right direction and back into the fray. Two minutes later Young Rory did it again.

This went on for some time. In fact, we all got a bit bored with it and went back to drinking with the Seaforths, everyone stepping aside as Terry hurtled past again and again. After about half an hour Terry finally managed to fell Young Rory with some cunning Japanese manoeuvre when, locked in each other's arms, they fell like a great tree onto the ping-pong table, and honour was satisfied. The Mess Steward then sobered us up with a hefty bill for damages. It remains in my memory as a bloody good evening and I still have a soft spot for the Seaforth Highlanders.

I don't know why it is that these stories keep coming back into my head. Perhaps it is because I am not meeting many Scots on this journey and the space is being filled by memories of those Scots I met and had fun with long ago. Whatever the reason they serve to remind me that the Scots have a great sense of humour and a love of music and dance. That kind of memory, plus a little history, can fill up a very long walk.

Dunfermline Abbey was established in 1128 by the saintly Margaret's son, David I, that great endower of abbeys. It contains the tomb of Robert the Bruce who, having died of leprosy, was buried here in 1329. The original Benedictine abbey was demolished during the Scottish Reformation of the 1560s, but the church is now the parish church of Dunfermline and a very splendid one with a great brass plaque covering the grave of the Bruce.

As proof that many historic tales are actually true, when the grave of the Bruce was opened in 1818 the body of the King was discovered, wrapped in sheets of lead. When these were unwound it was found that the breastbone of the skeleton inside had been sawn in two, obviously in order to remove the heart which the dying King Robert had asked his friend Sir James Douglas to take with him on pilgrimage to the Holy Land.

According to the legend, the heart of the Bruce was duly extracted and Sir James set off for Palestine, but when he got to Compostella in Spain he elected to join a local fight against the Moors. Sir James was killed in the battle, but not before throwing the King's heart on into the ranks of the infidel and plunging in after it with drawn sword. Somehow or other the heart of the Bruce came back to Scotland and now lies buried in Melrose Abbey.

Dunfermline lies in the Kingdom of Fife, a region which borders the north shore of the Forth and takes its name from a centuries-long royal connection. Charles I, the last monarch to be born in Scotland, was born in Dunfermline, and that grim figure, the Earl of Morton, lived at Aberdour Castle just to the east of the Bridge. Had I pressed on north from the crossing point I would have come quickly to Inverkeithing, which is one of the oldest burghs in Scotland. The Kingdom of Fife is full of history, but a lot of it is concentrated here in Dunfermline, a good place to continue the story of Scotland's kings because Malcolm Canmore and his wife Margaret were both buried in Dunfermline.

Canmore was followed by his younger brother Donald Bane, who ruled from 1093 to 1094 before being briefly deposed by Canmore's heir, Duncan II. Duncan had been a hostage at the English Court of William Rufus, but on the old King Malcolm's death he was released and came north with a small army of Norman knights. Donald Bane wisely fled to the Highlands, but once the Norman horsemen went home again he returned; Duncan was swiftly murdered and King Donald was back on the throne again by the end of the year. Donald ruled until 1097 and is the last King of Scots to be buried on Iona. Then came several less well-known Scots kings and in 1124 the accession of David I, whose work we have seen along the Border.

Dunfermline did well from that royal connection, but the kings were long gone by the 1650s when the town fell on hard times. In 1715 a local weaver, James Blake, returned from working in Edinburgh where he had been employed by a company of Huguenot damask weavers exiled from France after the Revocation of the Edict of Nantes, an Act which denied French Protestants the right to practise their religion. Dunfermline already had plenty of weavers, Blake had learned how to make fine damask, and a local industry began that flourished until the Industrial Revolution put an end to hand-weaving.

Fortunately that Industrial Revolution brought the town another great benefactor, Andrew Carnegie.

I cannot be the only one who owes a debt of gratitude to Andrew Carnegie. Before the present time, when any young person with a little hard work and a modicum of intelligence can go to university, most people got their further education in the local public library. Most of these libraries were built and endowed by Andrew Carnegie of Dunfermline. He was a benefactor to several generations and his work continues.

Andrew Carnegie was born in Dunfermline in 1835. His father was a hand-loom weaver and an early victim of technological progress, for when the power loom was invented in the 1840s he could no longer find employment and was forced to emigrate with his family to America. Young Andrew was then 13 and, although he had been a bright pupil at Mr Robert Martin's Academy in Dunfermline, when the family arrived in America, he too had to go to work. He began as a 14-year-old 'bobbin boy' in the textile mills of Pennsylvania, where for a 60-hour week he received pay of exactly $1.20, about 80p in modern money. By 1850 he had increased this to $2.00 a week, about £1.40.

Young Carnegie had the Scots' love of education. In what time he could spare from work and sleep he continued to study, and by 1853 he had become private secretary to the proprietor of the Pennsylvania Railroad. He remained with the railroad until the outbreak of the American Civil War in 1861.

During the hostilities, the price of iron soared to unprecedented heights and, when the war ended in 1865, Carnegie, now 30, decided to devote his energies to the iron industry. From then on his financial and business career soared like a rocket. He built bridges and railroads and invested in the developing oil industry before turning his

Robin Neillands on West Highland Way

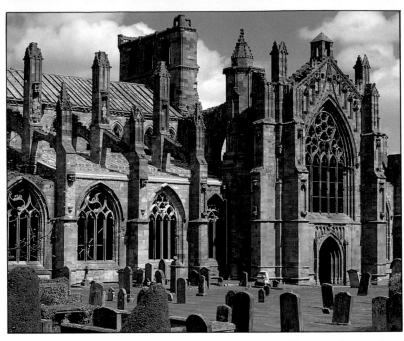

Melrose Abbey on the Borders

The Walkers: Rob, Keith, Geoff and Ginger

Loch Voil near Balquhidder

Stream crossing in the Highlands

Fleming's cairn, Rannoch

A view of Rannoch Moor

Rob on the Summit of Ben Nevis

The path to Suilven

Robin Neillands

Geoff near Cape Wrath

Geoff in Sutherland

Sandwood Bay

Arrival Cape Wrath

The Kyle of Durness

attention to the new metal – steel. By 1881 he was a multi-millionaire and by 1889 the annual profits of the Carnegie Steel Company exceeded $40 million a year – a fabulous sum for the time. In 1901 he sold his businesses to the United States Steel Corporation for a personal profit of $60 million. He then devoted himself to the implementation of his private belief, that rich men should use their wealth for the public good.

Between 1901 and his death in 1919, it is estimated that Carnegie gave away more than $350 million in public donations, particularly for the erection of public libraries, and 660 Carnegie libraries were built in Great Britain alone. Many of these are still in use, including the one at his birthplace here in Dunfermline, a town now littered with gifts and memorials donated by Carnegie to his native burgh. These include Pittencrief Park. As a boy, Carnegie had been ordered out of the Pittencrief Estate, and when he grew up and had the money he bought the estate and gave it to the town for use as a public park. A nice touch and a very satisfying gesture.

The main area of the Kingdom of Fife lies to the east of Dunfermline, and there is another interesting footpath there, the Fife Coast Path, which runs from Dunfermline to the castle at Aberdour, round Inverkeithing Bay. This is no distance and might have been fun, but I had the urge to get on with my own walk north into the Highlands.

To do that I had to get past Stirling. My route next day lay north and west from Dunfermline towards that fortress city, set around the rock above the River Forth and the battlefield of Bannockburn. My problem now was how to get there, for the most direct route was along a main road and – as you will now know – I don't like walking on roads. On the other hand, the rain was now tipping down and showed no sign of stopping. The Ochil Hills, which might have provided an enjoyable route to Stirling and lie just to the north of the road, were shrouded in mist, streaming with water and a bit off my route. There was no point in trudging along another main road in the rain and I wanted to get into the hills as fast as possible and do some proper walking. That decided, I got on a bus outside the town and went on to Stirling.

7

Stirling and the Bannockburn

As long as one hundred of us remain alive, we shall never submit to the English; it is not for honour or glory or reward that we swear this, but for liberty, which no good man gives up but with his life.

The Declaration of Arbroath, 1320

If geography alone could influence destiny, Stirling would be the capital of Scotland. A glance at any map will tell you that. Stirling lies more or less in the centre of the country, on the east-to-west axis, barring the main route from north to south, a fortress on the Highland Line along the river Forth. In other words, Stirling is a frontier town and looks like one.

South of Stirling lay the soft and prosperous Lowlands. Beyond that again lay the English Border. North of Stirling lay the Trossachs and the Grampian Mountains, and the high heather-clad country, the ancient land of the wild Gaelic Highlanders. All about the castle rock of Stirling lies the valley of the river Forth which, as Stevenson said in *Kidnapped*, 'bridles the wild Hielandman'.

Throughout history Stirling was, and to a large extent still is, the key to the country and the kingdom. At Stirling I went through the northern gateway of the Lowlands and stayed in the Highlands from there all the way to Cape Wrath passing every day through wonderful country. After passing through Stirling the grand times began.

The lock on that Highland gate is Stirling Castle, a splendid, stirring fortress, perched high on a ridge of rock above the town, overlooking that wide floodplain of the Carse of Stirling. South of the Forth and along the line of the Bannockburn stream lies the place where in 1314 King Robert the Bruce inflicted Scotland's only major reversal on the kings of England and ensured his country's independence for the next 300 years. Any visitor to Scotland must come to Stirling.

I got to Stirling on a bus and in pouring rain and I arrived in a very bad mood. I could see good walking country just off the road, and the distance from Dunfermline to Stirling would have been a good, long, day's walk, but the weather that day was ghastly.

However, by taking the bus I had gained a day to explore the town and the battlefield of Bannockburn, and when I had dumped the rucksack and emerged again from my hotel the rain had stopped. Apart from the odd shower later that day I had no rain at all for the rest of my journey. From now on it would be clear skies and sharp winds, but I had already developed an impressive tan, at least from the neck up. Scottish weather tends to be a bit on the damp side and I anticipated that my journey through the Highlands would be as wet as my passage through the lands to the south. This was not the case, and the walk from Stirling to Cape Wrath turned out to be one of the best journeys of my life.

This springtime drought was a blessing for it can rain a great deal in the Highlands, but there was, as ever, a bad fairy at the feast. It turned very, very cold and windy, and it remained like that for the next few weeks. Walkers in the Highlands have to be prepared for weather that is not only bad but very changeable, but the wind is the worst of it, blowing hard from the Arctic with nothing much to stop it cutting right through you. Within a couple of days I was on the phone to Geoff, telling him to pass on the serious news: that the wind up here was a killer, to insist that the gang bring their windproofs.

In this I spoke of what I had come to know, for I had my wonderful Sprayway windproofs and would have been in a bad way without them. All that lay ahead of me for the moment. For today I had all the historic sites of Stirling and Bannockburn to explore and a full day to do it in. For someone like me, who likes walking and history, that was just about perfect.

I began by walking out to the Bannockburn, which was not a good idea. The battlefield lies in the suburbs of the town, below the loom of the castle and I soon got lost. I do not know why it is but I get lost very easily in suburbs. Send me off on my own into the hills with a rendezvous five days later and a hundred miles away and I will arrive in the right place on the dot; turn me loose in a housing estate and you will have to come back and find me. In the end some children took pity on me and led me to the gates of the Bannockburn Heritage Centre.

The battlefield of Bannockburn is not very dramatic. There are no hills or significant physical features, while the Bannockburn is just a narrow stream, but battlefields are always interesting because simply by existing they tell you that the things you have read about in the history books are actually, or probably, true.

The battlefield is often the last piece of physical evidence we have left: the terrain, the obstacles, the rivers and hills may not have changed much over the centuries and the ground can usually be related to the old tales. This is the place where so-and-so actually fought and died, that must be the hill from where the king watched the battle. Given a little imagination – but not too much – and suddenly it all slips into place, not some long-ago and now-irrelevant story, but as a part of history, a step on the long staircase climbing from the past to the present.

This is not a question of romance. Wars and battles are not often romantic, but battlefields should evoke memories and stir your feelings, and the best of them do. A man would have to be very short on soul and totally lacking in imagination to stand on the D-Day beach at Arromanches or on the farm of La Haye Sainte at Waterloo or in one of the countless graveyards of the Somme and not feel that something terrible and significant once took place here. Battles occur when sanity runs out, and battlefields should be visited as silent witnesses to ancient tragedies.

Bannockburn takes its name from the little river that flows through here, a minor tributary of the Forth, but the battlefield itself gives little away. The issue at Bannockburn was settled by hard fighting rather than any refinement of tactic and terrain, but the story is well told in the Heritage Centre, one of many information centres I visited on my travels through Scotland, and one of the best. There is an excellent video presentation of the battle and the events leading up to it, though this did not explain why the English kings ever thought they had a right to rule in Scotland or act as the overlord of the Scottish kings.

I toured the exhibits and browsed among the books, and then I went out past the fine equestrian statue of Robert the Bruce that stands nearby. I wandered about in the long wet grass on the battlefield, thinking about the English and the Scots, and those 1,000 years of animosity that have somehow managed to link both nations together.

The conflict seems to rest on the fact that many Scots kings had Lowland origins and English connections, and when a dispute arose, especially over inheritance and succession as it did all too often, the Scots lords, when unable to agree among themselves, tended to turn to the king of England for arbitration. This might have seemed a good idea at the time but the price of arbitration was sovereignty.

The English king said, in effect, 'Yes, I will be the judge in your dispute, but only if you recognise the fact that I have the right to make a decision you will abide by. If you do that, you must accept me as your overlord.' One side or the other, in any dispute, was usually willing to agree to this condition, in hope of a favourable decision. Whether they intended to keep to the obligations of a vassal later on was quite another matter, but the more powerful English kings were determined to hold them to their word.

It was also a fact that the king of Scotland held lands in England. The kings of Scotland traditionally held the rich earldom of Huntingdon from the king of England and therefore had to do fealty for it. This act of homage caused the king of Scots as many problems and as much embarrassment as possessing the dukedom of Aquitaine caused the king of England in his relationship with the king of France – because the king of England *was* the duke of Aquitaine and, as such, a vassal of the French king.

So, when the king of Scots became the English king's vassal for Huntingdon, did he not become the king's man in all other things? A man only had one sword, so which was right? To wield it in defence of his independent Kingdom of Scotland against the invader, or remain the obedient liege man of his overlord of England? Centuries of Anglo-Scots warfare failed to answer that question.

There is not the space to go into all the problems caused

by the demands of homage in the medieval world, and the situation in Scotland is better explained by examining the events that led up to the battle here at Bannockburn. To do this we have to go back to the reign of Alexander III, one of Scotland's more successful kings. Alexander reigned from 1249 to 1286, he put a stop to the Viking raids on the north and west coasts of Scotland, and his reign closed in great prosperity. It also closed very suddenly, on a snowy night in March 1286, when the King, who had dined too well and drunk too much, rode his horse off a cliff near Aberdour in Kinghorn. This left his kingdom without a suitable heir.

To be exact there was an heir but she was just a toddler called Margaret, the Maid of Norway. The Scots Lords were not too keen on a foreign princess and a child to boot and they sent to Edward I of England to ask his advice. This was their first mistake, for Edward was little Margaret's great-uncle. He advised the Scots to send for her and get a Crown on her head as soon as possible. He then had another thought. . . .

There is always a temptation for the modern reader to regard medieval personalities as animated playing cards, who wear armour and funny hats and move stiffly as if to some pre-ordained gavotte, saying 'Verily' and 'Forsooth' and 'By my Halidom!' and not being like real people at all. If this were so the reading of history would be a boring business and the study of it lose all fascination. Think of them as people not that different from you and me, and it all becomes very interesting.

I can see the difficulty for someone without imagination, but given that minor gift the actions of people in history become fascinating and their motivation all too familiar. To put it bluntly, medieval kings usually had an eye on the main chance and their own advantage, and the Devil help anyone who got in the way. You can meet people like that in any office, and the world of politics is full of them.

What happened in Scotland is a good example. Having got the Scots to accept Margaret as their Queen, Edward then applied to the Pope for a dispensation which would allow little Margaret to marry his son, the young Prince of Wales, Edward of Caernarvon who, please note, was little Margaret's uncle.

Margaret's father, the King of Norway, actually agreed to this match and the little Princess duly sailed for Scotland. The ever-crafty King Edward's scheme then fell apart, for the little girl died of seasickness in the Orkney Islands and the whole issue of succession was open yet again.

However, King Edward had still been asked to arbitrate in this matter and there was an advantage for him in that role, not least in pressing his claim to be the Lord Paramount of Scotland. Since his ruling would be useful to any claimant, there were those who were willing to acknowledge this claim in return for his support. A number of candidates then put in a bid for the throne, and the shortlist was whittled down to just three: John Comyn, the Lord of Badenoch, a descendant of Duncan I, and two other lords, John Balliol and Robert Bruce, both of whom were distant descendants of Malcolm IV.

All these claimants came from Anglo-Norman families. Truth to tell, there was not a lot to choose between them, but the Scottish lords expressed a slight preference for Robert Bruce.

Bruce and Balliol were both willing to accept Edward I as Scotland's overlord. In November 1292, to Robert Bruce's great chagrin, John Balliol was acclaimed King of Scots and duly did homage for his crown to the King of England.

Balliol was not a great king and he did not rule long; his most lasting achievement was the founding of Balliol

College in Oxford as a centre for poor scholars from Scotland and the north. His rule in Scotland came to a swift end in 1296, when Balliol threw off his allegiance to England and concluded an alliance with France.

Edward I promptly invaded, defeated one Scots army at Berwick, then defeated another raised by Comyn, and laid siege to Edinburgh Castle, moving on after the garrison capitulated to invest Stirling and ravage the Lowlands. Balliol then surrendered and was sent prisoner to the Tower of London, and Edward returned triumphantly to the south, taking with him the sacred 'Stone of Scone' from Perth, the pillow of Jacob, on which Scotland's kings had been crowned for centuries, which now lies under the Coronation Chair in Westminster Abbey. It was not Scotland's finest hour.

While King Edward was ravaging Stirling and the Lowlands, young Robert the Bruce, now Earl of Carrick, invaded Annandale with a force of English soldiers. Giving no help whatsoever to his native land, he seized what he wanted and then made war on Comyn. Patriotism was a rare virtue in those days, and anyone who deposed Bruce's rival was Bruce's ally.

This treason did Bruce little good, at least in the short term. Edward left Scotland to be ruled by the Earl of Surrey, but Surrey did not rule in peace for long. Their great lords might have been subdued but the Scots soon stirred against the English, under the leadership of a simple Scottish knight by the name of William Wallace.

There is a lot of history in this chapter but I cannot help it. The walking will begin again soon enough in those snow-tipped hills I could now plainly see from the ramparts of Stirling Castle, but what happened hereabouts explains a lot about Scotland, and dispels some misconceptions.

The chief of these is that Scotland was always one

nation, right back through the mists of time, and largely inhabited by tartan-wearing, claymore-swinging, bagpipe-playing Highlanders. Now I was actually walking the ground, I could see that was not right. Here I was, in the early years of the fourteenth century and almost halfway up Scotland, and the Highlanders are not yet on the scene. As I was soon to discover, the Highlanders were not to play a part in Scotland's story for another 200 years, and that a brief one.

In the Middle Ages, and for a long while after it, the military and economic power of Scotland rested in the Lowlands and in the hands of men who, save a touch of accent, were not all that different from the gentle folk south of the Border. The military might of the Highlands was deployed for less than seventy years in the late seventeenth and eighteenth centuries, before it went down before the English and Lowland muskets and cannon at Culloden. The Lowlanders' hatred of the English was as nothing compared to their hatred of the Gael.

Well, we are not there yet, historically or geographically. We are in the early years of the fourteenth century and Scotland, which had been sold to the English by her lords, was about to be won back by the common people.

Wallace had a short career and ended on the mutilation block in London but he gave Scotland a breathing space, a chance to recover her nerve and realise what kind of a nation she was or wanted to be. The definition changes, but the difference now became clear: Scotland was not an English or a subject nation and never would be.

Resistance to Edward's suzerainty began almost at once, especially in Galloway, and gradually concentrated under the leadership of Wallace, the poor descendant of a Norman family who had settled near Paisley. Wallace's ragged bands were soon roving the Lowlands, hanging any Englishman they met, and in September 1297 Wallace led his forces to victory over the Earl of Surrey at the Battle of Stirling Bridge. After that triumph, Wallace became the 'Guardian of Scotland', in the absence of King John Balliol, still a prisoner in an English castle.

Wallace's victory has never been forgotten in Scotland. Robert Burns recalled Wallace when he wrote of those:

> Scots wha hae wi' Wallace bled,
> Scots, wham Bruce has afen led,
> Welcome to your gory bed,
>   Or to victorie.
> Now's the day, and now's the hour:
> See the front o' battle lour!
> See approach proud Edward's power—
>   Chains and slavery!

King Edward's power was approaching indeed. The King soon heard of Surrey's defeat and hurried home from Gascony. He then came north with a great army and, when Wallace met him at Falkirk in July 1298, the issue was decided in a few hours, the Scots defeated and Wallace gone, in flight to the mountains of the north. Gone perhaps, but his example remained, and, though King Edward ruled for some years in Scotland, his writ never reached far beyond a bowshot from his archers. In 1305 Wallace returned to the field, only to be betrayed, captured and taken to England. There he was given a travesty of a trial before being hanged, drawn and quartered at Smith-field.

I went to visit the Wallace Memorial at Stirling, flogging up the tower, a breathy climb of 246 steps, but well worth it for the great views from the top. The collection of relics inside includes Wallace's great two-handed sword and a set of sculptures showing Scotland's heroes, including Robert the Bruce, the victor of Bannockburn.

Robert Bruce made his decisive bid for the Scots throne in 1306, when he met his rival, John Comyn, for a conference at a church in Dumfries. The men fell out, one thing led to another, then the daggers came out and the upshot was that Bruce stabbed Comyn to death beside the altar.

Bruce then moved swiftly. Edward was in England, King Balliol was in prison and his rival Comyn was dead, so it was now or never. Bruce rode to Scone and five weeks later was crowned King of Scots. Edward mustered his army and came north yet again but Edward – the Hammer of the Scots – was an old man now. At the end of 1307 he died in his armour at Burgh-on-Sands on the Solway Firth, and his lands and claims passed to his son, Edward II, who was no kind of soldier at all.

The death of Edward I did not end Bruce's problems, for the English had allies in Scotland. He spent years in hiding or on the run with just a few followers, finding shelter with the Macdonalds in the Western Isles or fleeing across to the coast of Antrim in Ulster where, in a cave on the island of Rathlin, he had that memorable encounter with the spider and found the will to try, try, try again for the Scottish throne.

Whole books have been written about the Bruce and his times, but I have to get on with my walk, and the story of Bannockburn must be swiftly concluded. For this we must move on to June of the year 1314, when Edward II came north with a great army and met the Bruce's army at Bannockburn.

The Bruce gave his army's morale a considerable fillip on the evening before the battle. While making a reconnaissance between the lines, he was attacked by a heavily armoured English knight, Sir Henry de Bohun, but, riding on a small agile pony, Bruce avoided the point of Sir Henry's lance, spurred close to the knightly destrier and smashed in

Sir Henry's skull with one blow of his axe. 'I have broken the haft of my good battle axe,' the King lamented as he regained the cheering lines of the Scots Army.

The Battle of Bannockburn need not detain us long, but it was a Scottish victory, and a decisive one. The Scottish knights dispersed the English archers, the English knights were helpless before the steady advance of the Scottish *schiltrons*, and by nightfall the English Army was vanquished and Edward of England was fleeing for his life.

Bannockburn may have settled the issue but it did not end the war. Edward's northern lords continued to raid across the Border, there were periodic campaigns in Edward's name and he would not acknowledge the Bruce as King of Scots. Neither would the Pope, the ultimate overlord of all Christian kings, at least until 1320, six years after Bannockburn, when the Scots lords framed an appeal from the Scottish nation and sent it to the Vatican.

This appeal, the Declaration of Arbroath, was a flat statement of Scotland's position and the words of it ring down the centuries like a trumpet call. The Declaration begins with an account of Scotland's long history and the events surrounding the accession of their King Robert Bruce, but made it clear that their support for the Bruce was only part of it, for:

> If he should give up what he has started and make us or our land again subject to the English King or the English, we will drive him out as our enemy and a subverter of our rights, and make some other man our King.
>
> For as long as one hundred of us remain alive we will not be brought under English rule. In truth, it is not for glory, or riches, or honours that we are fighting, but for Freedom – for that alone, which no honest man gives up but with his life.

Hurrah, God-dammit, that's telling them; what a pity they don't write words like that anymore!

That was the Scots telling their King and the Pope exactly where they stood. The pale ghost of poor, forgotten, mutilated Wallace must have smiled. That was the voice of the people, rising above the self-interested claims of the mighty and ambitious. Like all splendid truths it holds true today.

Words do have a power. These words finally convinced the Pope that the Scots would not bend to the Lord Edward, whatever edicts or anathemas he might urge the Pope to put upon them. The Pope therefore ordered the English to recognise the King of Scots and the independence of the Scottish nation. This was not the judgement the English King wanted and he would not accept it, though all the other European nations, dukedoms and principalities soon followed the Papal example.

Edward II was murdered in 1327 and the Bruce followed him to the grave in 1329, leaving as heir his son David II, who was just six. In May 1328, a few months before the Bruce died, the English finally agreed to recognise the Bruce, his heirs and successors as independent rulers, renouncing all claims to sovereignty and specifically referring to the Bruce as 'the Illustrious King of Scots'. This agreement was a greater victory than Bannockburn, a final recognition that all claims of England on Scotland, claims dating back to the Norman Conquest, had finally been given up. Or had they?

That Anglo-Scots concord lasted exactly five years. Then Edward Balliol, son of that long-imprisoned and half-forgotten Prince, John Balliol, gave his oath of homage to the new English King, Edward III, and received in return an English Army with which to reclaim his father's kingdom. Then came the Scots defeats at Dupplin Moor and Homildon Hill, and the Anglo-Scots wars began again and went on for three more centuries.

I had a good morning mooching around Bannockburn and the Wallace Memorial, and then a good afternoon in Stirling, an old grey town set on and around the slopes of the hill that supports the castle. The attractions of Stirling could fill half a book, but I had three hours of them and still saw a lot. Best of all there is a Town Walk, and Stirling, like Edinburgh, is easily explored on foot.

I went first to the Church of the Holy Rude – or Rood or Cross – in St John Street, a kirk where a monarch we have yet to meet, James VI and I, was crowned King of Scots in 1567. This was the church of the City Guilds and is very well looked after. Near here lies Broad Street, site of the market and the Mercat Cross which is crowned by the statue of a unicorn known locally as 'The Puggy'; when I asked why I was told 'Because it is,' which is as good a reason as any other.

Stirling has wynds and curving narrow streets and some fine architecture like Spittals House in St John Street, where the Bruce used to lodge, and a town walk around the city walls which were erected, or re-erected, in 1545 when the Earl of Hertford came up here in the 'Rough Wooing'. This walk runs right around the walls and gives fine views to the north and over the Carse of Stirling, but one of the odd sights on Castle Hill is the old beheading stone. Now half-hidden behind a basket-like grill, this stone was used at the lopping off of a great many noble heads, including those of the Earl of Lennox and the Duke of Albany who fell out with King James I in 1425.

It is a puffing climb up to the castle but no visitor can really miss it. Stirling Castle is a medieval pile clinging grimly to a ridge of volcanic rock and still a garrison, the depot of that famous regiment, the Argyll and Sutherland Highlanders, who are currently celebrating their 250th anniversary, and their museum in the castle recalls a hundred gallant deeds. Mary Queen of Scots was crowned in the castle chapel, and the later Stuart kings often stayed here, protected by the ramparts from their outraged subjects. Stirling Castle has splendid State Rooms and grim dungeons and fine views from the battlements, and really needed more time than I had available.

If I had had more time there was a pilgrimage I could make. Before the last war, my grandmother lived in Fintry, a village in the Campsie Fells, some miles to the west of Stirling. From the castle walls and after a study of the map I could see a fine ridge walk from Stirling, right along the edge of the escarpment above the Forth, over the Touch Hills and the Gargunnock Hills and the Fintry Hills and finally down to the village on the Endrick Water. It would be a good day's walk, exactly the kind of walk I enjoy; but I did not go to Fintry. I had been there before.

My grandmother took me there just after the war, having tricked me out in my new kilt, anxious to show me off to the people she knew. That was when I learned another useful lesson for a traveller. Never go back. No one in the village remembered my grandmother. The man living in the house she had lived in was most unpleasant, Heaven knows why, and when she came away from his door, her back straight, she stood in the road, crying. She never went back after that, and I won't go back there either.

The mountains are in plain sight now, snow-tipped, challenging, a beacon calling me away towards Callander, the Trossachs and the land of Rob Roy Macgregor, and I want to get up into those hills as fast as my feet will take me. So early tomorrow I will lace up the boots and put in some miles on my path towards the Highlands. Another day at the most should get me there.

8

Across the Highland Line

I am told there are people who do not care for
maps; I find that hard to believe. The names, the
shapes of the woodland, the courses of the roads
and rivers, the prehistoric footsteps of man run
distinctly traceable up hill and down dale ...;
here is an inexhaustible fund of interest for any
man with eyes to see or a tuppenceworth of
imagination to understand with.

Robert Louis Stevenson, 1877

I set out early from Bridge of Allan on a dry, sharp, sunny
day – the first fully dry day of my trip. I could see that I was
leaving the Lowlands behind for there was Ben Vorlich up
ahead, with patches of snow on his heathery head, and
other mountains – bens – looming up on every side. I have
to say that I was very glad to see them, for while the
Lowlands has some splendid walking country and the
Borders are quite magnificent, ahead now lay some of the
finest walking country in Europe and, for me at least, a
terra incognita.

When I was reading up for this journey one of the
sentences that stuck in my mind was one which said that

134

the Highlands of Scotland were still undiscovered, un-mapped and unexplored by outsiders long after America had been opened up, when the rest of Europe had long since been turned over to pasture. It seemed unlikely at first reading but, as I read on and looked at other books, so it seemed ever more possible, for until well into the seventeenth century the Highlands of Scotland were dangerous ground, wild, virtually unexplored, the country of the clans . . . so what were these clans and how did those wild tribes last so long in the crowded continent of Europe?

Well, the first reason is that the Highlands always were and are today one of the most thinly inhabited parts of Europe. Indeed, if my experience is anything to go by, the Highlands today are emptier than they have ever been. It was usual to walk all day through the glens and never meet a soul. It was estimated at the end of the eighteenth century that the Highland glens could put about 40,000 fighting men in the field at the most, and that should have put the population at a total of about 250,000 men, women and the child born yesterday; but, since there was no census and the clans never put anything like that number in the field, no one really knows how many people lived in the Highlands in the heyday of the clans.

Whatever their various origins, and clans roots can be traced back to the Northmen, the Irish Gael and the Norman, the clan system was well-established in the Highlands by the thirteenth century and survived, virtually unchanged, until the early years of the last century: a quite remarkable longevity.

Part of the reason for this survival lies in the clan culture, which created a way of life quite different from that of the Lowland Sassenachs who lived below the Highland Line. The word 'clan' means 'family' but the clan was more like a tribe. Clan members did not all bear the same name or belong to the family of the chief. However, it was the practice for the children to be boarded out with other members of the clan so that they lived in a kind of extended family, all owing loyalty and rent – 'tack' – to the chief. With their herds of black cattle, their flocks of sheep and their fertile glens, the self-sufficient clans were by their own standards rich. Whatever else they needed they could obtain by trade or more pleasurably by raiding south into the soft farms of the Lowlands.

The Highland clansman has been presented to history as a gallant, romantic, even poetic figure, with his songs and stories and the music of the pipes, but they must have made uneasy neighbours. They were violent, dangerous, even murderous to outsiders, touchy of their honour and much given to theft and blackmail. A Lowland farmer in the seventeenth and eighteenth centuries would have felt rather like a Texan or Arizona rancher a hundred years later, awaiting the assaults of the Comanche or Apache, not knowing when the attack would come, but living with the thought of it all the time.

The chiefs were little better, and equally lawless, but most had a touch of gentility and, as the decades passed, they adapted a little to Lowland ways. A chief must have his claret and brandy, his shelf of books, his children educated, but he also had his piper and arms-bearer and his train of bodyguards, strong young men, all armed to the teeth and ready to fall on anyone who slighted their chief or his honour.

The chief had the power of life and death – or pit and gallows – the right to imprison his clansmen in a pit for sentence and hang them from his own gallows tree without reference to higher authority. Indeed, there is the story of a man sentenced to hang, and placed in the pit to await execution. When the time came, he made a lot of trouble, until his wife arrived at the edge of the pit and cried down to him, 'Angus, come awa' oot and be hanged and stop annoying the laird.'

The clan was also a military society with the chief as the commanding officer, his head tenants – tacksmen – as the officers, and the lesser tenants as the rank and file. This aspect remained to the end at Culloden, and was one reason why the Lowlanders, and the government, were always suspicious of the clans, and made numerous attempts to disarm and destroy them. The clan chiefs had access to an instant army of fit, hardy, resolute swordsmen and were quick and ready to use them; a Macdonald of Keppoch spoke for many a chief when he boasted that the value of his rent-roll was 500 fighting men.

In combating the menace of the clans the governments of the day, Scots or English, were aided by the chronic dissension between the individual clans and between the two great Highland groupings, those clans which supported the Catholics and the Stuarts – mainly the Macdonalds, Camerons, Frasers and Stewarts – and those who supported the Lowland government and the Presbyterians, most notably the Dukes of Argyll and the two great Campbell clans of Argyll and Breadalbane.

Whatever their affiliations, all Highlanders were well armed. Typically, they carried a musket and two smoothbore pistols or dags, carried on either side of the sporran. The finest pistols came from the village of Doune, which lay ahead of me now as I walked north from Stirling. For defence they carried a hide shield, or targe, and for close-quarter fighting a dagger, or dirk, and the great sharp broadsword or claymore, though some preferred the long-hafted Lochaber axe.

Thus equipped, the Highlander was a hardy soldier and an efficient fighting machine, at least on his own rough ground. His one tactic was the charge to close quarters where he would lay about him with sword and dirk. If that charge could be held, then the clansman was in trouble, for he was above all an individual fighting man, with no idea of drill or tactics or the skills and discipline that hold a battalion together.

For a clan battle rough ground was required, preferably hilly, but always with tumbled terrain to offer shelter from cannon-fire and cavalry. The lightly shod, nimble, kilt-clad Highlanders could sweep across such ground from a well-chosen position on the heights, in a screaming, sword-waving charge, then pour in a volley of musketry, throw away their muskets and pistols and close in with sword and dirk. It took a stout heart and iron discipline to make infantry stand against such tactics, and this should be remembered later when we get to the field of Culloden.

Highlanders, then, were hard and dangerous, but they were not without virtues. They were loyal, brave, kindly and hospitable, and in that at least they have not changed. They also inhabit a country of breathtaking grandeur that was drawing me on as I left the outskirts of Stirling and took the road north to Callander and the Trossachs.

From the Bridge of Allan I went across the M9, my last motorway for a few weeks, and up on the old military road that jigged about by the minor road that passed Keir House and took me to the village of Doune, past the crenellations of Doune Castle, once the home of that James Stewart who is better known to Scotsmen as the 'Bonnie Earl of Moray'. James, the 2nd Earl, was supposed to be one of the many lovers of Mary Queen of Scots, and in 1592 a party of Gordons, led by the Earl of Huntly, murdered him by Queensferry and cut his body almost to pieces.

This is a pleasant walk through rolling country and along the banks of the Teith and into the village of Doune, which lies about five miles up a green valley from Bridge of Allan. Doune was once famous for the manufacture of pistols, and most of my way there could be made in safety along the track of a dismantled railway which runs beside the road for much of the route.

In the middle of the last century, even until Dr Beeching wielded his axe on the railways in the 1960s, the Highlands must have been seamed with small railways. Their dismantled tracks run everywhere among the glens and provide a marvellous alternative to waymarked footpaths and a merciful relief from busy roads. The mountains were now looming up all around me, and the day was warm, so I had a beer in Doune and I walked on in the afternoon beside the River Teith and so to the town of Callander. That was quite far enough for one day. I had arrived at the gateway to the Trossachs and I wanted to take a look around.

Callander is a pretty place, set under the 876m-high bulk of Ben Ledi – the 'Mountain of God' – and a holiday spot with at least two claims to fame, maybe three. It is the eastern gateway to the glorious country of the Trossachs, which lie just ten miles to the west; it is the capital of Rob Roy Macgregor country, and in the 1950s and 60s it provided the setting for 'Tannochbrae' in the popular TV series, *Dr Finlay's Casebook*. Callander prefers to keep quiet about the latter incarnation, while making a great song and dance about Rob Roy Macgregor, whose life story is told in the excellently organised Rob Roy Centre in the middle of town.

Rob Roy was born in 1671 at Glengyle, a glen in the Trossachs near the head of Loch Katrine, and, whatever history has to say about him today, at the time he was referred to by his neighbours as 'the notorious robber and rebel, Rob Roy Macgregor'.

He was quick to strike with sword or pistol and soon obtained the job of guarding his neighbours' herds of black cattle. To be exact, he offered the neighbours protection from theft – if they paid him not to steal. Those who declined to pay found that their cattle tended to disappear, and this practice has credited Rob Roy with inventing the word and practice of 'blackmail'. On the other hand, perhaps Rob Roy was destined to that end, for few other courses were open to anyone called Macgregor at the end of the seventeenth century and for a hundred years thereafter.

The Macgregors were not typical Highlanders, or so it must be hoped. They were an extension of the worst and best of them, notorious for fighting and raiding, killing and looting, famed for their skills as poets, pipers and swordsmen. They raided and warred on all their neighbours and on anything resembling authority and they kept it up for generations. Sword in hand, they sallied out from their home here in the Trossachs and the Braes of Balquhidder and they kept it up until every man's hand was against them. Finally, the clan was proscribed.

In 1597 Letters of Fire and Sword were issued against the entire Macgregor clan, making all of them outlaws. This had never happened before and it led to a kind of Highland genocide. None might bear the name Macgregor, or wear their badge or shout their warcry. If more than three Macgregors were gathered together their lives were forfeit, and other clansmen were offered rewards to kill and slay them, to do away with the Macgregors, root and branch.

Their lands were taken from them and given, inevitably, to the Campbells, who profited greatly over the centuries from the ruin of other clans. This persecution did not last for a few weeks or until a pardon could be sought, but for over two hundred years. The proscription against the Macgregors was not lifted until George III repealed the Act on 22 May 1775, as part of his Government's attempt to woo more Highlanders into the ranks of the Army to fight in the war with the American colonies.

Somehow the Macgregors survived. The most famous of

them all was the one who lived hereabouts, Scotland's answer to Robin Hood: Rob Roy Macgregor. Even the locals seem to have their doubts about Rob Roy, for the exhibition at the excellent Visitor Centre in Callander is entitled 'Rob Roy – Hero or Villain?' Daniel Defoe wrote a book about him while Rob Roy was still alive and subtitled it, 'The Adventures of a Highland Rogue', and Rob Roy does not appear to have quarrelled with that description.

Rob Roy spent his life fighting or robbing anyone in reach, but his particular enemy was the Duke of Montrose. In 1712 the Duke gave Rob money to buy cattle, only to have Rob depart over the hills with the cash and never come back. The local Watch laid Rob Roy by the heels three times, and three times they saw him escape from the tolbooth and return to his old ways, stealing cattle and raiding farms. The Rob Roy Centre at Callander does not gloss over the fact that the local hero was a professional thief.

According to a leaflet produced by the Tourist Board, 'Rob Roy was brought up in the cattle business'; I expect the same thing was said about Butch Cassidy and the Sundance Kid, for Rob's business was other people's cattle. He was the son of Lieutenant-Colonel Donald Glas of Glengyle – not Macgregor, please note, for that name was not permitted – an officer who had served in the armies of Charles II. All went well enough until 1697 when a series of hard winters brought great hardship to the Highlands and Rob Roy decided to revive the family fortunes by raiding south into the Lowlands. This led to his first run-in with the law. Then came the little matter of the Duke of Montrose's money, and it was the Duke who had Rob declared an outlaw in 1713.

He remained on the run for the next seven years. During that time he is credited with fighting for the Old Pretender at Sheriffmuir in 1715, and taking part in the so-called rising of 1719, when a body of Spanish troops came to the Highlands in an attempt to rouse the clans. By 1720, though, most of Rob Roy's thefts had been forgotten or forgiven and he returned to live openly around Balquhidder. In 1725 General Wade arranged a formal pardon. Rob Roy died in 1734, having lived through the great decline of the clans, from the Glencoe massacre to the failure of the '15, and had only been twelve years in his grave when the clans went down before the English in the last great fight on Drummossie Moor.

I spent most of the afternoon mooching about Callander, poring over my maps and working out my route for the following day, when I had a long bash over the mountain to the Braes of Balquhidder. Then I fell into conversation with a couple at the hotel and was offered an evening ride around the Trossachs, at least as far as Loch Katrine, a place which I had never heard of before but is one of the scenic gems in this part of the world.

That is another of the tricks of foot-powered travel, the knack of ingratiating oneself into the cars of other people if you want to see anything that lies off the route. Asking about getting somewhere on foot won't do, for most people think in terms of driving and will say, 'It's only five minutes down the road – about four miles.' If you are on foot, four miles is an hour there and an hour back and therefore out of the question. When we rode our bikes from Istanbul to Jerusalem I can recall asking an Arab on the Jordanian frontier how long it might take to get to Amman. 'About an hour,' he said. Since I knew it was at least 40 miles away I then asked him how far it was on a bike and he had no idea. I was actually sitting on my bike when I asked the first question and I thought he might have noticed. People today think in terms of car travel and you just have to get used to it.

The Trossachs is splendid walking country, yet another area I have noted down in my book as one to return to, like the Borders and the Ochil Hills. We went along the side of Loch Venachar to Brig o' Turk, which is more or less in the middle of the Trossachs and lies close to Ben Venue and Ben A'an and that cattle-droving road that runs up into the Highlands through Glen Finglas, a route which, had I not been staying further east, would have taken me north through this splendid mountain country to the shores of Loch Voil.

This was also Macgregor country, and the signs remain: Rob Roy's birthplace is now a private house, but you can see it from the road in Glengyle, and there is a Clan Macgregor graveyard close by and another one near Portnellen by the edge of the loch. Loch Katrine tends to hide itself away, and we were just too late at the Trossachs pier to catch the evening cruise on the SS *Sir Walter Scott*, a lake steamer built at the end of the last century, a very elegant vessel which sails about Loch Katrine in the summer months. Well, no matter, the spring evenings are long in these northern parts and we took a couple of hours more about this splendid countryside before heading back for Callander and dinner.

Now came a long day's walk, my first real bash since the one up to Dunbar, and I was glad of it. The trick of a long day is an early start so I was up at seven-thirty, at the breakfast table by eight and on the road by half-past, heading at a smart clip along the old railway track towards the Falls of Leny. This was a glorious day, perhaps the best walking day of my trip so far, along the western edge of Loch Lubnaig up to Strathyre, about nine miles but easy ones on a smooth and level track. The sun shone, there was no one about, the traffic was all on the main road on the far side of the loch and the countryside was stunning. There were as yet no cars by the footpath to the

Falls of Leny so I took a look at those, a fine, spurting sight after the recent rain, and then pressed on quickly towards Strathyre.

Strathyre is just a little place but a walking centre. As I went in I met a pair of walkers who had come here down the track I must now follow, up over the hill to Glen Buckie. This was fortunate because the start of the footpath at Strathyre is just a muddy mark on the bank and not easy to find. Fortunately it soon widens out into a steep forest ride. The OS map was accurate and before long I was up and away through the forest of Strathyre, climbing steadily up the hill, happy to note that the legs were strong and the breath adequate, up and up, out of the forest and onto the ridge that looks back and down to Loch Lubnaig, a breezy spot with wonderful views.

It took an hour or so to gain the top of the ridge. Once up here the regular outlines of the forestry plantations again came in useful, for there was a roughly rectangular one on the far hillside and a farm that could only be Ballimore, and so that must be the Glen Buckie burn. There was no real point in trying to pinpoint my position on a June day like this. All I had to do was press on to the west and I must descend into the Buckie glen, but a little practice when the day is fine hones the technique for those times when the weather is bloody awful and the visibility is nil.

I find going downhill rather more difficult than going uphill, but this was one of those exhilarating days. I went down the hillside in great strides, boots sinking into the soft grass, sending a bow-wave of sheep before me until I picked up the footpath again, found the ladder over a stone wall and came out on the lane that leads north to Balquhidder. I went along the lane, swinging my stick at the dandelion clocks, on, over the bridge and up to the tiny church and ruined kirk that stands by the road at Balquhidder.

Balquhidder stands at the eastern end of Loch Voil. It is, even by Highland standards, a beautiful spot, but I went there for Rob Roy. The Braes of Balquhidder was Macgregor country, though they had to share it and fight for it against the MacLarens and the Campbells. Rob Roy put up a very good fight and died in his bed, but his sons were not all so fortunate. His youngest son, Robin Oig, who clearly followed in his father's footsteps, was hanged in Edinburgh in the 1750s for kidnapping a young lady and holding her to ransom, and when David Balfour and Alan Breck Stewart came this way in *Kidnapped* David records that the eldest son, James More Macgregor, was already awaiting trial for some other offence in Edinburgh Castle.

Well, whatever their lives, in death the Macgregors came together, and Rob Roy and his family lie buried in the kirkyard at Balquhidder, Rob Roy's gravestone bearing the defiant words 'Macgregor, in spite of them'. The little ruined kirk here is worth exploring and I put the rucksack up against a wall in the sun and roved about the gravestones of the MacLarens and Macgregors, thinking that there must be worse places to rest at the end of a vigorous life.

I had come up the glen and over the hill from Callander, about 15 miles or more as best I could tell. Now I had a problem. My immediate destination was Crianlarich, a hamlet which lies on the West Highland Line and the West Highland Way, a footpath which I hoped to follow at least as far as Glencoe. I also wanted a ride on the West Highland Line Railway because it was exactly a hundred years since the first section of the line opened to Fort William, and this was a good excuse for a newspaper feature. All I had to do now was get to Crianlarich.

There was a path over the top from Balquhidder into the valley of Loch Tay and so to Crianlarich, but that would take more time than the day had left. On the other hand, it was still only mid-afternoon and I was not tired. Besides, Loch Voil looked beautiful and if I went west along it surely there would be a way over the top further down? There is a hotel at Balquhidder and a couple of B&Bs, and I could have stayed on there, so I went to the hotel for a cup of tea and a chat with the owner who, inevitably it seems, was English.

Where are the Highlanders? Certainly they are not all that common in the Highlands, at least to the passing stranger. I had yet to meet one, and it was not for want of trying, but at least this Englishman was full of information. I could indeed go west down the glen, for there was accommodation down there and a path, a very popular path beyond that, which led over Ben More and so to Crianlarich. We unfolded the next map, and I was secretly pleased that yet another map could now be put away. We put the two maps together and saw a couple of routes over the top, both right for my purpose.

The most obvious and most direct route lay almost due north from Balquhidder, a forest track through the Kirkton glen that emerged on the tops to become a footpath and lead past some shielings down to the village of Ledcherrie in Glen Dochart, a glen between Crianlarich and Loch Tay. This was about six miles, with a mountain in between, and would take me about four hours, allowing for the fact that before too long I would start to tire. It looked a good route, and once in Glen Dochart there was yet another of those abandoned railway lines which would take me west to Crianlarich. That was about another seven miles and that was a poser, for that was too much distance in the day.

It was now about five in the evening and if the worst came to the worst I could always deploy my tent and sleep out. Otherwise I could just keep going, ever more slowly, until I could not walk any more or I arrived in Crianlarich, whichever was the sooner. But if I did not get there today, who cares? If I did not get there today, well then I would get there tomorrow.

The real reason was that I wanted to see more of the Braes of Balquhidder and this lovely country by Loch Voil, so pushing on could wait. I set off slowly west, along the shores of Loch Voil, walking into the rays of the setting sun that were turning the waters red, and an hour or so later, a bit weary but very content after a wonderful day's walk, I was sitting in the bar of the hotel at Monachyle Mhor with my nose in a pint of beer.

I had a very good evening at the Monachyle Mhor Hotel. I recommend it to anyone who is lucky enough to pass this way, through the glorious Braes of Balquhidder. The hotel is set in an eighteenth-century farmhouse just north of the road and looks out to the meeting place of Loch Voil and Loch Doine and the tumbled hills behind. The hotel's food is famous locally – the dining room was already packed when I arrived – the owner and his wife are, inevitably, English, and all the staff were young people from New Zealand. Many of these Highland hotels and hostelries are staffed in summer by young New Zealanders – I think they feel at home with all those sheep about.

There were also a number of local people, and even a couple of Highlanders, who were full of advice on local footpaths but not over-familiar with the local maps, as is usually the case. The locals already know the local area and have no need of maps and are usually quite convinced that the path you want is glaringly obvious and the fact that there is not a sign of it on the map did not faze them at all. They were also full of information on other things, like sheep.

The local shepherd, a young man in his early twenties, looked after 2,000 sheep, a mixture of Cheviot and Scots Blackface, and said that if I was at the farm down the road by about ten next morning, when he stopped by for a cup of tea he would show me the drove road up the glen to Crianlarich. He also advised me never to kill a midge … 'they are like a family; kill one and a million will come to the funeral'. So far, thank God, I had not even seen a midge.

The Monachyle Mhor is well used to walkers and I could have my breakfast at a very early hour so I stuck to my routine and was out on the road before nine. The first leg of the walk had me heading west beyond Loch Voil to the smaller Loch Doine and the River Larig, heading towards the farm beyond Ardcarnaig and my rendezvous with the shepherd. There was a constant stream of cars flooding past up the narrow road, and when I had gone a couple of miles and consulted my map again I saw the reason why. The carpark by the side of the road was full of cars from which a great many people were extracting boots and rucksacks and a great range of outdoor kit before setting off up the hill to reach the 1,174m top of Ben More and bag another Munro.

'Munro-bagging' is a great Scottish hill-sport, the sort of activity that can and often does keep a keen hillwalker busy for years. A 'Munro' is any Scottish or Irish mountain 3,000 feet high or more, and Scotland has a great many of them but, as more and more scientific means are employed to assess the heights, the number varies. There is another small complication for the hill heights are now given in metres and to the nearest metre. Therefore, a height of 914 metres for, say, Foinaven in Sutherland, means that Foin-aven might be just over 3,000 feet or just under. This urge to get it right has caused a drastic reduction in the number of Munros, but there are still more than enough to keep the walkers flooding into the hills, and before too long the number might go up again. I am anticipating letters on this point when this book appears; just try to be funny, please.

The current estimate is that there are 277 Munros in

Scotland. When Willie Shand completed his tour round all the Munros in 1968 he climbed 280 and brought a rock down from every summit to build a cairn in his garden. This is counting only the major, solitary peaks; add the outlying 914m-high ridge tops as well and the total might well exceed 500.

When Sir Hugh Munro published an article in the first edition of the *Scottish Mountaineering Club Journal* in 1891, listing 'Munro's Tables: giving all the Scottish Mountains over 3,000 ft in height,' he made the number at that time no less than 538 but soon added a qualification:

'The decision,' he wrote, 'as to what are to be considered distinct and separate mountains and what may be counted as "tops", although arrived at after careful consideration, cannot be finally insisted upon.'

Personally, I don't really think it matters. If bagging Munros gets more people into the hills and they behave sensibly I am all for having as many Munros as possible. As the doyen of Scottish hillwalkers, Tom Weir has said 'The major thing about the Munros is not the number but the enjoyment to be obtained by just being on the high tops. Just to bag them for bagging's sake is to miss a lot. After all, even Munro didn't complete them. He missed out on three.'

Sir Hugh Munro was a Scots landowner, born in London, who spent much of his life as a King's Messenger, carrying secret documents around the world. That job still left plenty of time for walking and climbing in the hills. He died in 1918, in that epidemic of Spanish 'flu which swept Europe after the Great War, but he has a splendid memorial in his Tables, though I wonder if he ever imagined what he was starting. There is now a Munro tie and a Munro dinner; some people devote their lives to bagging his Munro-qualified hills. The average time to get around the lot is about ten years, but some people do the

Scottish Munros in a couple of months. On the other hand, Tom Weir can recall two people who took 55 and 66 years respectively. On this breezy Sunday morning Sir Hugh was being remembered all over Scotland, as people set out to follow paths up to the summits he had listed long ago.

I had no intention of climbing Ben More or indeed any other Munro other than Ben Nevis. I duly met my shepherd and we had our cup of tea and another look at the map. 'There was fresh snow on the tops this morning,' he told me, 'but in the valley where you are going you will have no trouble.'

These Scottish hill farmers are remarkably kind to walkers; English farmers please note and copy. We went out and he pointed out the way, first up one of those drove roads the farmers drive up into the glens to get at their sheep and then over the top and down to the outskirts of Crianlarich. The only damn nuisance was that the path lay at the junction of several maps which had to be fitted together in the wind. Although I could have managed fine with just a compass, I always like to know where I am.

This was another good day's walk, up the drove road until it petered out, and then following the rushing burn uphill to the top, splashing over it from time to time as it cut to and fro across my path. There was more than one Munro on the way to Crianlarich with the 1165-metre Stob Binnein on my right hand offering a route to the 1,174-metre summit of Ben More. Both of these were dusted with fresh snow. Hoody crows flew about, wagtails skipped ahead over the stones of the burn. Apart from the birds there was not a sound but the soughing of the wind and outbursts of bleating from the sheep. Perfect.

I walked up the glen all day, stopping to eat my packed lunch on a sun-warmed rock, snuggled down in a hollow out of the chill wind, and came over the hill and down into Glen Dochart exactly where I intended, near Benmore

Farm. There I turned left along the road for Crianlarich.

I don't like road walking, but you will know that by now. Luckily, there was yet another disused railway line here, running between the road and the loch, so I ducked under the fence and walked along that, pushing the branches and brambles aside with my stick. I passed a ruined castle out on an island in the lake and after about half an hour saw ahead of me a railway bridge that must be the one carrying the West Highland Line to Rannoch and the north. In another few minutes I had arrived at Crianlarich and was fully in the Highlands at last. It felt good to be there, and weeks of wonderful walking lay ahead.

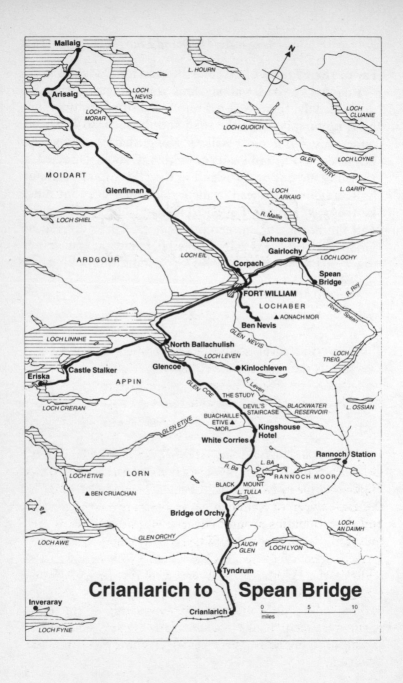

Crianlarich to Spean Bridge

0   5   10
miles

9

The Highland Way and the Highland Line

Now the shrill sound of the railway whistle breaks the stillness of Morar and Mallaig, new glories of West West Highland scenery are opened up for the insatiable tourist.

Glasgow Herald, 1901

Crianlarich is the crossroads of the Western Highlands. At Crianlarich the West Highland Way footpath and the West Highland Line railway come together; beyond Crianlarich the great sweep of Rannoch Moor opens up to the north, and the mountains around Glencoe and Fort William are only a day's march away. When you get here, you have arrived. Whenever I reach Crianlarich I feel myself to be really in the Highlands, and so it was this time. I stood outside the hotel next morning, zipping up my gaiters, sucking in lungfuls of pure air, wondering if the tearoom was open on the station platform and whether I should have breakfast there before catching the train for Tyndrum.

From Crianlarich to my next intended nightstop at the Kingshouse was a distance of at least 26 miles and probably rather more. Though the route was flat, the countryside stunning and the legs strong, that was a trifle too much for one day. The obvious intervening stop, at Bridge of Orchy, was both too close to Crianlarich and too far from Glencoe and Fort William, which I hoped to arrive at next day.

Besides, I had a commission to write an article on the West Highland Line. It seemed to me that even though I had made several trips on this most attractive railway over the years, I could not legitimately write a feature to celebrate the 100th anniversary of the line's opening in 1894 without travelling on at least part of the route. Well, that is my excuse anyway. I therefore decided to take the train up to Tyndrum and thereby lop six miles off that day's distance.

Even before Dr Beeching wielded his notorious route axe, Britain was not over-endowed with famous scenic railway lines. Britain has little to match the Canadian Pacific trip through the Rockies or that ride on the 'Ghan' to Alice Springs, or the Blue Train run from Jo'burg to Capetown, or even that rickety train-ride from Tana to Tamatave in Madagascar, all railway journeys that attract train buffs from all over the world.

Even by such standards, though, the West Highland Line, which runs from Glasgow to Mallaig and Oban, can be rightly described as one of the Great Railway Journeys of the World. To qualify for inclusion in that distinguished category a line must offer scenic beauty along the way and hellish difficulties during the construction. It also helps if those natural obstacles to laying the track have been overcome by human ingenuity and some original feats of engineering. If the line can also offer a few quirks, so much the better.

All these elements are present along the West Highland Line, but the beauty of the countryside is the constant factor: the wilds of Rannoch, the views of Loch Eil, the monument to Bonnie Prince Charlie at Glenfinnan, the famous Glenfinnan Viaduct, the views from the line at Arisaig out to the offshore islands. Walking is a grand way to see the Highlands, but the West Highland Line is not to be ignored. At just over a hundred years old, the line even has history.

The West Highland Line opened for business on Thursday 11 August, 1889, when the first engine pulled out of Queen Street Station in Glasgow and began to puff north to Fort William. That, however, was not the start of the story.

The nineteenth century was the Railway Age, a time when lots of small private companies opened up rail routes in the hope of commercial advantage, long before the creation of British Rail. These early ventures included many in Scotland, where their abandoned tracks were now proving useful on this walk. The West Highland Line was an offshoot of the North British Line, and the idea of constructing a route to the Western Highlands and Islands to provide access for sportsmen and tourists, and a route to market for the West Coast fishermen, had already been around for over fifty years. Until then, access to the Western Highlands had been on the old roads constructed by General Wade or by steamer to the West Coast ports – and this, please note, at the end of the last century.

The problems were not merely those of finance and terrain. The steamer companies and the other railway lines were worried that any new route would affect their profits. There was a rail route to Oban via Callander – I had just walked along it – and another to Inverness, but the route to Fort William and Mallaig, though still unsurveyed, was known to be difficult. Nor were the estate landowners helpful, being worried that a line would upset their rural tranquillity and disturb the grouse and red deer. The arguments went on for years, but in 1889 the first of two Railway Acts was passed, authorising the construction of the line.

They did not hang about in the Victorian Age. Four years later, the first main section of the line opened, from Glasgow to Fort William, after all manner of technical problems had been encountered and solved. One major obstacle was swampy Rannoch Moor, where the ground would not support the track. The line had to be supported by a bed of timber, laid like a giant raft; the guidebook says that the line 'floated across the Moor' and it still does, on the original trackway.

The work went on in the midge-plagued summer and the freezing winter, laying track, building stations, blasting a way across the mountains, erecting bridges, boring tunnels. More than 3,000 mainly Irish navvies were employed on the work; they had to be fed and housed, and the difficulties increased as the line forged on to the north.

The line climbs steadily from sea level to Crianlarich, where it divides, with one track heading west for the port of Oban. The line for Fort William must now cross Rannoch Moor, first skirting Glen Orchy, round the famous Horseshoe Curve and away past Loch Tulla to Rannoch Station, the most isolated spot on the line. Then it goes on across the Moor and into the Lochaber country, avoiding Glencoe but cutting round Glen Spean to Spean Bridge, round the back of Ben Nevis and down to Fort William.

Getting the line to Fort William completed the first stage of the construction, and the President of the West Highland Line, the Marquis of Tweeddale, duly joined the first passenger service to inaugurate the line in April 1894. The trainload of dignitaries was met at Fort William by the

Cameron of Lochiel and most of his clan, and the rest, as they say, is history.

Well, not quite. It took a further six years to run the line on for another 40 miles to Mallaig. On the way the navvies had to blast out another eleven tunnels, build the 1,000ft-long Glenfinnan Viaduct, and float more sections of the line over the peat bogs. The construction of the line saw the first significant use of the new wonder material, concrete, which was used by the main contractor, Robert MacAlpine, and earned him the nickname of 'Concrete Bob'. In the end the line reached Mallaig and all the effort was worth it.

As the *Glasgow Herald* records with that opening quotation, the West Highland Line opened up the West Coast of Scotland to the traveller and tourist, brought a measure of prosperity to the fishermen and crofter who could not get their produce to market, and created a marvel of engineering and a scenic route that is unparalleled in the British islands. Anyone who comes this way must take a trip on the West Highland Line, and that I now had to do.

I was in luck. There was a train up to Tyndrum at ten that morning, so I had plenty of time to sit in the station tearoom with the other walkers and have another breakfast before the train pulled in. Like many of the stations on the line, Crianlarich is not manned, but if you hang about on the platform at train-time and hold up your hand, the train will stop. On this morning there were plenty of people on the train and plenty getting off, so I heaved on the rucksack and bought a ticket from the guard. Ten minutes later I got off again at Tyndrum; had I opted to walk, that distance would have taken me about two hours. It was now half past ten in the morning and I had a good day's walk ahead, all the way to Kingshouse on the West Highland Way.

*

Scotland could support a good many more long-distance footpaths, if the powers-that-be should invoke the 'Auld Alliance' and put Scottish footpaths together on the French fashion, using them to display the historic and natural attractions of this country, providing them with an adequate number of access points and plenty of inexpensive accommodation. This has the advantage of putting money into the pockets of the local people, so helping them to stay on the land, and bringing life to small rural communities. Remote places in Scotland, England and Wales could use such encouragement.

As it is, at time of writing, Scotland has just two long-distance footpaths, the Southern Upland Way and this West Highland Way, plus one or two shorter routes that hardly qualify for the title. The West Highland Way runs from Milngavie on the outskirts of Glasgow all the way north to Fort William, a distance of 95 miles. This is a good one-week walk for a fit, well-equipped hillwalker, and one which is rightly popular. I met a lot of people who have done it and all of them raved about the trip.

The Way was Scotland's first long-distance footpath, opening in 1980 and is now one of the Great British Walks, followed by hundreds if not thousands of walkers every year; the people in the villages along the Way do very nicely from the money the walkers spend in passing. Crianlarich is about halfway, and from there to the north must surely be the most attractive section of the entire route. The scenery alone would see to that.

The Way out of Tyndrum follows a wide, clear track all the way to Bridge of Orchy, a small hamlet at the eastern foot of Glen Orchy. From there to Kingshouse it follows the old military road, one of a number of roads built across the Highlands in the 1730s to get cannon and cavalry into the mountains and overawe the clans. The latter ambition was not too successful for the clans rose up again in 1745 to fight for the Young Pretender, but the eventual outcome of Wade's work was beneficial. The General's roads make perfect walking routes while the tourist traffic howls off down the newly laid tarmac roads nearby.

According to the guide, this part of General Wade's road to Glen Orchy was built by the Buffs (3rd Foot) and Rich's Regiment, between 1750 and 1752. The roads are not very wide, about farm track width, but then they must have seemed like motorways. They were designed to be wide enough for troops of cavalry, commissary wagons and three-pounder cannon, the field artillery of the day, the kind used at Culloden.

This military road cuts across the mouth of the Auch Glen, with the Horseshoe Loop just to the east and then contours around Beinn an Dothaidh to follow the railway line through the pass to Bridge of Orchy, where it crosses the river. The Way then heads through the woods and down to Loch Tulla, the railway line veering off to the north-east, while the Way skirts the southern end of the loch, crosses the Victoria bridge and climbs up through a plantation towards the Black Mount. The wide vastness of Rannoch Moor is now unfolding to the east, like a great, red-gold carpet.

Words cannot do justice to the scenery hereabouts. Even to attempt a description risks falling into raptures, and I am not very good at lyrical descriptions anyway. I can recall one winter morning years ago, when we were encamped on the plateau above Aviemore, and Terry Brown, my Commando 'oppo', dragged me out of my sleeping bag to marvel at the view. It was just after dawn; the mountains around were covered with snow, the glens between them were thick with mist, and all of it, mist and snow, had been turned deep pink by the rising sun.

'Look at that,' raved Terry. 'It's ... it's ... what do you think of *that*?'

'Very nice,' I said.

It was nearly the end of a beautiful friendship.

'Very Nice?' shrieked Terry. 'Very *nice* . . . is that the best you can do??'

Hard words, like 'Unfeeling clod' were then hurled at my head.

'Christ!' I said feebly. 'What do you expect at five in the morning? Wordsworth?'

'You are an oaf,' said Terry.

Maybe I am, but I could rave about Rannoch. The truth is that I like moors more than mountains. Mountains make me feel hemmed in, almost claustrophobic, while the sense of space you can get on an open moor I find almost thrilling. As a compromise give me ridges – smooth, open grassy ridges – and I will walk content. Rannoch may not be the biggest moor in Scotland but scenically it must be the most splendid. It lies above the 300-metre mark and covers an area of some 60 square miles, an expanse of purple heather and golden blanket bog, ringed by mountains, seamed and silvered by threading streams, speckled with the blue waters of a hundred lochans. Rannoch is glorious in summer, but it must be hell in winter on that bleak and empty moor. . . .

I met one or two walkers over the next few miles, some clearly out for an afternoon stroll with the dog from the nearest carpark, others dressed in the full hill-bashing number, and five days or so into a trip along the Way. All conceded that May was the good month for the trip, before the midges sharpened their fangs and fell upon them. Besides, the weather today was good and looked likely to last.

'It's a canny day,' said one walker by way of greeting, and that just about summed it up. This good weather was a bonus, for it can rain more than somewhat hereabouts. The annual rainfall total on Rannoch can reach 118 inches!

After an hour or so, I crossed the Black Mount, strolling past a number of plantations and over the River Ba, with snow-capped hills nudging in to my left. The Black Mount is not much of a mountain, but in Scotland a mount is usually an upland plateau, which is what this is, a place where the cattle raiders of Glencoe used to hide their booty until the pursuit had passed. The Way undulates along in a pleasing fashion at a little over the 300-metre mark up to the crest of the hill.

This is the highest point on the West Highland Way at 441 metres and there, up on my left as the road crossed the crest, was a distinctive cairn. The cairn is quite unmarked, but was erected as a memorial to Peter Fleming, brother of Ian Fleming of James Bond fame, a great writer and an intrepid traveller. Peter Fleming travelled in Mongolia and the Eastern steppes in the years between the wars, and wrote about his travels in a fine book, *News From Tartary*. He then went off on an amusing if abortive expedition to find Colonel Fawcett in the Amazon jungle, and died up here of a heart attack in 1971 while out for a day's shooting on the Black Mount.

There is no plaque on the cairn. Even here the vandals have been at work, pulling stones from sides of the cairn to create holes and gaps the weather will soon exploit. I tried stuffing a few rocks back into the gaps to make a rough repair before splashing downhill through the mud, and taking up the Way again for my nightstop at Kingshouse.

From this crest the Way descends past the carpark and ski-lift of the White Corries ski-area, now quite deserted as summer came on. Skiing in Scotland is now a major winter industry, a far cry from what it used to be thirty years ago when we came up to ski at Glenshee in the Grampians and put the fear of God up the locals.

In those now distant days the great curve of the Devil's Elbow barred the road from Blairgowrie to Braemar in winter. We would take the transport as far as we could, then march up to the Elbow and camp, stripping off in the snow to slip into our windproofs. You had to be a real enthusiast to ski at Glenshee in those days, for the skiing facilities consisted of a single rope tow, and the weekend queues were considerable. That may have been the problem, for boredom swiftly set in, and a bored Commando is a terrible thing for he then plays dangerous, swiftly invented games.

First there was Commando Paralleling, which is not the usual graceful type of parallel skiing but two skiers tying themselves together before plunging down the slope. Broken ankles are almost guaranteed in the process, even before you hit the heather.

When that palled there was Pyramid Skiing. For this, three or more skiers get into their bindings and as many as possible then climb on their shoulders. Our record was a pyramid of 16 Marines; as it grew, the slope below us cleared of civilians.

Once the Pyramid is formed the rest of the party push the base skiers forward to the top of the slope, and shove them over. You have to be seriously insane to do this. The Pyramid picks up an alarming amount of speed, Scotland's ski-slopes tend to be short, steep and rocky and terrible crashes at the bottom of the slope were inevitable. Jumping from the top of the Pyramid was considered bad form but was not exactly easy either. Funnily enough, I don't recall anyone getting seriously hurt, and I also recall that we did this sort of thing when stone-cold sober.

Scotland's skiing has come on a lot since the days of the Racing Snowplough. Forgetting the rule about never going back, I returned to Glenshee some years ago. They had ironed out the kink at the Devil's Elbow and a maze of lifts now covered the slopes we used to plunge down. Smartly dressed skiers abounded. I don't suppose they would let anyone go Pyramid Skiing at Glenshee today. There is a full range of lifts and runs, shops and facilities, but it is not all good. When I went onto the slopes that afternoon they seemed over-supplied with sullen, out-of-control, truculent drunks. We may have been lively thirty years ago, but we could hold our liquor, stay out of trouble, and laugh. Where did all the laughter go, I wonder?

From the White Corries carpark the Way runs off to the main road and then veers over to the inn at Kingshouse, a place I was quite glad to reach after about 20 miles on the trail. It seemed to be deserted, give or take a camper or two pitched in the field near by, and as I stopped by the front door, which is actually at the side, there seemed to be no one about at all. Then I went round the back, to the stone terrace by the burn, and found the pub was packed.

The Kingshouse Hotel claims to be the oldest inn in Scotland. This may or may not be the case but it has certainly been there for a very long time and must have seen a lot of history pass the door; refugees from Glencoe, clansmen hastening to join Prince Charlie, Redcoat infantry and rumbling cannon heading for the garrison at Inverlochy ... the Kingshouse has history and is now a comfortable inn, a most useful combination.

It was not always comfortable. When Dorothy and William Wordsworth stayed here in 1803 Dorothy wrote in her diary, 'Never did I see such a miserable, such a *wretched* place,' and Dorothy Wordsworth was both used to the hills and indifferent to comfort. Perhaps the views were some compensation, for the setting is superb with hills and peaks and rolling moorland running off on every side.

The customers of Kingshouse today largely come from the hillwalking and climbing fraternity and they are not over-concerned with comfort either. A bunk, a beer, a steak and chips, more beer, and a lot of hills in the immediate vicinity are their most pressing requirements, and all this the Kingshouse can provide.

By early evening the grassy fields and the banks of the burn near Kingshouse were dotted with tents. The back bar is stone-flagged and equipped with wooden benches and relics of climbing expeditions. These range from stones off Everest to bits of old ropes and pitons, all slung together rather than carefully displayed. That night the bar was full of people in hillwalking kit, all shouting happily about their day, and the din was considerable.

After dinner I got a beer, found a table and spread out my map. The West Highland Way still had more to offer me on the next day, but after an hour or two it went off over the Devil's Staircase, up the boundary wall of Rannoch and over the hill to Kinlochleven. I am sure there is a good reason for this but I cannot think what it might be. If this were France and somewhere as beautiful and as significant as Glencoe lay anywhere near the Way, then the Way would surely divert and go through it.

This is where the footpaths of France score time and again over the footpaths of Britain. The British footpaths offer a walk; the French footpaths offer a longer walk and an education. Think about it. Think of all the places that must lie below the South Downs Way and the Berkshire Ridgeway, just two long walks that stick rigidly to the hill and pass by many beautiful and interesting places. Well, there is always room for self improvement. As the sun started to fall away to the west I went out to sit on the banks of the burn and thought about the massacre of Glencoe.

The story of the massacre of the Macdonalds of Glencoe is too well known to need full coverage here. John Prebble has written a full and marvellous account of the affair in his book *Glencoe*, and anyone who has not read that is missing a wonderful and tragic story.

The basic facts are these: After the expulsion of James II from his Kingdom in 1688 and James's final defeat at the Battle of the Boyne in Ireland in 1690, King William of Orange required all the Jacobite clans to submit to his rule and swear an Oath of Allegiance by New Year's Day 1691. Certain clans, most notably the Campbells, were already on King William's side. The Campbells had raised a regiment of Foot from the Campbell clan – the Earl of Argyll's Regiment – to fight in King William's service, and many of these Campbell clansmen, not least one of the Captains, Robert Campbell of Glenlyon, had lost all they had in raids from the Macdonalds of Glencoe.

William of Orange did not give a damn about his English – or British – Crown. He viewed Britain as a source of men and money for the Dutch wars with France and Spain. All he wanted from the Highlands was peace and quiet while he campaigned on the Continent, and stout-hearted recruits for his regiments. This required the submission of the clans who had been out against him in 1689 under the leadership of John Graham of Claverhouse, a man better known to Scots history as 'Bonnie Dundee'.

Viscount Dundee had been killed leading the clans at the Pass of Killiecrankie, and without Dundee all resistance collapsed and the clans went home. On the way home the Macdonalds of Glencoe ravaged the lands of Captain Campbell of Glenlyon, reducing his family to penury. Once back in their glens, the chiefs sent messengers to France, asking King James to release them from their Jacobite Oath of Allegiance, so that they might in all honour submit to King William. This release was a long time coming.

The clansmen knew, and so did King James, that if their submission was not swiftly forthcoming, King William was determined to punish them. Eventually, King James sent word releasing the chiefs from their oath, but it was not until midnight on 30 December 1691, twenty-four hours before the deadline, that McIain, the chief of Glencoe, arrived at Inverlochy, the present Fort William, and asked the Governor to administer the Oath of Allegiance to King William.

Colonel John Hill, the Governor of Inverlochy, could not do it. The oath must be sworn before a magistrate, and the nearest magistrate was Campbell of Arkinglass. Arkinglass lived in the Campbell stronghold at Inverary, two or three days' journey away, a long trip for an old man in bitter winter weather. In the event, McIain did not swear the oath until 6 January, but his attempt to do so on 30 December had been registered and reported by Colonel Hill and his oath was accepted by Arkinglass and sent to Edinburgh. It was, however, now too late to prevent the crime that had already been planned. The Government had decided to make an example of a Highland clan, and the clan chosen for attack was that of Glencoe.

In early December 1691, half of the Earl of Argyll's Regiment had come up to Inverlochy and were only awaiting orders to fall on a recalcitrant clan. The King's orders to this Campbell regiment were quite specific:

> To act against the Highland rebels who have not taken advantage of our indemnity, by fire and sword and all manner of hostility; to burn their homes, destroy their goods and cattle and cut off the men.

It only needed a pause until the soldiers knew which clans had failed to take the oath, but the Macdonalds of Glencoe, long-time enemies of the Campbells, had already been selected by the Campbells as their favourite for extirpation. The good news arrived in London on 11 January, 'that Glencoe has not taken the oath at which I rejoice. It will be a work of charity to root out that damnable sept, the worst in all the Highlands.'

Thus wrote the Master of Stair, the King's Deputy in Scotland. Five days later orders went to Scotland, ordering that the Macdonalds of Glencoe, 'that sept of thieves' should be attacked with all despatch. Stair's orders to John Hill, the Governor of Inverlochy, were even more stark. 'Let it be swift and sudden,' he wrote. 'Deal with them as you find their consternation and the circumstances allow but by all means be quick.'

King and politician had set the train alight and the fuse now passed to the military. Stair's orders to Inverlochy arrived at the fort at the end of January and were handed to the Deputy Governor, Lieutenant-Colonel James Hamilton. He promptly sent two companies of Argyll's Regiment to billet themselves on the Macdonalds of Glencoe, under the command of that ruined captain, Robert Campbell of Glenlyon.

At this point a pause is called for. Massacres were no new thing in the Highlands. The clans had been massacring each other for generations, and singing and boasting about it afterwards. Had the Campbell infantry simply fallen on the Macdonalds of Glencoe and cut them down in that time-honoured Highland fashion, the rest of the High-landers would have hastened to take the Oath – which most had already done – shrugged their shoulders and said 'Hard Luck'. The continuing horror surrounding the massacre in Glencoe in February 1692 springs from other causes.

First of all, it was an act of political murder and an attempt at coercion by fear, executed on men, women and children regardless of guilt, and ordered by the King and his Ministers in Government in defiance of any law, natural or statute; Adolf Hitler and his acolytes could not have done worse.

The men who ordered this atrocity claimed to be gentlemen and behaved like barbarians. Even at the time, people were both shocked and disgusted, and the familiar attempts to pass on the blame or cover up the crime did nothing to dampen public condemnation. It was a crime, pure and simple.

Well, perhaps not so simple. What stuck in Scottish throats and in particular in Highland throats, was that this was murder under trust. When the Campbell soldiers fell on their Macdonald hosts they had been sharing the same table and living under the same roofs as their victims for over two weeks, in apparent amity. This fact was crucial to the execution of the massacre, and the orders to Robert Campbell of Glenlyon from his commanding officer, Colonel Robert Duncanson, might have been written by Himmler:

> Sir,
> You are hereby ordered to fall on the rebels, the Macdonalds of Glencoe and put all to the sword under seventy. You are to have a special care that the old fox and his sons do on no account escape your hands. You are to secure all avenues that no man escape. This you are to put in execution at five o'clock precisely; by that time I shall be with you with a stronger party. If I do not come at you by five, do not tarry but fall on.
> This is by the King's special command for the good and safety of the country, that these miscreants be cut off, root and branch.

In response to these orders, early on the morning of 13 February 1692, the Campbell soldiers fell on their hosts with sword, bayonet and musket. Old MacIain was shot in the head as he struggled to dress, his house looted and burned, his cattle driven off. His wife was robbed, stripped and beaten and turned out into the snow. The Campbells killed men and women and children and, although the toll in the actual massacre was only 38, about a tenth of the clan, no one knows how many died later of their wounds or of cold and exposure in their flight across the frozen hills to safety in the neighbouring glens.

As terror, it worked. Any recalcitrant clansmen soon learned the fate of Glencoe and swarmed from their glens to take the oath. In Edinburgh and London and Paris, the news of the massacre had a less useful effect. King William was a Dutchman and had not been on the British throne long enough to start slaughtering his subjects like this. Many wondered who this Dutchman was, that he should come from another country and start his reign like this; King Charles of blessed memory had lost his head for less. Parliament was outraged, or pretended to be outraged, and all business stopped while the Members digested the news from Scotland and demanded an explanation from the King and the Government.

In the end, inevitably, scapegoats were found. The Argyll Earl of Breadalbane, who had urged the massacre on the Master of Stair, was the first to be blamed and imprisoned by the Scots Parliament. It did not take the King long to decide that his orders were no mandate for slaughter by Argyll's Regiment. Then the Master of Stair was accused of exceeding his authority by setting the troops on.

It was all a mammoth whitewash. Of course the King could not be blamed, and he graciously forgave the Master of Stair, now a viscount, for his excess of zeal. The Earl of Breadalbane was released from prison on the King's orders, and that was that. The hoodie crows picked at the dead in Glencoe, and the other clans sheltered the survivors and trembled in fear of a like fate. Captain Robert Campbell of Glenlyon died in Bruges four years after the massacre, but his heir later took 500 Breadalbane swords-men to fight for the Stuarts in the risings of 1715 and at the Sheriffmuir – such is the irony of battle – the Glenlyon men were brigaded with the Macdonalds. The Macdonalds of Glencoe crept back to live in their glen and lived there for another 150 years. Then the sheep came, and since the 1840s Glencoe has been much as it is today, wild and lovely but empty of people.

Some lasting good did come out of it all. In debating the conduct of the Campbell soldiers, the British Parliament set down clear rules for the conduct of armies, so that the plea of 'only obeying orders' could never again be advanced as a defence:

> Though the command of an officer be absolute, yet no command against the laws of nature is binding; a soldier, retaining his commission, ought to refuse to commit any barbarity, as if a soldier should be commissioned to shoot a man passing by innocently upon the street, when no such command will exempt him from the punish-ment for murder.

These rules, or something very like them, remain in the Rules of War until this day and every soldier worth the name stands by them.

The following day was bright and clear. When I came out of the Kingshouse, the sound of coughing came from every tent, the hoodie crows were wheeling about, like black rags against the sky, and the air was as cold and fresh as Highland water.

In that clear light I could see every fold and crinkle on the slopes of Buchaille Etive More, the 'Great Herdsman of Etive', that cone-shaped peak that stands between Glen

Etive and Glen Coe. Climbers were already scrambling up that dangerous peak as I followed the track of the old military road and the West Highland Way to the foot of the Devil's Staircase. The Way crosses the road at the top of Glencoe, from where the Staircase forges directly up the hill. There we parted company, for the Way runs over to the aluminium smelting town of Kinlochleven, and my way lay west, down through Glencoe.

The path through Glencoe is by any standards a fine route, though it took a mile or two before I could get off the road. This can be done just by the waterfall at a group of rocks called 'The Study', which stands in the Pass of Glencoe proper. From there I could descend to the river and so to the floor of the Glen, and I walked on beside the winding Coe to the foot of the valley for a welcome coffee stop at the Visitor Centre. Glencoe is grand and beautiful and a splendid morning's walk, but there is none of that half-expected sense of foreboding. With people and dogs and a wedge of shortbread to go with the coffee, it seemed a cheerful place.

The Macdonalds have long gone, and none of the few buildings and shielings that dot the glen today existed at the time of the Massacre. It happened and it is over and that is all. I climbed on the Signal Rock, from where the Chief would summon his clan, and looked at the memorial and took some photos. Then I pushed on out of the glen to the shores of Loch Leven and the bridge at Ballachulish. I had a long way to go that day and I had to keep moving.

10

Fort William and Ben Nevis

Some people, by the dispensing power of the imagination can go back several centuries in spirit and put themselves in sympathy with the hunted, houseless, way of life that was in its place upon these savage hills.

Robert Louis Stevenson, 1873

When I emerged from Glencoe, walking past the loom of the breast-shaped hill called the Pap of Glencoe and onto the shores of Loch Leven, I was faced with another of those hard choices. Should I return up the south shore of Loch Leven and pick up the West Highland Way at Kinlochleven for another stint over the hills to the end of the Way at Fort William? Or should I go the other way, westwards down beside Loch Leven to Ballachulish where this loch joins with Loch Linnhe? Then I could leave Appin and cross over into Lochaber by the new bridge.

Having done my stint on the West Highland Way, I felt no particular desire to flog back up the glen and rejoin it. Kinlochleven is not very pretty, and if I put my foot down I could get up to Fort William along the shores of the sea-lochs and see a thing or two along the way.

Therefore I ambled along the nice smooth path beside the loch, heading towards the high iron bridge at Ballachulish and thought about stopping somewhere for tea or even the night. Years ago I might have had to. When I first came this way, more than thirty years ago, there was only a ferry at Ballachulish, a successor of the one that had brought those Campbell soldiers from Inverlochy to Glencoe in 1692. The ferry could only shift a few cars at a time and the people waiting had to endure the playing of a very tuneless piper who, clad in his full regimentals, would pace up and down beside the cars making a terrible din until the passengers paid him good money to shut up.

I have probably given terrible offence to those who love the bagpipes, and revealed myself as untrue to my origins. This is not so. I love the pipes, but they take some playing, though the technique sounds simple. The piper breathes air into the bag and expels it through the drones by squeezing the bag under his arms, stopping the vents with his fingers. It sounds simple if you say it like that, but anyone who has tried to play the pipes will be lucky if the first effort sounds no worse than the wails from a trodden-on cat.

The bagpipe is a medieval instrument and is still found in many places especially in those with Celtic connections. The medieval version is still found in Brittany and various parts of France where it is known as the 'cornmuse'. There are other kinds of pipes, the difference usually lying in the number of drones. In Germany the pipers are called *grosserbock*, and versions are found in Ireland, in Spanish Galicia, in Czechoslovakia, even in Iraq. For that I have the assurance of the Bagpipe Society, who added that Scottish pipers, having obtained the high ground, are now very conservative; a Scots piper can be thrown out of the band for playing vibrato.

The old piper has gone from the ferry side at Ballachulish. Now there is a bridge and the cars whizz north across the loch for Fort William in a matter of seconds. Fortunately, the walker cannot rush. The quotation at the start of this chapter comes from an essay by Stevenson with the wonderful title, 'On the enjoyment of Unpleasant Places', and those who pause here, just under the bridge, will come across just such a place, marked with another memorial to the wild old days. This is where James Stewart, called James of the Glens, was hanged by the Campbells for the 'Appin Murder', the shooting of Colin Campbell of Glenure, the Red Fox, an event used by Robert Louis Stevenson for one of the dramatic scenes in *Kidnapped*.

To this day no one really knows who shot the Red Fox by Lettermore in Appin in 1752 except that it was not James Stewart of the Glens and was probably not Alan Breck Stewart, David Balfour's Jacobite companion in that stirring Highland tale. I had always thought that the entire incident was a pure invention by Stevenson, but not so; Alan Breck Stewart did exist, Colin Campbell was indeed ambushed and shot, and the Campbells duly tried and hanged James of the Glens for the deed on the gallows at Ballachulish on 8 November 1752.

The Campbells were determined to hang someone for the Appin Murder, and James was the most obvious candidate. It was his land that the Campbell was about to seize when someone shot him off his horse. The bones of James Stewart are buried in a little graveyard a few miles down the road to Oban and Castle Stalker, but they swung in the gibbet here on the Gallows Hill by the Ballachulish ferry for many years before they were taken down and decently interred. Visiting Ballachulish in 1880 Stevenson wrote that 'We had no difficulty in finding the cairn that marks the site of his death' and another memorial marks the spot today.

I had a look at that and then I crossed the loch, quickly and easily by the new bridge, and set off up the road to Fort

William. The road to the old Inverlochy is a fair step but a flat route, with the yachts and boats on the loch to keep my mind off the heat in my boots, and the hills ahead to draw me on. It took the rest of the day and a half-hour's rest out of my boots, drinking tea in a hotel, but by early that evening I had arrived at Fort William in Lochaber and stood at the foot of the Great Glen. My tasks now were to explore Fort William and – weather permitting – to ascend Ben Nevis.

This latter ambition was my main reason for coming to Fort William. Ben Nevis is Britain's highest mountain at 1,344 metres. It looms over the town when seen from a distance and is a peak which, in all honour, I could hardly avoid. I am getting too old for physical gestures but I have a small rule for these walks, that if a good mountain bars my path or lies just by the trail I must have a go at getting up it. This resolve has taken me over the Plomb du Cantal in the Auvergne in the middle of a spring snowstorm, across the Sierra de Gredos in Spain in the heat of summer, falling down the far side and doing myself no good at all, and, on my last long walk, up Carrantuohill, the tallest mountain in Ireland, which I climbed in torrential rain and when not at all well. Perhaps I am a bloody fool after all.

Anyway, here now stood Ben Nevis and somehow I had to get up it. I don't actually climb using the full rope and piton number. At the most I scramble up on all fours, trying to ignore any nearby void, but most mountains have a pretty way up and that is the one I look out for. In the case of Ben Nevis there is a footpath to the top from the farm at Achintee, and according to the local people the up-and-back from there would take about six hours.

The young lady at the hotel who told me this became quite alarmed when she heard what I intended. She insisted on telling me that it was hard work, that I should not go at all if the weather was foul and that she would call out the Rescue if I was not back by, say, five in the evening. I thought that a bit excessive; I'm not such a bloody fool as all that. Besides, thousands of people go up Ben Nevis every year and only a few fall off. The ascent does, however, require good weather and I wanted a clear day to do it.

At dawn next day the weather had closed in again, making a trip up Big Ben less than appealing, for the views from the top are the main attraction. I was also pretty tired. I don't seem able to do these long stints day after day without it taking a toll, and I had come quite a long way in the last couple of days. I decided to wait for clear skies and give Fort William a closer look.

Fort William is not a pretty town. It is a combination of railhead, port, industrial centre and tourist trap, with a particular role as the setting-off point for visits to the Western Isles and the Western Highlands. I began my day with a vast breakfast at the Alexander Hotel, followed by a visit to the nearest outdoor shop to buy a pair of gaiters, essential wear in the boggy tops of the Highlands. This was a useful stop, for the young man in the shop had walked from Kinlochbervie to Cape Wrath and was full of advice: 'Allow longer than you think you'll need,' and enthusiasm, 'It's a bonnie spot and Sandwood Bay is a wonder.'

This was encouraging and thus encouraged I set out for the West Highland Museum. This is a fine museum, full of interesting things I wanted to see, like the musket that killed the Red Fox, swords and muskets collected from Culloden Moor, the helmet of the Marquis of Montrose, all sort of other curiosities, and details of the old fort at Inverlochy which now lies under the railway station. That reminded me that I needed to do a longer stint on the West Highland Line. The upshot was that I decided to award myself a couple of days off and take a look at some of the places on the west coast of Scotland, beginning with a trip down the West Highland Line to the port of Mallaig.

The railway station at Fort William occupies the site of the original fort, the one built by General George Monck in the 1660s and called Inverlochy. This was destroyed by the Camerons of Lochiel after the Restoration of Charles II, and when it was rebuilt by Colonel John Hill they decided to name it after King William, their new Dutch King.

From Fort William to Mallaig by rail is only 33 miles but somehow it seems much longer. The train rattles along beside Loch Eil, around the bends, over the bridges and the great viaduct at Glenfinnan, past the column erected in 1831 to mark the spot where Prince Charlie raised his standard in 1745. I must start to consider Prince Charlie, and where better to do it, but first on to Arisaig and, with the offshore islands of Rum and Eigg and Skye in sight out to sea, onto the end of the line at Mallaig.

I had about twenty minutes to see the town before taking the train back to my nightstop at Arisaig House. This is just about enough time, for Mallaig is not very big. Ferries sail from here to Armadale on the Isle of Skye, a short trip across the water, and the fried fish shop in Mallaig sells haggis and chips, but that is about it. The rail journey is the thing that matters and in fifteen minutes I was back on the train for the brief hop to Arisaig, remembering to tell the guard where I wanted to get off. Happily, the system works. The train stopped at Bleasdale, the car was waiting to greet me and within five minutes I was in the Arisaig House Hotel and ready for the lap of luxury. Two days out of the boots suddenly seemed like Paradise.

From previous experience I can thoroughly recommend a spot of luxury after a few weeks on the trail. After climbing Ben Nevis my route would take me away from the west coast and up the Great Glen to Inverness and Cromarty and beyond. I would not return to the west coast until I reached Lochinver, and that meant missing out a great many beautiful West Coast places that lie to the south of Sutherland. I could not leave this part of the Western Highlands without taking a closer look at the coast and, with the weather so good (having cleared the minute it was too late to tackle the Ben), this was a chance not to be missed. The rainfall on the west coast is regular, heavy and deeply depressing, and the opportunity to see it in sunshine was not one to pass up. Besides, I wanted to look at Glenfinnan.

The statue on the column at Glenfinnan is not of Charles Edward Stuart, eldest son of James II and better known as Bonnie Prince Charlie, but of an ordinary Highlander. It stands on the spot where the Prince hoisted his standard and began that last desperate venture of the ill-starred Stuarts which led to the destruction of the clans and the Highland way of life. The Prince was just 25 when he landed at Arisaig on 19 August 1745, the same age as his Hanoverian cousin, the Duke of Cumberland. He had been born in Rome and had never set foot in the land claimed by his father, but here he was, in need of an army, and he expected the Jacobite clans to support him.

The Prince was not welcome. The chiefs of Clanranald and Lochiel begged him to go home again, but the Prince said 'I am home' and they had no answer to that. They went away to round up their people, and those of their clans who were unwilling to join the muster were harried from their homes by the threat of setting fire to their thatch. Only slowly did the Rising gain momentum. A deputation went to raise the Macdonalds of Skye but their Chief wisely refused to declare for the Prince. Four thousand clansmen from the Macdonalds of Sleat were absent from the Prince's army and many other clans stayed in their glens, having been advised to do so by Duncan Forbes of Culloden, the Lord Advocate of Scotland.

The first to come in were 150 men from the Macdonalds of Clanranald, followed by the pipers of Lochiel leading 600 Camerons. So it went on, day after day, in the late summer of 1745, as the Prince advanced to meet his people; a flash of steel on the hill, a rant on the pipes and another group of men came through the heather to join his growing array, which never reached 10,000 men and was probably only half that by the time the end came at Culloden.

Still, the Prince took Edinburgh but not the castle, and scattered the English at Prestonpans and advanced into England as far as Derby before his luck began to run out. The retreat that began there never stopped, although the clans scattered another English force at Falkirk in January 1746 before falling back behind the Highland Line. So it went on, gallant but hopeless, to that day of cold steel and cannon fire on Drummossie Moor which saw the downfall of the Prince and the clans and all their Jacobite hopes.

I will come to that eventually. The next day was devoted to a car tour down the west coast, from peaceful Arisaig to the wonderful seclusion of the Isle of Eriska, past Ben Cruachan and Castle Stalker and all the little corners of this glorious coast. I spent that night at the Isle of Eriska Hotel, another luxurious Highland watering hole, where several of the staff were keen walkers, but by the following afternoon I was back in Fort William with my boots on my feet, refreshed and ready to ascend the Big Ben.

Fort William, or the 'Black Garrison of Inverlochy' as it was once called, was built to overawe the western clans, and a glance at the map shows why it was strategically important. The fort stood at the head of Loch Linnhe, a sea-loch thrusting deep into the heart of the Highlands. That meant the fort could be safely supplied by sea. From Fort William strong columns of troops could march up the Great Glen, with an overnight halt at Fort Augustus, and so to Inverness, or foray out into the lands of the Macdonalds or the Camerons with comparative ease. The garrison at Fort William was a stone in the throat of the Highland clans and I would follow the old military road up the Great Glen to Inverness. First though I had to get up the Ben. To that task I now applied myself, starting with another look at the map.

Ben Nevis is the tallest mountain in Britain but it is not a pretty one, like Helvellyn or even Snowdon. It is a great, square, bulk of a mountain, one of a mountain mass that rears up between the Fort and the Great Glen, and runs east to Glen Spean and Loch Treig. The mountain attracts climbers and hillwalkers and fell runners and in September every year there is a race to the top and back for which the current record stands at 1 hour 25 minutes and 34 seconds. The best of luck to them; I intended to go up the slow but steady way.

The local people I had talked to all told me different things. The guidebook says four hours up and down is sensible, though that looked like a cracking pace to me. Everyone else suggested seven or eight hours or said they hadn't done it yet but were saving it for another time. This got me brooding and muttering under my breath because before I set my mind on doing something I like to have a target, something to measure myself against, for, though I am not competitive at all, I like to compete with myself. In the end, I resolved to get up to the top of Ben Nevis and back in six hours ... maybe a bit less. This will break no records and may even curl the lips of the hard men, but it would do me. Just to do what I set out to do would be sufficient.

Besides, one of my fondest recollections connected with the Ben is watching a TV film which intended to show a winter ascent of Ben Nevis. This project seemed to involve a cast of thousands and a great deal of money. The leading climbers were assembled, the Royal Marines had their base on the top, the helicopters were standing by, radios hummed and chattered from base to summit, a host of bearded gents in hard-hitting gear were opining on this and other mountains climbed, but no one seemed keen to actually have a go at Ben Nevis on this particular day, probably for the very sensible reason that the conditions made it downright bloody dangerous.

The cameras returned to the scene at intervals throughout the day where the hanging-about and the 'shall-we-shan't-we' had been going on for hours. Then, suddenly, a Frenchman appeared at the top of the mountain, pushed his way through the throng (*'Excusez-moi, merci, eh bien*, etc ...') and announced that if nobody had any objection he would ski down the face of the mountain.

There was amazement among the hard men, a murmuring and a forecast of woe, but the Frenchman shrugged and said the skiing down mountains was his, how-to-say, *violin d'Ingres*, his hobby. The TV producer looked mightily relieved (something to film at last, thank God), the cameras were trundled forward for a preview of the route – eeek! – and the Frenchman duly put on his skis and leapt off the top to a chorus of indrawn breaths.

His route to the glen below did not resemble the normal ski slope; it resembled an abyss, a descent seamed with ice gullies and black rock, alive with possibilities of pain and sudden death. Our hero skied the bits he could ski, including places where I kept my eyes shut. When it got too hairy even for him, he produced a line, belayed himself to a rock and abseiled down to the next patch of skiable snow. I doubt if the whole thing took five minutes. Then he was at the bottom, out of his skis and wandering off, leaving the hard men looking amazed.

If it was going to take me six hours up and back, an early start was advisable. I got up at seven, watched the

Breakfast News and weather forecast – 'a fine day after a cloudy start' – while stuffing myself with food, and then set out briskly for the top.

There are three ways to the top of Ben Nevis, one from the north side of the town, leaving from the Victoria Bridge and heading up past the whisky distillery, one from the farm at Achintee and one from the Youth Hostel in Glen Nevis, which runs up a zig-zag path to join the route from Achintee. These all end up in the same place, combining about halfway up for the final ascent, and one or other of these paths attracts walkers by the thousand every year. There are also climbing routes for summer and winter ascents, and the young man in the outdoor shop told me, with that wild climber's glint in his eye, that the ice climbing on Ben Nevis can be grand. By that I assumed he meant dangerous.

As I never climb anything steeper than bus stairs I was content to walk along to the farm at Achintee, go through the gate there and address myself to the path that ran diagonally up the hillside ahead. This proceeded at a graceful incline for a mile or more, a wide path edging up the side of the 711m Meall an t-Suidhe mountain, that screens this western side of Ben Nevis, past the path that comes up from the Youth Hostel from which a number of people were now emerging to start up the Ben.

By nine-thirty I was a good way up the hill and going well, though passed as if I was standing still by a man even older than I am who told me, without pausing for breath, that he did this every year and that I had better hurry before the weather closed in. Since I was already hurrying this advice was unwelcome, but I could see what he meant.

I sometimes wonder if weather forecasters think of doing something obvious during the forecasting round, like looking out of the window. The day had started pin-bright and sunny at seven, but even I know that when days start like that, it is usually raining cats and dogs by eleven. So far the day was just turning into a sullen morning with lots of lowering cloud and great wisps of mist fanning across the slopes ahead of me, but the clouds were creeping ever closer. Well, at least the path was obvious. I had all the hard-hitting gear and I was not going to turn back now, short of thunder and lightning.

This walk up Ben Nevis is really just a good old-fashioned bash. The mountain is not attractive, or even striking, but the advantage of getting to the top on a good day must be the stunning views from the top which run for miles over Lochaber and Appin – or so I am told. By ten o'clock, and staring hard, I could just see the hand in front of my face. At about half past ten, when I was having a breather, I was passed by a couple with a dog making their way up, and by a man who did it every year and told me it was his birthday. There really is one born every minute. His hair and clothes were already streaming with moisture, he told me that it was snowing on the top but he had to hurry as he was meeting his wife back at the farm for a birthday lunch.

I flogged on. The path ran across a plateau, wide and open and easy to follow, but I nearly missed the turn-off onto the steep track that led up the side of Ben Nevis proper and I certainly missed the lochan that is up there somewhere on the plateau, at least according to the map. On and up, into the first patches of snow, and then over one or two snow bridges across steep gullies, dirty, well-worn crossing points which were about to collapse but looked good for a day or two yet.

There is a trick to all this. The big trick is to keep moving. It does not matter if you move slowly, but if you have to stop every few minutes for a breather you have no business on the mountain at all. Take short steps, take advantage of every small rock and foothold, press on until you have your second wind, but keep moving. It helps if you can get the mind busy on something other than the raw air in the lungs and the pain in the legs. If you can do that and keep moving you will make good time.

As I was now getting nicely wet from the mist I stopped to put on the windproofs and was reminded of the other big snag with this kind of mountain walking. If you are in no particular hurry it does not hurt to stop and rest now and then, to savour the view, pull out the hip-flask, or pore over the map. The snag is that you instantly get very cold. There was not a lot of wind but it was very cold and getting colder as I got higher. I would have liked to have stopped and joined up with another walker or a party, but the second I stopped the sweat started to freeze on me and I got very cold and clammy indeed.

I was above the snowline and walking on a well-trodden path when suddenly it stopped or ran out or somehow disappeared. It was a virtual white-out, with visibility of a few yards at best and that over steeply sloping, hard-packed snow. I cast about a bit but could see no discernable track. Then I met the couple with the dog again, equally lost but thinking that the route lay somewhere to the right. I don't go in for instinctive direction-finding and since I didn't know where I was the compass was no good for this sort of work. I therefore decided to go ahead, walking very slowly in the mist but always uphill, working on the theory that there must be a summit up there somewhere.

I don't put this forward as a good idea. Walking in white-out can be dangerous. I can recall walking with Paul Traynor in the Pyrenees in just such a white-out and we walked right off a ledge. We only dropped about six feet, into a lot of soft snow, but it might have been a thousand feet for all we knew. This time, however, the theory worked. The wind got up and blew the cloud about, the mist shredded and I could just discern a host of boot-prints, all heading in the same direction, up a wide snowfield with some sharp cornices over the void to my left. Then I met a man muffled up in a balaclava, coming down carefully swinging an ice axe. 'Keep going,' he said. 'It's about another hundred metres,' and so it was.

Roaming about like this in the snow and mist put me in mind of those times when we used to go soldiering in Scotland, and of one of the more eventful days in my life, in a blizzard and white-out somewhere above Coire Cas in the Cairngorms.

Then, as now, we were flogging up the glen in deteriorating weather, the entire gang, Terry Brown, Stan, Lou, Joe Cartwright, Geoff Laven, Ginger Simpson and a score more, all names to make strong men tremble . . . and me, of course. We went on, dim shapes in the swirling snow, until shouts from ahead told us to stop, pitch our tents and wait out the weather, which sounded very sensible. Pitching the tent was not easy in that howling wind and on the edge of a void, but we were soon inside, holding onto the tent poles and trying to keep the flaps down, when Lou decided to fire up the Primus and get a brew on. Within seconds he had set his Bergen rucksack alight.

The rucksack sat in the middle of the tent, wreathed in flickering flame like a Christmas pudding, while we lay around mesmerised, waiting for the tent to catch fire. Then Lou let out a yell, seized the rucksack straps and dived headlong out of the door. Trailing smoke and flame, he vanished down the mountainside, looking just like Halley's Comet, until there came a loud 'PH-Twock!' from far below as Lou impacted into a snowdrift.

We all scrambled out of the tent – which promptly blew away – and leapt down the slope to where Lou and his rucksack were smoking gently in the snow. We were all standing about, having a laugh, when there came a shout of 'Stop it!' from above and an open wallet slid down out of the mist, shedding five-pound notes. Stan promptly stopped it by whirling his ice axe round his head and driving the spiked end through the morocco leather and into the snow.

This was a mistake. The wallet belonged to our Commanding Officer, who did not take kindly to getting his wallet back with a bloody great hole driven through it. The CO chewed on Stan for some time and Stan, who did not care for officers at the best of times, returned from his wigging muttering 'Ungrateful sod,' under his breath.

By this time the second tent had blown away. Royal Marines are not easily daunted, and the orders now came to dig snow holes. Snow holes are quite comfy if you have enough snow, and the construction is simple. You dig a short tunnel into a snow bank, then hollow out a small cave, which you then enlarge into two bunks, with a central space for cooking and stowing the gear. You then light a candle. Reflecting off the snow crystals, the candle flame will give more light than a chandelier, and, that done, you get into your sleeping bag, break out the whisky, open up the paperback, and there you are, snug as a bug in a rug, until the weather perks up outside.

We divided into our usual 'me and my pal' pairs and dug our holes along the face of the *coire*. Terry and I dug a small, standard-issue hole and resisted the temptation to be more ambitious. Getting houseproud is the snag with snowholing; snow is a useful substance and you must resist the temptation to start squirreling away inside, making the hole bigger, hacking out shelves and a hanging cupboard and a guest room, even a fitted kitchen, if you get quite carried away.

Having dug our hole, set out our sleeping bags and moved our kit in, Terry and I went for a stroll along the slope. Snow was flying out of all the other holes, for the rest of the troop had decided to build interconnecting tunnels.

At first we had a good sneer at this but then we heard the laughter and began to fear we might be missing something. So we started to dig towards Geoff and Joe and they started to tunnel towards us, both sides keeping direction by periodic yells. After about ten minutes of hard tunnelling Geoff yelled, 'Give a shout and I'll shove my axe through.'

I rested my cheek against the snow, gave a yell and 'Thwock!' the sharp, spiked end of Geoff's ice-axe shot out of the snow and missed my throat by a hair's breadth ... I could rest my chin on the haft. We had a good laugh at that – well, everyone else did. I claimed an extra-large whisky and we all crawled in together for a good moan about the officers.

I miss those rambling conversations. I remember lying enthralled when Gerry Fellowes told us the saga of buying a fridge, and someone else told us in graphic detail about his visit to a VD Clinic in Algeria where no one spoke a word of English and he had to explain the problem in mime. The topic that day, and I can recall it now, was Great Movies we have Wept At.

''Ere, do you remember when we was on the Para course and we went to see *Carousel*?'

'Ah ... terrible. That bloke cleaning a star.'

'Wept buckets.'

'I remember him singing "My Boy Bill" and Robbie was sobbin' away. . . .'

'Bloody liar.'

'We came out in Oxford, in broad daylight, with red eyes, six big hairy Commandos, all with their mascara running. . . .'

'What about that time in *South Pacific* when Jakie had that girl and the lights went out. . . .'

'I'd have wept if I'd had that girl and the lights went on. . . .'

'What about *Bambi*?'

(*Chorus*) 'Wa'aaaa.... don't mention *Bambi*, you brute.'

Ah, well, 'Halycon Days' as Lou used to say. To be honest and exact, Lou never learned to pronounce it 'Halseeon'. He used to say 'Hal-i-Kon Days' and we all still do, forty years later.

Thinking about all that kept me busy on the plod to the summit. On the top of Ben Nevis is a cairn and a kind of box on stilts which is a shelter in case of emergency; it would have to be a real emergency to get me into it. It looked like the sort of cell used to punish recalcitrant prisoners in the Gulag Archipelago and far less cosy than a snow hole.

According to the map there are a couple of these boxes on the summit and an observatory and a ridge lined with tops – Carn Mor, Carn Dearg, Carn Beag Dearg – all over the 1,000m mark and all therefore Munros ... if it is legitimate to head along a ridge from top to top and tick off a Munro as you reach each one.

Further to the east and just visible above the mist was another summit which might have been Aonach Mor, but I was chilling down nicely now and rapidly losing interest in the view. Then, thank God, the couple with the dog appeared. This was essential because I had not flogged up all this way without having my picture taken posing by the cairn, to convince Geoff, other unbelievers and those of little faith that I had indeed made it to the top of Britain's highest mountain.

Photo taken, I now had to get down again and if I wanted to get up and down in less than six hours I would have to get a move on. I am one of those who find going down almost more trouble than going up, for all the weight comes on the knees, and after a couple of miles of steep going they start to complain a bit. Moreover, the track down Ben Nevis, if clear enough below the snowline, is very rough, littered with large stones and usually steep, not the sort of place where it pays to hurry.

However, I have my pride. Six hours or less I had said it would take, and six hours or less it should be. I went down the snow slope in a series of long strides, only fell once and found the track in the mist easily because a large party were just coming off it and starting to roam about on the snow. 'The summit is up ahead,' I said, adding the fatal words, 'You can't miss it.' It was now about noon and to beat my set time I had to be down by two, which meant going it a bit. I therefore went at it a bit, running where I could, walking at a fast clip wherever possible, skipping round people plodding up, sweating like a trooper and thinking this was daft. And it is daft, but if I had any sense I would not be doing this sort of thing at my age.

There is always a moment in one of these ventures when you are sure you will do it easily and slow down. Then comes the thought that you have slowed down too much and will miss the deadline by a couple of minutes and will have expended all this effort for nothing. That was the case when I got round the last corner of Meall an t-Suidhe. I had about a mile to go to the farm gate and less than fifteen minutes to do it in. So I ran. Maybe not like the wind but at a fair full-striding clip. I may be 58 and I may be daft but I was going to get to that gate on time if it killed me, and I got there with six minutes to spare. Then I flopped down on the grass and said to myself 'Never Again'. It felt good though.

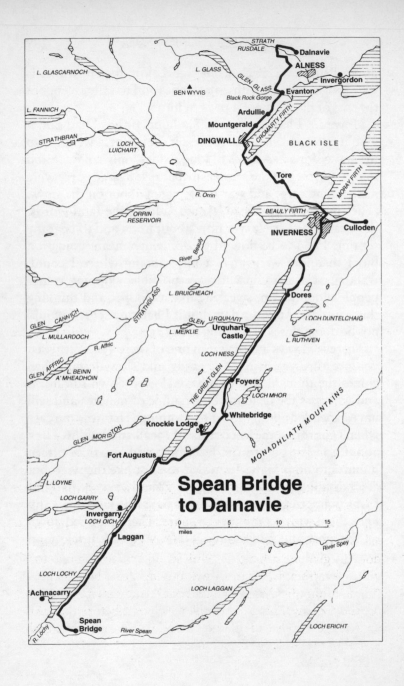

Spean Bridge
to Dalnavie

11

The Great Glen

If you had seen these roads before they were made,
You would lift up your hands and bless General Wade.

Anon

On the following day I was a very, very, tired old walker.
In fact, I was absolutely shattered. Perhaps *drained* is a
better word for it. The leg muscles were fine and I hardly
ached at all, but there was this empty feeling inside me.
That intimation of mortality that seems to occur more and
more often these days had returned to remind me that if I
must go rushing up and down mountains today, I will
surely pay for it tomorrow.

Getting out of bed was courageous. I managed that and
a shower and then I mooned about the room packing the
rucksack. I nearly fell over swinging it on. In fact, I had to
ask one of the young chambermaids vacuuming outside the
door to give me a hand on with it, and there's shame for
you. Nevertheless, I had to get moving, for I had spent a
full day shinning up the Ben and back, and taken two days
off the trail swanning about the west coast before that. At
an average distance of 20 miles a day, that meant that I had
lost about 60 miles of travel on my road to Cape Wrath. It
would not do.

This meant that I could not spend another day groaning in bed, which is what I wanted to do and what my body was demanding. From previous experience I knew that it would be a few days before yesterday's bash was finally put behind me, but I also knew that some exercise would probably help. I would not go too far but if I could do a few miles today it would help my progress to the north and cut the distance up the Great Glen to Inverness if I could put even 10 miles under my boots by nightfall. I therefore ordered another cup of coffee, spread out the map on the table and began the daily brood.

Fortunately, for the next 60 miles or so to Inverness I had flat terrain and easy paths. My route now lay north and east, up the Great Glen, or 'Glen Albyn' as the OS map subtitles it, to Inverness and the battlefield of Culloden. Under normal circumstances that would be a three-day hike, allowing some time for mooching about and seeing the odd site, but if I could go, say, 10 or 12 miles today, I could hope to be in Inverness in three days, by pushing it a bit thereafter. Nothing to it, I said to myself.

Nevertheless, I did not want to cover distance just for the sake of it. If you have to hurry, you don't want to walk. Yesterday had been a bash and there would be more bashing once Geoff and the gang joined me in Inverness, but for the moment there were things to see and understand along the way, sights I wanted to look at, like the famous Commando Memorial at Spean Bridge. The task now was to get up there and see them and arrive in Inverness in three days' time. Easy.

The Great Glen, Glen More, or 'Glen Albyn', is a natural fault that splits Scotland in two, on a south-west to north-east axis. The glen is fairly wide and largely filled by three lochs which were linked early in the last century by Thomas Telford's Caledonian Canal. This canal proved a wonderful boon to the Scottish fishing fleet, which thereby gained a safe route between the Atlantic and the North Sea without the dangers inherent in sailing through the stormy Pentland Firth and around Cape Wrath.

The fishing fleets have now declined, but the canal remains a popular waterway with yachtsmen and the cruising fraternity and, more usefully for people like myself, has a quiet towpath, ideal for walking up to Loch Lochy. Beyond that was yet another of General Wade's roads, the one linking the forts along the Great Glen, and that would take me up the quiet, south side of Loch Ness to Inverness. It all looked fairly easy, so with that decided I heaved on the pack and set off across Fort William for the foot of Neptune's Staircase.

Thomas Telford started building the Caledonian Canal in 1803. It took 24 years before the work was completed and it remains a splendid artefact, 22 miles of canal and 24 locks. Neptune's Staircase is a series of eight locks at Corpach outside Fort William, which lift the canal up 64 feet from sea level in a series of giant steps. Seen from the top or bottom it looks most impressive, and when I arrived a series of craft, fully rigged yachts and a couple of inshore trawlers, were in the locks and being transferred up or down. I found the towpath beside the lock and nobody said I could not use it. In about ten minutes I was out beyond Corpach, heading north up the Caledonian Canal, with Ben Nevis and Aonach Mor looming up to my right, and today they were standing out clearly against a cloudless sky.

The distance along the towpath from Corpach to Gairlochy is about seven miles. It took me over two hours for I was not walking well or moving fast and the views to Ben Nevis and the surrounding mountains would have made anyone linger. The canal is flanked by the feeder River Lochy and if the day was clear but chilly on the hill, down in the canal cut I was out of the wind and pleasantly warm.

If I had to stop and take a rest every so often, I think I made pretty good time under the circumstances.

At Gairlochy I had a decision to make: either to head for Achnacarry or turn up the road for Spean Bridge and the Commando Memorial. The reason for either or both diversions was the same, for between 1942 and 1945 Achnacarry House was the home of the Commando Basic Training Centre, the toughest battle school in the world, and the memorial at Spean Bridge is a place of pilgrimage for anyone who has ever worn the green beret.

All Commando volunteers recruited in the United Kingdom had to pass through Achnacarry. The School gained such a reputation that when I wrote my book on the Commandos many of those recruited abroad to replace casualties in the operational Commando units told me that they were not 'real Commandos' because they had not passed through Achnacarry. I don't agree with them, but I know how they feel. I joined the Royal Marine Commandos in the 1950s and while our training was tough there were still enough Achnacarry-trained Commandos around to tell us that we were having it soft – and we believed them. The point about Commando training is not just that it made you physically tough but, much more usefully, it also made you mentally tough. I make no claims for either quality, but this is a fact best illustrated by telling of the time which my cronies still refer to as 'The day Robbie fell off the cliff.'

For the record, I did not fall off a cliff. I never got that far. It was the last week of training and we were doing 'rocky landings' off Plymouth with a big sea running. I was bowman in the dory and my task was to leap ashore with the bowline and hold the boat on while the rest came ashore. I jumped, but before I could find a belay the waves took the boat out again. The line plucked me off the rocks and into the sea; the next wave brought the boat in again and *ground* me between the rocks and the keel.

What happened after that is either still clear in my mind or a total blank. I remember lying on a beach with someone washing the blood from my face by pouring seawater on it from a steel helmet. This can make the eyes water a bit. I then lay there among the nailed boots, puttees and rifle butts while my fate was discussed. Every time I lifted my head, blood ran into my eyes. It was eventually decided that I should go back to camp and report to the sick bay. How was I to get back? That was my problem.... 'You want to be a Commando, don't you?' A field dressing was wound over my head and I was sent off to the road.

I finally got back on a bus, a terrible sight, ignored by the other passengers and forbidden to sit down by the conductor because I was soaking wet. My main worry was the state of my rifle, which I had managed to hang on to in the sea, but was full of sand and seawater and no doubt starting to rust. I also kept falling down, but that failed to get much sympathy either. I bled all the way into Plymouth and I bled all over the bus station and I bled all the way out to the Commando School at Bickleigh. There I was given a roasting by the Sergeant of the Guard for going about in public in a filthy condition and without a beret on.

That done, I was taken to the sick bay where two SBAs, Royal Navy Sick Bay 'tiffies', took my clothes off, unwound the bandage from my head and whistled. 'It looks as if someone has stuck a potato peeler into your head and dragged it about,' one said. Then they started to stitch me up. I don't recall much after that for a while, until I was sent in to the doctor.

Naval doctors, always called simply 'Doc', were always good for a laugh or a bit of straight talk. I have never met a nicer, more down-to-earth group of people.

'It's like this,' he said. 'We have put a lot of stitches into your head and splinted up that broken finger.' That was the first I knew I even had a broken finger. 'I also think you have broken your right wrist or sprained it very badly and you will soon be covered in bruises. If you don't hurt now that is because you are still in shock, but when the shock wears off you will be in a lot of trouble. You may also have a bit of concussion, which is why you keep falling down. From the look of you, you should thank your lucky stars you're not dead.'

This was cheering me up no end.

'Now, what I ought to do,' he continued, 'is to send you into hospital for more X-rays and observation. I expect you would like that?'

Stupid question.

'However, if you go to hospital, they will keep you in. Then you will be back-squadded and will have to do the Commando course again ... and you only have three days to go. So, it's your choice. If you agree and promise to let someone know if you start to spit blood and don't do anything bloody daft, I will give you five hours light duty and some pain-killers and you can go on "Exercise Restcure" and get your green beret.'

That was laying it on the line, and, naturally enough when he put it like that, no contest; five hours later I marched out with the squad on 'Restcure' and three days later was a bold Commando. The point is that it was my choice. The great Commando saying was: 'it's all in the heart and the mind'. I looked and felt as if I had been run over by a tank but I could stand and I could function, so go to it, lad. Besides, as soon as I decided to press on, everyone in camp rallied round. The lad had decided to give it a go and that was good enough; how can we help?

The Guard Sergeant collected my rifle and took it to the armourer who took it to bits and had it back in an hour, oiled and glittering. The Sick Bay tiffies washed out my sea-soaked, bloodstained clothes and took them to the galley where the cooks dried them in no time by popping them in an oven. I was then taken to the back of the kitchen and given an enormous meal of steak and chips – that the cooks live better than recruits was another lesson I learned that day.

The MO gave me pain-killers that would have tranquillised an elephant, and while I was eating my steak the RSM arrived, looked me over, took me to the back of the Sergeants' Mess and gave me a very large rum. Then the Training Officer came round, took a look and said, 'My word, lad, you have done a good job of it,' then took me to the back of the Officers' Mess where he gave me a very large whisky. I was tottering back to my hut when I ran into the MO who said, 'By the way, don't drink with those pills.' By the time the squad came back I was higher than a kite.

In all this there was not a word of sympathy – 'If you can't take a joke, lad, you shouldn't have joined,' was another Commando saying – but there was a great deal of practical kindness and I have never forgotten it. The point is that *physical* toughness had nothing to do with it. I was a wreck. All it took was the *mental* toughness, the decision not to give in; after that it became easy.

One final point, to prove it's not personal. Exercise 'Restcure', as the name implies, was the final, sleepless, three-day scheme when we put all the training together and went through our paces. Since I could not do much, I spent the time on guard or dogs-bodying for the instructors. This gave me time to watch my squad at work and notice for the first time how good they were. They may have been immature, uncultured youths and not much good at cocktail parties, but by God they could soldier.

All Commando recruits arrived at Spean Bridge station and then marched the seven miles to Achnacarry. They had just over one hour to do it in and anyone who failed to arrive on time caught the next train out. That was the only punishment at Achnacarry; if you dropped out or fell out or went off the whole Commando idea, they threw you out, RTU'd – Returned to Unit. There was no other punishment. All the training involved live ammunition; 45 recruits were killed at Achnacarry in various live firing exercises.

Apart from a lot of hard physical training, including the notorious speed-marches, a mile in ten minutes for up to 15 miles, in full kit with platoon weapons, there were tactical exercises by day and night all on the 'Me and my pal principal' where two men 'oppos' or 'opposite numbers' worked, ate, slept and soldiered together. The training went on for six solid weeks with no stopping for Sundays or bad weather – the weather around Achnacarry can be very bad indeed but, as the instructors pointed out, 'The war does not stop on Sundays and the Germans keep on fighting in bad weather, so. . . .'

All the recruits were trained soldiers before they arrived. The result of this was to produce a Commando soldier, a rather different type of animal, tough, resourceful, fierce in battle. The Commandos carried the war to the enemy where and when no one else could. They fought at Lofoton and Vagso, in the Adriatic and Yugoslavia, at Dieppe, and D-Day and all the way beyond the Rhine to the Elbe. They fought in Italy, at Commachio and at Anzio, at Salerno, in Sicily, in North Africa and in Burma. Then the war ended and they were not wanted any more.

So the Army Commandos were disbanded and the Royal Marines took on the role. Our history records only one year from the end of the war until the present day when the Royal Marines Commandos were not in action somewhere in the world, in Korea, Palestine, Malaya, Suez, Cyprus, Borneo, Aden, Ulster, the South Atlantic and the Gulf.

Commando soldiers may not be able to do everything

but they will always have a bloody good try, and men who think like that can work miracles and win wars. If from this you gather that I am proud and grateful to have been one of them, you are dead right. They also gave me the best friends a man could wish for and some very happy years.

My intention had been to dump the pack at Spean Bridge station and see if I could speed-march up to Achnacarry House in the original time; it would have been without pack and kit but I am not a spring lamb any more and it would have been something. Slogging up Ben Nevis had put paid to that idea, so instead I decided to pay my respects to the Commando Memorial that stands on the hill above Spean Bridge, a couple of miles to the east.

I had not seen it before outside a postcard and I found it splendid. It shows a tight group of three Commando soldiers in battle dress and fighting order, armed with rifles and fighting knives, each about nine feet tall and standing on a plinth which bears the Combined Operations motto, 'United We Conquer' and a bronze plaque telling a little of their history and the fact that 'This country was their training ground'. It is one of the most impressive of all military memorials, and a constant stream of cars and coaches were pulling up to disgorge admirers.

I liked it, but there is another Commando memorial which I like almost as much in the crypt of Westminster Abbey. This again is a statue of a Commando soldier, bearing a proud but simple message taken from the Second Book of Samuel: 'They performed whatsoever the King commanded'.

I spent a lot of time up by the Commando Memorial, wondering if I should go to Achnacarry, still the home of the Cameron of Lochiel, or go into Spean Bridge. In the end Spean Bridge won, and down I went, past the church that carries a memorial plaque to Colonel Charles Vaughan, who was the Commandant of the Commando School during the war. Then into the village for a look at the railway station where the volunteers used to get their first taste of what was in store for them. They were ordered to jump out onto the railway line, not the platform, and make their way across the track and up onto the other platform and then onto the road to form up for their seven-mile bash. This was not an easy thing to do after ten hours on a cramped wartime train.

Spean Bridge has a good Commando Museum and a Commando Bar and leaves visitors in no doubt that the memory of the Commandos is cherished hereabouts. I had a good mooch around those and, still feeling frail, had an early night to prepare myself for a good 25-mile bash on the morrow up to Knockie Lodge. 'If They can do it, I can do it,' as we used to say long ago.

My first objective next day was to push up the road towards Fort Augustus, 15 miles north and east, at the head of Loch Ness. Once I got off the busy main road and back on General Wade's military alternative, I made good time. Scottish walking is not often on those narrow English-style footpaths, at least in my experience. There are plenty of footpaths in Scotland but on my cross-country version I walked more often on fairly wide rutted roads not unlike farm tracks, which are good going and offer fine views.

It is perhaps not too soon to explain the difference between cross-country walking and walking a long-distance footpath. The first point is that the distance itself is nothing to do with it, and the second point is that you don't need a laid-down route. What you need is a start and finish and a theme. With those three things fixed, you then plan a route between the first two that enables you to explore the third. My three points were a start at Kirk Yetholm, a finish at Cape Wrath, and history. Before starting I planned the route on a rough basis to take in certain strategic places, like Abbotsford and Glencoe, but the daily walks were often planned on a daily basis. The only skills required are a modicum of ability with map and compass and the fitness to walk 20 miles. Given those, anyone can do it.

I went along at a good clip, by the edge of the loch and then along the old railway line, looking back to the peaks and ridges on and around Ben Nevis, looking north to the hills above Loch Lochy, and, apart from a group of pony trekkers, saw not another soul until I came along that section of the Caledonian Canal that links Loch Oich, the small loch beyond Loch Lochy, with the much larger Loch Ness, the lake of the Monster. This brought me to Fort Augustus, a very pretty spot indeed, and I had got there in just under six hours, not bad going for an old man in a delicate condition.

The main road from Inverness to Fort William dodges about from one side of the canal to the other, and at North Laggan, near the head of Loch Lochy, it moves over to the north side of Loch Oich, and then back to the south shore up to Fort Augustus, and then along the north shore of Loch Ness. Since both sides of the loch are equally hilly, forested and steep, I cannot imagine why this is so, but from Fort Augustus good old General Wade has been at work and left a fine empty military road running along the south side of the loch all the way to Inverness; this road was completed between the risings of 1715 and 1745. Although I was tempted to follow the modern road up the north side of Loch Oich past Invergarry to see the Well of the Heads and Urquart Castle, in the end I stuck to the towpath of the canal and it took me easily into Fort Augustus.

Fort Augustus is a relaxing little place with not a lot to see or do except visit the old Benedictine Abbey Church and sit in the sun by the locks watching the craft go

through. Fort Augustus was named after the second son of
King George III and built as a garrison after the 1715
rebellion. My decision to make this walk in May was now
starting to pay off, for as the days wore on and I got further
north, the evenings were getting longer and longer. That
meant that I could take my time over a long day and enjoy
plenty of rests, which I seemed to need, though after a
fairly stiff day I was starting to feel myself again. There are
no two ways about it; the best way to recover from
excessive exertion is a bit more exercise and lot of tea.

I felt I had done quite enough for one day when I arrived
at Fort Augustus, but I had to go a few miles more to my
next stop at Knockie Lodge. I therefore spent part of the
afternoon resting and drinking tea before I pushed on up
the hill for something stronger at Knockie Lodge. At
Knockie, Tigger, the in-house Labrador, who regards
taking guests for walks as his duty, recognised a kindred
spirit in suitable boots and was clearly disappointed at my
lack of interest in an evening stroll around the neighbouring bens.

I was feeling much better and ready for another long slog
on the morrow, all the way to Inverness, where I was to link
up with Geoff, Keith and Ginger. I was in the middle of the
Great Glen and deep in the Highlands, the weather was
glorious, but it was time to call Geoff and check that the
gang were indeed going to meet me as agreed, outside
Inverness station in four days time, not later than noon. I
should have known better.

'Ah well,' said Geoff. 'There's been a bit of a problem. . . . I don't really see how we can leave here until
Saturday. . . .'

'What?' Not again. This was our third long walk and
Geoff had yet to make a rendezvous on time.

'But,' he continued, 'if we drive all day, we will be in
Inverness by the evening.'

I doubted that, and I said so, firmly. Geoff's driving is very close to low-flying but there is no way that any reasonable man can drive from the Thames Valley to Inverness in one day and arrive fit for the hills. Besides. . . .

'It's that bloody Rugby Club again,' I said. 'It's the Club Supper, isn't it? Friday Night is Ratfaced Time with the Old Neanderthals . . . right?'

'Well . . .' said Geoff, '. . . a bit, but I also have a business meeting on Friday afternoon. By the way, Keith isn't coming; he's got 'flu.'

I know a protective aside when I hear one but this was a real surprise. Keith may sometimes look as if he is at Death's Door but he is never ill and would fight his way out of the coffin to go on a good walk with a bunch of chums. Clearly, this was serious. Besides, Keith was bringing the other tent to shelter us on wild nights far from home when the going got tough and the sleet was sheeting down. I reminded Geoff of this.

'We are not staying in tents,' said Geoff firmly, 'and neither are you.'

'But what . . .?'

'You can walk your feet off all day if you like,' said Geoff, 'and I will walk with you, but come the evening time it's into the car and on to a comfy B&B for a shower, a meal, a few drinks and a soft bed. We are too bloody old for sleeping on the ground, and anyway we don't have to.'

Put it like that and who am I to argue? Geoff had done all the planning on the stage from Inverness to Cape Wrath and was therefore in charge – if he ever turned up. I am not too keen on roughing it either if I can help it. As we used to say in the old days: 'Any damn fool can be uncomfortable' and this walk was not planned either as a backpacking trip or an endurance contest.

I had already noticed that there was plenty of accommodation in the Highlands and my excessively heavy rucksack full of hard-hitting gear had yet to be fully deployed. All we had to do now was achieve a link-up. With Geoff involved this could be as complicated as docking a rocket ship to a space station, and called for a similar use of technology.

We had to go into a long and expensive rethink on the telephone before we had the new arrangement in place, but since it worked I will pass it on. I was to go into the Tourist Office in Inverness and book us all into a bed-and-breakfast for the Sunday night somewhere north of the Cromarty Firth. The name, place and directions would be passed to Geoff. We would then make our own way to this rendezvous, keeping in contact throughout Saturday and Sunday by periodic resort to public telephone boxes and Geoff's car phone. That arranged, I could now press on up the Great Glen with a fairly easy mind. Pity about Keith, though.

The Great Glen virtually splits the Highlands in two. It runs from the Firth of Lorn, all the way north and east to the Moray Firth, a distance of about 65 miles. Some 45 miles of this trench are filled by three lochs, of which Loch Ness is the largest and by far the most famous, thanks to the legend of the Loch Ness Monster, a legend which scientific investigation and common sense have quite failed to dent. Indeed, the Monster industry grows; visitors can go into the legend in depth at the Official Loch Ness Monster Exhibition Centre and literally into the depths of the loch in a Monster-hunting submarine. There are Monster hats and tee-shirts and Monster toys and Monster things to go in the bath. The Loch Ness Monster – Nessie – now supports an entire Highland economy.

The only snag is that the Monster's appearances are somewhat infrequent. The best place to improve the chances of sighting the Monster is in the waters off Urquhart Castle on the north shore, where Nessie still tends to appear if the Monster trade looks like dropping off.

Every couple of years or so, some otherwise sensible person will come staggering into a hotel, or more often these days onto television, and swear that 'This great, big, loopy, horrible ... *monster*' had bounded along the surface of the loch, or even across the main road ahead and given them a terrible turn. Far be it from me to say 'Rubbish!' Like many people, I wish there really *was* a Monster in Loch Ness, but until I see it for myself, well, as they say in the Highlands, 'I hae me doots.'

That said, the Monster has a good provenance. Quite apart from these regular sightings, tales of the Monster go back a bit. The first mention came as long ago as the seventh century and tells us that around AD 589 St Columba was making his way down the loch on his way to Aberdeen, when the Monster attacked his boat. This must be true because St Columba was a saint and saints never tell horrible lies. Sightings continued down the centuries and the reports show certain similarities. All the accounts report a long neck, lots of coils or humps, and the Monster cruising out of sight faster than a motor boat – hence no clear pictures except one, and that one was recently declared a hoax, as it was noticed that the date on which it was taken was 1 April 1934. However, the photo was taken after a spate of similar sightings.

The Monster really came to fame in 1930 when a newspaper reported that three fishermen had seen it from their boat. There were 33 sightings in 1933 alone, including one of the Monster on land, crossing a road near Dores, only 200 yards ahead of the witnesses' car. The Monster or some monster swirlings in the water were caught on film in 1934. In 1941, in the middle of the Second World War, the Italian Air Force claimed to have killed the Monster during a bombing raid along the loch, the brutes.

In 1952 the record-breaker John Cobb was killed on the loch while attempting to achieve the world water-speed record. A memorial to this event stands by Urquhart Castle. After his death the story went around that his craft had collided with the Monster. After the war, technology took a hand in the search, and in the last decades the Monster has been tracked by sonar beams and by underwater cameras and chased by scuba divers and submarines. From time to time someone comes up with a photograph, but the quality is never good and the outlines far from sharp. Nessie must be the only celebrity in Britain unwilling to have her face in the papers.

Whether there actually *is* a Monster in Loch Ness is a matter of opinion; personally, I would like to think that there is, but a bit of definite proof would come in very handy. Even so, anyone passing by Loch Ness, whether they admit it or not, will be keeping a look out for the Monster. This is a good thing for apart from the Monster there is rather too much loch. Loch Ness is not the longest loch in Scotland – that honour goes to Loch Awe – or even the deepest, for Loch Morar claims that title, but it is still pretty big, 24 miles long and up to 800 feet deep. There is still not a great deal to see there, apart from boats far out on the loch and a few Monster-like ripples on the surface that end up just being ripples.

I set out from Knockie Lodge early next morning, early enough to surprise a group of red deer hinds browsing beside the road, the first deer I had seen on this journey. I wanted to get back to the loch to walk the flat General Wade road for a bit up to Inverness, but I elected to get there across country, cutting down to the Wade Bridge at Whitebridge, one of the finest of his works, and taking the track from there past Dell Lodge and Dell Farm and then down the banks of the River Foyer. This is a very lovely stream, quite spectacular in parts, with rapids, waterfalls and gorges, past the Falls of Fiers, which were pretty low after only a few days without rain, and so out again to the edge of the loch and General Wade's road.

Boswell and Dr Johnson make their appearance again here, for they came down this road on their *Journey to the Western Isles*, failing, like me, to catch a glimpse of the Monster. The Doctor would certainly have recorded it, but the good Doctor neither reports a sighting nor refers to the legend, which is rather strange, for the Doctor always had an eye for the unusual or the curious. Still, he did come trotting along this very road and I found it exciting and encouraging to think that I was following in his path, albeit in the opposite direction.

Once out on the military road, the day passed in a dream. There was the blue loch sparkling on the one hand, and deep, shady woods coming down to the road on the other. Most of the traffic was on the far side of the loch, a distant hum, no more. I saw a couple of red squirrels leaping about in the trees and startled another group of hinds who went bounding off into the undergrowth with not even the snapping of a twig to mark their passing. The sun shone, the banks above the loch were a carpet of primroses, and if one car went by every hour that was the most of it.

I went on, the Skull Cinema fully engaged in thinking about the Monster, my eyes constantly diverted by the scenery, and early that evening I found myself entering the suburbs of Inverness. There was a bit more of the Caledonian Canal here and rather too much pavement, but the streets were quiet as I plodded into the centre and out across the River Ness that pours through the centre of the city, and so, wearily I grant, I came at last to the Mercury Hotel. The Mercury seems to cater mainly for business people rather than those with large rucksacks, but perhaps I had novelty value. The staff competed to carry my pack to the lift and told me dinner would be waiting whenever I was ready, and how about a drink from the bar? What nice people you meet when you go walking.

12

Culloden to Cromarty

As far as I could distinguish, at a distance of
twenty paces, the English appeared to be drawn
up in six ranks, the first three kneeling and
keeping up a terrible running fire upon us.
The Chevalier de Johnston, Culloden, 1746

Culloden! The name has a ring to it like the stroke of
Doom, tolling the death-knell of the clans. Culloden put an
end to Stuart hopes and all those long-cherished Jacobite
dreams, but it did more than that. It wiped out generations
of clan love and loyalty with a furious blaze of musketry
and cannonfire. That loss and not the defeat of Bonnie
Prince Charlie, is the true tragedy of Culloden.

The name Culloden is a good name for a battle or a
battlefield but Culloden seems to be a new name or an
English one. At the time, and for a while after it, this
bloody but brief engagement was known in the Highlands
as Drummossie Moor, named after that flat patch of
heather and gorse where this fight took place, on the cold
snowy morning of Wednesday 16 April 1746. Stevenson
has Alan Breck calling it so in *Kidnapped* and that was
written more than a hundred years after the battle.

However, it has always been the English custom to name a battlefield after the nearest castle or great house near by, hence Agincourt rather than Tramecourt or Maisoncelles. The nearest great house to Drummossie Moor was and is Culloden House and there is a Culloden Moor so we can settle for that. It lies a few miles east of Inverness and I got to Culloden by walking out from Inverness along the road to Nairn, with the Moray Firth and the Black Isle and the snow-tipped mountains of the north looming up to my left. After a while I found signs pointing to 'Culloden' and made my way there around the edge of the battlefield, passing under the line of flags that mark the positions of the Jacobite and Hanoverian armies. A path across the moor led me up to the Battlefield Centre, which offers a good presentation on the battle and, almost as usefully on this brisk spring morning, a hot cup of tea.

Culloden was the end of it all. Although the moor is attractive where it is not featureless, unlike Glencoe, Culloden has an air of doom about it. You do not have to be a soldier to see at a glance that this was no battlefield for the clans. If that is clear at a glance today, then what persuaded Prince Charles Stuart to fight here, with all the odds against him and none of that necessary advantage of terrain? When I first came to Culloden many years ago trees and plantations covered much of the battlefield, but all that has recently been cleared away and the ground is much as it was in 1746. Culloden Moor is flat and open, the perfect killing ground for an army equipped with cannon and cavalry and fighting an army equipped with only infantry and total reliance on the sword.

By the time he arrived at Culloden, eight months after arriving at Arisaig, Prince Charlie had an army containing about 5,000 clansmen, some Irish volunteers, a few Englishmen and a number of French officers. His men were inadequately armed. The clansmen had muskets, swords and pistols, while for support he had a small number of horsemen – the word cavalry would be an exaggeration – and a few cannon without any trained gunners to man them. The task was hopeless.

Coming up from Nairn that morning under their commander, the Duke of Cumberland, were more than 8,000 English soldiers, most of them infantry of the line, plus eight companies of Highlanders from Clan Campbell. Cumberland was an experienced soldier, the victor of Fontenoy in 1745, the second son of King George and the cousin of Bonnie Prince Charlie. His well-equipped, professional army included 2,400 cavalry and Colonel Belford's artillery train of ten three-pounder field-pieces, light cannon capable of firing both round-shot and canister.

The Jacobites were wet, tired and starving. The English Army was equally wet but otherwise in good order, their ranks filled and their confidence replenished since their recent defeats at Prestonpans and Falkirk. They had received special training with the bayonet, each man being directed not to fight the Highlander in front but to thrust at the one on his right and take that enemy on his unshielded side, where the stout leather-clad Highland targe was not available for a parry or protection. If the English infantry could keep their nerve and hold their line when the Highland charge came in, their victory was assured.

The fight on Drummossie Moor did not last long. The first shot came from one of the Jacobite cannon. That fired a couple of shots at the English line, one cannon ball skimming over the opposing artillery and killing a man in the rear rank of the infantry which now stood like a red wall across the moor. Then Colonel Belford brought his batteries into play and the calvary of the clans began. Belford had ten guns and trained gunners to serve them and they played at will on the Highland line. Within ten minutes Belford had silenced the Highland guns and was able to turn his attention to the clansmen.

Belford's guns did terrible execution. Whole files of men went down before them and the Highlanders had no means of replying to this cannonade. They had nothing to sustain them but blind courage, loyalty to their chiefs and the hope that someone would take charge and order them across the moor with sword and dirk. The clansmen stood in the slanting sleet, under the cannon fire, staring at the Prince, waving their swords and crying 'Claymore?' begging him to order the charge.

Until that order came they stood there and took it, their ranks being even further galled when the Campbells came round on their right flank and begin to enfilade their line with musketry. The Jacobite line could not endure much more of this, and if the order would not come, they must move without one.

After half an hour under artillery fire, Clan Chattan charged across the heather at the centre of the English line. Hot on their heels, the other clans came on, the Macdonalds of Clanranald, Glengarry and Keppoch, 3,000 men or more, running across the open moor, screaming in to the attack with sword and dirk, urged on by the ranting music of the pipes.

Belford saw them coming through the smoke and sleet and switched his cannon from round-shot to grape, greeting the clans with a hail of musket balls. The Redcoat infantry brought their muskets up, took aim and began to fire volleys into the Highland line: 'the fire of small arms began from right to left, which for two minutes continued without cease like continual thunder equalling the noise of the loudest clap.'

The Highlanders went down before this fire, but the clansmen who survived still came on, shouting their warcries 'Loch Moy' and 'Dumaglass', and where they reached the Redcoat line and struck home they did fearful slaughter. Splitting heads to the chin, lopping off arms, hacking with the claymore, stabbing with the dirk, stopping to fire at the Redcoat line with musket and pistol before running in with cold steel, those who could stand attacked the English line. One man of Clan Chattan killed twelve English soldiers and cut his way through to the rear of the English Army before he was shot down. Major Bean, also of Clan Chattan, hacked a path through two English battalions before someone fired a musket into his back. His piper, having played the clan into battle, laid his pipes aside a hundred yards from the English and went into the fight with drawn sword.

Macgillivray of Dumaglass, the first Highlander to reach the English line, led his clan into the ranks of Bligh's and Sempill's regiments before he was bayoneted and brought down. This was not like Falkirk or Prestonpans. This time the English did not flee. They stood their ground and met the clans with discipline, musketry and the bayonet.

All across the moor the Highlanders were coming forward to the English line, fighting for their Prince in the only way they knew, at close quarters, matching cold steel against cannon and musketry. 'I must own,' wrote one English solder after the battle, 'that the Rebels behaved with the greatest resolution.'

It was not enough. The English line was penetrated here and there, but it was not broken and the English infantry did not yield. They matched the claymore with the bayonet and when the Highlanders drew back to regroup or take a breath they opened fire on them again with musket and cannon. Before ten minutes had passed from that first assault the ground between the armies and before the Redcoat line was littered with the dead and wounded of the clans. Those who survived were now falling back, but some came on again when their chiefs commanded it.

'My God,' cried Macdonald of Keppoch, who was lying on the heather in front of the English line, both legs broken by a sweep of grape-shot, 'Have the clansmen of my name deserted me?' His men of Keppoch turned back into the fire of the English line, where Macdonald died and his brother with him and many more besides. Keppoch's proud boast had been 'a rent-roll of 500 fighting men' – most of that rent-roll died with him on Drummossie Moor that morning.

It was gallant and glorious and quite wonderful, but it was a slaughter and that was not glorious for a dream died here. Some 1,500 clansmen fell on Drummossie Moor that day, nearly a third of those engaged, and hundreds more died of their wounds or were slaughtered and murdered in the days and weeks that followed.

Meanwhile what of the Prince? He sat his horse and rode about the field, watching in horror while his army was shot down. The Prince was no general and he lacked the good sense to listen to those who knew more about soldiering than he did, like Lord George Murray, but he had his courage and his share of honour. He would have led his horsemen out against the English cavalry now flooding across the field, to give some support to his broken infantry, but his officers took the bridle of his horse and led him away. From that day on his life was a tragedy. He left behind the ruin of his House; the clans took the road from Drummossie Moor that led inexorably to the destruction of the Highland people and their old way of life.

The Prince wandered in Scotland for a further six months before a French frigate came into the Western Isles and took him back to France. A reward of £30,000 was offered for his capture, a fabulous sum for the time, but no one betrayed him, not for money, not from fear. He was passed from hand to hand, house to house, cave to cave, while the Highlands he had roused against the House of

Hanover went up in fire and pillage all about him.

That gallant, well-remembered lady, Flora Macdonald of Skye, risked her life and lost her liberty for aiding the Prince, and never got so much as a letter of thanks for it, though he left her a lock of his hair which still rests in Dunvegan Castle. Some time in this flight he took to the bottle, and remained on it until he died in Rome in 1788, fat and drunken, a far-from-Bonnie Prince. Maybe that, too, is the sadness of it, that such a Prince came to such an end and all for nothing.

Putting the battlefield of Culloden back the way it was, clearing away the trees, was a good idea because it is now possible to work out what happened and see the ground as it stood in 1746. The clansmen were buried in a mass grave now marked with headstones naming the various clans, and there is a separate grave for the fifty or so English dead. Flags mark the opposing lines, at no great distance apart, and the hopeless bravery of the Highland charge is plain for all to see.

Well, enough of that for now. As we shall soon see, the blame for the final destruction of the Highland way of life cannot be laid only at the door of the English, but that still lies ahead, both for this story and for the clans. I had another cup of tea at the Battlefield Centre and then made my way down the road to Culloden House.

Culloden House is now a fine hotel, and the building that stood here during the fight on Drummossie Moor is not the same as the one that stands here today. Even so, if you stay around Culloden you should stay at Culloden House as our present Prince Charles did recently, partly for the house's historical connections and partly for the owner, Ian Mackenzie, who is a Scot, very hospitable, an expert on the battle, and a dowser.

I don't know how the subject of dowsing came up but

come up it did during a drink before dinner. Ian let on that he was a dowser; I confessed to Ian that I had always wanted to try dowsing, and he told me anyone could do it and promised to show me how. Lessons began during dinner, to the ill-concealed alarm of some of the other guests, when Ian appeared at my side clutching a metal coat-hanger and a pair of pliers. He then proceeded to cut the coat-hanger into two L-shaped pieces, placed them in my hands and said, 'Away you go then.'

Away I went then, or rather the coat-hanger did. Without any assistance from me – I swear – the rods swivelled slowly in my hands and came to rest pointing inexorably at the radiator. 'There you are,' said Ian. 'Would anyone else like to have a try?'

The other guests quailed. Everyone took a great interest in their plates while I dowsed the soup, the water glass and the wine bottle. Ian then went on his evening 'Mine Host' tour, telling unlikely tales of haggis hunts and haggis traps to the American guests. That done, we retired to the drawing room and talked about Bonnie Prince Charlie.

At the time of the '45, Culloden House belonged to Duncan Forbes, Scotland's Lord President of the Court of Sessions, the country's leading judge. Like most Scots, he was not in favour of the Jacobite cause and when he heard of the landing at Arisaig he urged the Government to arm the friendly, pro-Hanoverian clans and send troops at once to the Western Highlands. His advice was ignored and his future perilous, especially in 1746 when the Jacobite Army retreating from England arrived in the area and camped in the grounds of his house. The home of a Hanoverian supporter was lawful booty, but the house was protected from pillage by the Prince's personal writ. It did not enjoy similar protection from the English when the battle was over.

After the battle, seventeen wounded Jacobite officers

took shelter in the cellars of Culloden House. There the servants cared for them until a patrol of Cumberland's Army took them out and shot them by the stables. Such atrocities were taking place all over the area, on the battlefield, on the surrounding farms, on the roads north and west to the glens and mountains and in the town of Inverness. Any Highlander the Redcoats found was shot or hanged, together with a good many people who had neither been in the fight nor supported the Prince. Just to have a Scots accent was a dangerous thing hereabouts in the bloody days after the battle.

Duncan Forbes spoke out strongly against this brutality and slaughter. As his country's leading advocate and a known supporter of King George he might have hoped to gain attention, but the killing went on for months. Forbes even went to London to request clemency for the clans, only to be turned away from Court. The money he had spent from his own pocket raising troops for the King was not refunded, and he died in 1747, almost bankrupt.

His house was largely destroyed by fire in 1753, and the present building is in the Georgian Palladian style attributed to Robert Adam and dates from 1772. It retains many elements of the former house, including the stump of the old gallows just outside the main gate, and there are lots of good strolls in the garden and the surrounding countryside. I had a good time at this historic and hospitable house and hope to go back some time. Meanwhile I had to get on, for the next stage of the journey, the thrust for Cape Wrath, was now about to begin.

That evening I rang Geoff and got some good news. Keith had emerged from behind Death's Door and was on again for the walk, and the three of them – Keith, Geoff and Ginger – were intending to leave on the morrow ... in two cars. Two cars seemed excessive and I said so but Geoff said that he was in charge north of Inverness and I was to shut up. I therefore shut up and set off next morning for Inverness, the Black Isle and the Cromarty Firth.

Inverness is a fair town, the capital of the Highlands. The town lies below the heather-clad slopes of the Monadhliath Mountains, is split by the River Ness and fronts onto two Firths, the Inverness Firth and the Beauly Firth. There is a castle and a lot of narrow medieval streets and far too much sprawling suburb, but you can hear Highland voices at Inverness and there are a few places there worth exploring.

The castle by the river is the third to stand here. Robert the Bruce destroyed the first, Mary Queen of Scots hanged the governor of the second for refusing to let her in, and the Jacobite Army blew it up in 1746. The present, much-restored version, houses the Sheriff's Court. The Town Museum shares premises with the Tourist Board, and after a look at that I found a B&B across the Cromarty Firth where we could all stay on the Sunday night, and that was about it.

Dr Johnson and Boswell came through Inverness on their way to the Western Isles and the Doctor seems to have liked the place. It is curious that although he must have passed right by Culloden on his way here from Nairn he does not seem to have visited the battlefield; at any rate there is no mention of it in his Journal.

He does record that here he first heard people talking *Erse* – by which he must mean Gaelic – and mentions that the English spoken in Inverness is the purest, and the language of the town had long been considered 'peculiarly elegant'. The present visitor would be hard pressed to hear Gaelic spoken in the Highlands today, except perhaps in the Hebrides.

When talking of Inverness, Dr Johnson praises the Scots love of education and literature, but he then spoils that favourable comment by remarking that 'until the Union made them acquainted with English manners the culture of these lands was unskilful and their domestik life unformed; their tables were as coarse as the feasts of Esquimeaux and their houses as filthy as the houses of Hottentots.' I cannot think how he formed this opinion, and to attribute the Scots' love of culture to the influence of England is an amazing statement. From Inverness the Doctor and Boswell took horse and went off down Loch Ness towards Fort William, and I went the other way, north across the Black Isle.

I could not discover how the Black Isle got its name, but since it is still heavily wooded no doubt that is the cause, since the term 'black' usually means that a place was forested with pines. Another point is that the Black Isle is not an island at all but a peninsula which, with the other peninsula to the north of it, creates the great natural harbour of the Cromarty Firth.

The Home Fleet once had a great base here at Invergordon, the scene of a mutiny over pay between the two World Wars. The old naval dockyard is now a base for the refitting and repair of North Sea oil rigs. My original intention was to take the train from Inverness to Dingwall since the only practical routes across the Black Isle lay along main roads and across two bridges and I saw no point in a long walk in heavy traffic. However, when I got to Inverness station, an event changed my mind.

Inverness station on a Saturday morning is a departure point for hillwalkers. The place swarms with them, sitting about with maps and Munro's Tables, waiting for trains to hither and yon, and I felt quite at home amid their anoraks and rucksacks. I bought a paper and a plastic cup of coffee and sat down on my own to await the train ... and then it happened.

A man sat down beside me, leaned close and asked, 'Do you have love in your heart?'

I took one look and whatever love I might have possessed was replaced by another emotion: stark fear, I think it was.

My interlocutor was very large, very drunk and heavily tattooed. I recognised the tattoos as the mark of one who has spent many years in the slammer, a graduate of the Barlinnie Hotel. 'Love' and 'Hate' tattooed on the knuckles, a line with 'Cut Here' dotted around the throat, a small blue butterfly on each earlobe and a blast of bad whisky when he leaned close to tell me of the last person he had met, who had no love in his heart and had ended up in traction.

I seem to attract people like that. There could be a hundred people in the bar but the one the yob will pick on is me. This has happened so often over the years that I have learned to be resourceful. If they are smaller than me, I hit them; if they are larger, I cringe.

I would have run for my life or the nearest policeman but there was no chance of that. My new friend had my arm in a vice-like grip and, while exploring for my loving heart with the other hand, he managed to find my wallet.

This was madness; I was being robbed in broad daylight and in mid-morning. I have been mugged before, but this was an insult. Everyone on the platform seemed to know what was going on. They were all wearing those 'Rather you than me, mate' expressions that meant there was no help there either.

Then it got bizarre. My friend handed me my wallet and said 'I know you have love in your heart and leave it to you.'

'Leave what to me?' I asked.

'Your wee giftie,' he said.

'How wee a giftie would you settle for?' I asked.

He waved a knuckle or two in my face and said, 'Could you make it a pound?'

A pound!

A pound is a small price to keep out of traction but I don't believe in pushing my luck. As my chum took the money and reeled off towards the bar, I took to my heels and fled from the station towards the Black Isle. I may be a poor judge of character but I don't think he had love in his heart.

So, in the end I walked across the Black Isle to Dingwall. Dingwall is a fine little town, though I don't recommend the walk. The views promised better days ahead, for the skyline was barred by tall, snow-tipped mountains, a spread of forests and some deep glens. From the map I could pick out Ben Wyvis, another Munro at 1,046 metres, and the other dark mountains of Easter Ross. Once I got beyond the Cromarty Firth I would be in the real Highlands again and much further north than I had ever been. I could hardly wait to get there and start tramping up the glens from Dalnavie towards Strathcarron and the mountains of Sutherland.

I had some lunch in Torc and missed a bus and swore a bit and thought of hitching a lift, but in the end I punished myself for being a wimp by walking all the way, butting ahead into a clear, stiff northern breeze that made stopping for any length of time a chilling experience.

In Dingwall I first tried to get rid of my rucksack before making a tour of the town, eventually leaving it at the railway station. The station bore a brass plaque which said that between 1915 and 1919 the station buffet had served no less than 134,864 cups of tea to the soldiers. That's very precise. Outside the station stands a memorial to the men of the Seaforth Highlanders who were recruited hereabouts and went to fight in France during the Great War, the memorial cross being the gift from the village where they were billeted before going into battle.

Dingwall is a soldier's town, a solid, quietly prosperous sort of place that ought to be famous, for this was the home-town of General Hector Archibald Macdonald (1853–1903), a man known to his contempories as 'Fighting Mac'.

I have a great deal of sympathy for Hector Macdonald, who started life in the ranks and came to a tragic end after decades of devoted service. Macdonald was born in a croft at Rootfield near Dingwall. By the age of 12 he was helping his father on the farm, but he was made for a soldier and at 17 he enlisted in the 92nd Highlanders, later the 2nd Battalion, the Gordon Highlanders. He soared rapidly to the rank of lance-corporal and sailed for India in 1871, where within two years he was a sergeant. When the Commanding Officer of the 92nd presented the stripes he told Macdonald that 'A sergeant in the 92nd Highlanders is at least the equal of a Member of Parliament, and I expect you to behave accordingly.' The CO was not disappointed.

In 1879, during the First Afghan War, Colour Sergeant Macdonald distinguished himself in action against the enemy near Kabul. The story goes that soon after the battle, General Roberts – 'Bobs' – offered him the choice of a commission or the Victoria Cross. Macdonald took the commission, saying that he would win the Victoria Cross later. He was duly gazetted in 1880 and finished the war with a fine reputation and a chestful of medals.

In 1881 Macdonald was in action again, in the fight at Majuba Hill during the first South African War, where he was taken prisoner by the Boers. In 1885 he was in Egypt, marching to the Sudan in the vain attempt to save General Gordon at Khartoum. He fought in various Sudan battles with great distinction and received the DSO. He returned to the Sudan later and was with Kitchener in the campaign that led to the victory over the Dervishes at Omdurman.

Kitchener never admitted it, but by common consent in the army Macdonald saved the day at Omdurman, when at the crux of the battle his Brigade was surrounded by the Dervishes and outnumbered seven to one.

'Fighting Mac' received the order to retreat, but he had wounded men to guard and replied, 'It'll nae do; I'll see them damned first and we maun fight it out,' ... and fight it out they did.

In 1900 Macdonald arrived in Cape Town as Major-General commanding the Highland Brigade – the Black Watch, Seaforths, Gordons, Argylls and Highland Light Infantry (HLI) in the next Boer War. Here matters did not go so well. His Brigade was badly cut up at Magersfontein and again at the Modder River and it was here that his personal downfall began. Rumours began to spread in the army that Macdonald was homosexual and had had a relationship with a Boer prisoner. Nothing came of these stories at the time, but the stories would not go away. In 1902, when Macdonald was serving in Ceylon, a letter appeared in a local paper openly accusing him of homosexuality.

Homosexuality was not uncommon in the Victorian army but wise men repressed it; both Kitchener and Gordon seemed inordinately fond of boys, but their conduct and behaviour survived close inspection. Perhaps Macdonald was indiscreet; perhaps his humble origins went against him.

In 1903 a Ceylon schoolmaster accused him of 'habitually misbehaving' with schoolboys aged 12, and the fat was in the fire. The Governor of Ceylon ordered him home to face an enquiry, and after that he was ordered back to Ceylon to face a court martial. Macdonald was passing through Paris when the story broke in the newspapers and he took what was then seen as the honourable way out. He put a pistol to his head and blew his brains out in a Paris hotel room.

After his death, as is the way of the world, everyone was very sorry. More than 30,000 people visited his grave in Edinburgh within two days of the funeral, and the people kept coming for months, covering his grave with flowers. Dingwall too has remembered its most famous son, and there are two memorials to 'Fighting Mac', as well as a good display on his life and service in the Town Museum.

I could have stayed in Dingwall that night, but it was light until nearly 11 p.m. and these long Highland evenings made me feel like getting on, so I took the high road out of town, walking along the hill above the Cromarty Firth, looking ahead to the seven or eight great oil-drilling platforms that were moored in the waters of the Firth. As the gloaming settled down, they became festooned with lights and stood like great Christmas trees with their feet in the water.

After leaving the town behind I could not find anywhere to stay. I therefore had to keep on walking, ever more slowly as the evening drew on, past Mountgerald and Ardullie with the walls of the Fyrish Memorial crowning the hill ahead, and the blue waters of the Firth to my right. There was enough interest in the views to keep me going until I crawled wearily into the straggling little village of Evanton and found a bed at the Novar Arms. I had come a long way that day and seen a lot of things, and I was tired. What I needed now was a good dinner, a glass or two of wine and an early night. It was not to work out like that.

13

Across Easter Ross

When the bold kindred in the time long vanish'd
Conquer'd the soil and fortified the keep,
No seer foretold the children would be banish'd,
That a degenerate Lord might boast his sheep:
Fair these broad meads – these hoary woods are grand,
But we are exiles from our Father's land
                              'The Canadian Boat Song' (Anon)

Sunday morning in Evanton is not the liveliest time of the
week. That title belongs to the Saturday night when the
Novar Arms Hotel hosts a *ceilidh*. I was unaware of this
fact when I tottered up to my room after dinner and was
lying on my bed, boots off but fully clothed and sound
asleep when the sounds of revelry reached my ears.

First I tried the usual tactics, trying to ignore it and
hiding my head under the pillow, but it was no good. The
beat of the music came throbbing up through the floor. The
next tactic is the old one: if you can't beat 'em, join 'em. I
got up, had a shower and went off to the bar. This was a
mistake. I did not get back to bed until well after midnight
and next morning I felt very, very poorly.

After the Saturday night *ceilidh* a heavy air hung about
the Novar Arms Hotel next morning. It took a certain

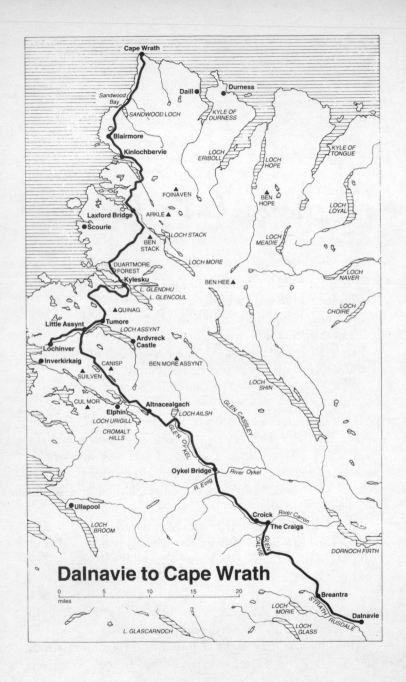

Cape Wrath

Sandwood Bay
Daill ●
Durness ●

SANDWOOD LOCH
KYLE OF DURNESS

● Blairmore
● Kinlochbervie

LOCH ERIBOLL
LOCH HOPE
KYLE OF TONGUE

FOINAVEN ▲
BEN HOPE ▲
LOCH LOYAL

● Laxford Bridge
ARKLE ▲
LOCH STACK
LOCH MEADIE

● Scourie
BEN STACK ▲
LOCH MORE

DUARTMORE FOREST
● Kylesku
L. GLENDHU
L. GLENCOUL
BEN HEE ▲
LOCH NAVER

QUINAG ▲
LOCH CHOIRE

Little Assynt
Tumore
LOCH ASSYNT

● Lochinver
● Ardvreck Castle

● Inverkirkaig
CANISP ▲
BEN MORE ASSYNT

SUILVEN ▲
LOCH SHIN

CUL MOR ▲
● Altnacealgach
LOCH AILSH

● Elphin
LOCH URIGILL
GLEN OYKEL
GLEN CASSLEY

CROMALT HILLS

Oykel Bridge
River Oykel

R. Einig

● Ullapool
Croick
River Carron
The Craigs

LOCH BROOM
GLEN CALVIE
DORNOCH FIRTH

Dalnavie to Cape Wrath

Breantra

0   5   10   15   20
miles

STRATH RUSDALE
● Dalnavie

LOCH MORIE

L. GLASCARNOCH
LOCH GLASS

amount of door banging and running up and down stairs before the landlady appeared and brought me breakfast. After that and lots of coffee, the next stop on the road to recovery is a good walk. There was nothing left to do that day but head east along the Forth and then over the hill to Strath Rusdale, on what promised to be my last leisurely day before the real mountains began. I had all day to get to Dalnavie and no need to rush, so I took my time about leaving.

Just west of Evanton the Glen Glass river pours through the Black Rock Gorge. I crossed the bridge there and made my way past the grounds of Novar House before turning past the Mains of Novar and up the steep wooded hill of Cnoc Fyrish to the Monument. Scotland is spattered with military monuments, usually dating from the Great War and consisting of a kiltie with bonnet and bayonet. The monument that crowns this hill above Alness is like a crenellated wall and was erected in the early 1800s by the local laird, another soldier, Sir Hector Munro of Novar, to commemorate his exploits at the siege of Negapatam, a city in India which the General had captured in 1781. Rather more usefully, the memorial provided work and income for some of the local people in a time of great poverty and widespread unemployment.

It took just over an hour to flog up to the memorial, but the views made the effort well worth it. To the north lay the mountains of Easter Ross, tipped and plastered with the late spring snow, while at my feet to the south lay the bell-shaped mouth of the Cromarty Firth, dotted with those oil rigs which, seen from above in daylight, looked just like those Martian fighting machines described by H.G. Wells in *The War of the Worlds*.

Alness, the little town and port below the Cnoc Fyrish has become a major centre for the refurbishment of oil rigs which come in here between drilling operations in the

North Sea and take up the slack left hanging when the Invergordon Naval Base closed down. Invergordon was the scene of the last Royal Navy mutiny back in 1928 when the Government decided to cut the sailors' pay, which was not very generous in the first place. As mutinies go it was a quiet affair, but it was suppressed with the usual rigour and a complete lack of sympathy for the problems of the lower deck.

My plan now, as agreed with Geoff, was to descend the hill and pick up the road that ran up Strath Rusdale towards Strathcarron and the north-west, the route we must follow as closely as possible in our *direttissima* towards Cape Wrath. If I could make a few miles up that road that would be time and distance saved tomorrow, for Geoff would drive me back to the point I reached today and we would start walking again from there.

It all seemed pretty straightforward, and the path along the top of Cnoc Fyrish fell away easily down the side of the hill through the trees and out to the little road that runs from Alness to Loch Morie. Apart from a startling moment when a man on a mountain bike came hurtling silently past from behind and scared me half to death, I made the road without trouble. There I found another track which, according to the map, appeared to lead down to the River Averon – or Alness – and thence to a bridge across the river into Strath Rusdale.

This it did. I found the path under some power lines and went down to the banks of the river, but then came the snag. Half the bridge had been swept away by the spring floods and the half that was left looked rickety and very unsafe. There was a notice at the near end advising people to stay off. Well, maybe, but at times like these, needs must.

I could not wade the river which was deep and fast and strewn with rocks so I clambered out on the bridge and carefully picked my way out to the end. That still left a gap of twenty feet or more to the far bank and I saw no easy way across the black, swirling water. I was stuck and would have to move upstream.

Back again on the near bank, I brooded over the map and elected to follow the river up to where, I hoped, it would narrow or have a bridge. I must have forgotten what happened on the Teviot some weeks ago for it happened again here. After a mile or so I ran out of towpath, then out of bank and finally out of dry ground. Before long I was forced to wade out into the stream, because I could not get up the slope or force my passage along the river bank, through a tangled maze of fallen trees and branches. With the river roaring past and a heavy pack on my back this was not advisable, but I was too bloody-minded to turn back.

I must have been flogging along like this for an hour or more, driven mildly frantic by the sight of a good flat footpath on the far shore. Then I found a steep bit of grassy bank which I could, with luck, manage to get up, though I was now very wet and pretty tired. I scrambled to the top and arrived in what were obviously the private grounds below Letty House. From there I skulked through the trees to a field full of horses, which came galloping up to sniff me over and then, wonder of wonders, my troubles were over. I came onto a path which led to a bridge over the river and yet another path. In half an hour or so, by about one in the afternoon I came out onto the Strath Rusdale road at Mains, just west of the village of Ardross. I was soaked to the waist and pretty muddy, but all was now right with my world.

I turned north and began to walk briskly up the glen, hoping to dry out before I went too far. This is one of the great advantages of Rohan clothing: it offers minimal protection from the chill winds so you have to keep moving, but it dries out in no time. By the time I had gone a couple of miles I was dry again and enjoying the views.

The agreement with Geoff was that I would wander along west, and north, and Geoff would eventually arrive and collect me *en route*. I therefore walked up the road for about four miles or more until the metalled track ran out. A number of cars came along and I stopped to wait for each one, full of anticipation for a flash of headlights and a wave of the whisky bottle. By the time I got as far as I could go that day, Geoff had not appeared.

I therefore turned back down the road, walking rather slowly now. I spent the next two hours or so retracing my steps, first into Ardross and then along to the crossroads and the Brown's farmhouse B&B at Dalnavie. I had just slipped off the rucksack and was thinking of asking Mrs Brown for a cup of tea, when the dusty bonnet of Geoff's car appeared around the corner of the wall. The gang had arrived at last and the push to Cape Wrath could begin tomorrow.

Over tea, Keith told me about their departure from the south. This had been scheduled for 10.00 hours, but when Keith arrived at Geoff's house at 09.45 hours there was no sign of Ginger, and Geoff was blundering around the kitchen in his dressing gown, looking like death.

Ginger staggered in an hour later, pale and wan after a long night at the Rugby Club Supper, and it took another two hours of tea-drinking, interspersed with minutes feebly stuffing gear into rucksacks before they were ready to say goodbye to Eileen, pat the dogs, Pickle and Kizzy, and set out for Scotland. I restrained myself from gloating over all this. They had then roared up to the Border and, after a night stop at Biggar, were looking more or less all right. They had in fact made very good time, and seemed ready for a good walk tomorrow.

Inevitably, Mrs Brown, our hostess, and her husband the

farmer, were not Scots. The Browns had sold a small farm in Yorkshire for a much larger one up here in Ross, and what with the sheep and the 'set-aside' they were doing all right and were very hospitable. We had a huge tea and I had a doze and then we went into Alness and got lost.

Geoff and I then had a bicker about his map-reading and we found a restaurant beside the Cromarty Firth where seals came to haul out on the sandbanks and £10 a head bought us a feast. That done we went back to the B&B and Geoff and I had another bicker over the sleeping arrangements. Since these arrangements were crucial I will explain them now.

Nobody wanted to share a room with Keith. This is no reflection on the waking Keith, who is charming and funny. Well provided with good books he is willing to share and fairly house-trained, awake, Keith is a gem. Asleep, Keith snores.

Now, most people snore sometime in the night but not the second they nod off. With luck you can usually hope to nod off before they start trumpeting, but with Keith you don't have a chance. Keith starts to snore as soon as his head hits the pillow and he snores in and out, without pausing for breath. It goes like this:

'Well, I'll put the light out now . . . all right, Keith?'

'Yeh . . . all right, Rob.'

'Well, g'night, Keith.'

'G'night, Rob ... ZZZZZZ ZZZZZ SAWWW GRRRE ... UMPFH.ZZZZZ ... (Grunts, snorts, gasps, gargles, horrible strangling noises) ZZZZ GRR RUMPH ACH ACH ARGH ZZZ ...'

'Keith . . . for God's sake . . . KEITH!'

'Wassa marra . . . urgh... humph.'

'You were snoring . . . LOUDLY.'

'Oh, was I . . . Sorry, Rob ... ZZZZZ, GEE-WHRIIR ZZZZZ. . . .'

He can keep this up for hours. I knew all about Keith's snoring because I had suffered it many times before. When Keith and I walked across the Pyrenees, an exhausted, hard-bitten bunch of hillwalkers got up before dawn and fled the Goriz hut without breakfast just to get away from his one-man din. Unfortunately for me, Geoff had found out about Keith's snoring at Biggar, and my crafty suggestion that I should share a room with Ginger and thus get to know him better did not work. 'Keith is your mate,' said Geoff, 'and you can bloody well sleep with him.' Fortunately for me, Mr Jones the farmer found a spare room. I had that, Keith slept on his own, and Geoff shared with Ginger. Ginger snored. Loudly.

It is a truth universally acknowledged that if four people have to get up and get moving in the morning they will take four times as long as one person will do on his own. On my own I was on the trail by nine at the latest. Once the merry men arrived, a half-past-ten start was considered good going. I had my breakfast and a brood over the map and snarled at Keith and paced up and down the yard muttering. Finally I could stand it no longer. I marched up to Geoff and Ginger's room, flung open the door . . . and reeled.

Their room looked as if it had been raided by the Drug Squad. Everything was upside down, every drawer was open, clothes and kit were strewn everywhere and both mattresses were propped against the wall.

'What in the name of. . . .'

Geoff's head appeared from under one of the beds. 'Not a word, Rob,' he said. 'Not a single word. This is serious . . . Ginger has lost his teeth.'

I cannot remember how we found Ginger's teeth, but by about noon on a very cold grey morning we were finally on the move from Strath Rusdale walking fast across a land of stark beauty, but one quite empty of people. Keith and I, who were to walk the route that day while Geoff and Ginger went ahead to find food and some overnight accommodation, were soon wondering where all the people had gone.

An hour beyond the start-point for that day we were in a wilderness of gorse and heather, dotted with small lochans and threaded by burns, following the well-marked drove road north and west to Glencalvie and the Craigs. We passed a ruined house or two and a shepherd's croft, but saw not a soul that day, not even another walker. The explanation for this absence of people came next day, in the church at Croick, the epicentre of that long and shameful Scots tragedy known as the Highland Clearances.

When I walked across Ireland in 1992 my route brought me to the town of Ballina in County Mayo, one of the places devastated by the Great Irish Famine of the 1840s. That tragedy I had at least heard about before I left England which is one of the reasons I went to Ballina. My knowledge of the Highland Clearances, the bulk of which took place at about the same time, was absolutely nil before I got to the place where they took place. The Clearances were almost as bad as the Great Famine, equally effective in driving the people off the land and, above all, a betrayal of an entire people by those who had laid claim to their loyalty, and exploited it for centuries.

The Highland Clearances came about because the people were in the way of the landowners' prosperity. The point is that the landowners were the chiefs and the people they drove out were their clansmen. It happened over time and it was done by Scots to Scots, and the English had no great part in it.

As we have already seen, after the '45 and the defeat at Culloden, hard times swept the Highlands. The kilt and pipes were banned, the clans disarmed, the clansmen recruited into the ranks of the British Army and the old clan system hastily suppressed. This destruction of the clan system left the chiefs with no great need for armed clansmen. What the chiefs needed now was money.

They had discovered Lowland ways. Now they wanted houses in Edinburgh, French fashions for their wives, a public school for their children and cash in the bank. They no longer needed warriors at their back. By the late eighteenth century the chiefs had discovered a fresh sort of wealth, far more profitable than the meagre tack rents they could get from their clansmen, who lived at best on or near subsistence level. The clansmen could no longer raid the Lowlands and made a thin living grazing goats and black cattle in the glens and on patches of land cleared on the hillsides. They survived in a simple fashion, but there was no money in it. Then the lairds discovered the profits that could be made from the wool and mutton produced by flocks of the hardy Cheviot sheep.

The 'Great Sheep', as the Highlanders called it, came from the Cheviot Hills on the Border. It had once been thought that this animal, though a fine producer of wool and mutton, was not hardy enough for the Highland winters. However, it was introduced progressively into the Highlands from the 1780s and did well enough, but it needed sheltered grazing, and the best grazing was in the glens, which were occupied by the common people.

Well, in that case, the common people would have to go. Commercial sheep farming was common in the Highlands by the end of the Napoleonic Wars and the people went down before the sheep less swiftly but more surely than they had before Belford's cannon at Culloden. The first resistance of the people came here in Strath Rusdale in 1792, a year known in Highland history as The Year of the Sheep.

The people of Strath Rusdale came from Clan Ross, and the laird was that General Sir Hector Munro who had built the monument on Fyrish Hill. Munro's sheep were soon competing for the grazing with the Rosses' black cattle and in 1792 the clansmen decided to drive the sheep away. Munro was the local magistrate and his response to the eviction of his sheep was to send in the army, accusing the country people of riot and sedition. The troops turned the sheep back into the glen and the magistrates arrested five of the local people who were tried in Inverness and sentenced to transportation. Fortunately, they escaped from prison before they could be shipped abroad, but the landowners had tasted power.

The events of 1792 taught the landowners that they could do what they liked with their clansmen. The clansmen had no leases for land they had lived on for 500 years. When they asked for one, hoping to gain security of tensure, their rents were raised to more than they could pay, and those who could not pay were evicted. The Great Sheep continued to flood the glens of Ross and the people were driven out, burned out, harassed, kept under legal pressure or faced with ever higher rents until they began to despair. Eventually they had to leave, some for the slums of Glasgow, others for the laird-free lands of Canada, New Zealand and Australia.

The lairds and chiefs saw no shame in this. This was the time when the doctrine of *laissez-faire* ruled the economic life of the British nation, and the lairds took full advantage of it to work their will and increase their profits, knowing that the Government would not interfere. The other reason for their lack of compassion was that they thought – Heaven knows how – that their actions were for the general good of the nation. The lairds and the magistrates usually referred to the Clearances as 'Improvements'. Naked self-interest often needs a cloak of hypocrisy. It was considered a fine thing to be an 'Improver', even when what you were actually doing was driving poor people from their homes and land.

Keith and I had a good day, a long walk across the hills, past the tumbled stones of long empty crofts. At the time of the Sheep about 400 people lived hereabouts, but now the land is virtually empty. I did talk to one man we met out walking his dog but he told me he worked on a North Sea oil rig or on repairing them in Alness. There is no work now in Strath Rusdale and no men there to do it if there were. At least the walking is good, beside the Blackwater and through the woods on to the higher land that leads up to the Craigs where Geoff and Ginger, having found a place for dinner, were waiting to take us off for the night.

Next morning we were out again, though by mid-morning rather than the crack of dawn. That walk brought us to Croick, which is hardly even a hamlet but was the centre of the Clearances of the 1840s. The murmuring of the dispossessed grew louder down the decades and their anger came to a head here in Croick parish in 1845, a hundred years after the chiefs had led out their clans to fight for Bonnie Prince Charlie.

The people of Glencalvie, the glen by Croick, who came mostly from Clan Ross, had lived in Glencalvie for over 500 years, serving their chief in the clan regiments, paying tack for their land. Then in 1842 the Great Sheep arrived and the common people suddenly discovered they had no rights to the land and must leave at once. Where they went was not the laird's problem: the laird, William Robertson at Croick, had left the dirty work to his land agent – or factor – James Gillanders. In May 1845 Gillanders evicted some 90 people from their homes in Glencalvie. His men destroyed their pitiful cabins to make a sheep run. Men and women, children and babies, young and old, had been driven out with nowhere to go, and so they were offered shelter here, in the churchyard at Croick. They were allowed to sleep among the gravestones, exposed to the rain and the chill.

The tragedy at Croick has been well recorded and was even well reported at the time. Hearing of the forthcoming evictions, the minister at Croick had written to William Delane, the editor of *The Times* and Delane had sent a reporter to witness the events.

The journalist's account is still preserved in the church at Croick and makes sad reading: 'Through the actions of the Factors in these glens, hundreds of peaceable and industrious peasants have been driven from their means of support to become wanderers and starving beggars ... a brave and valuable population has been lost.'

There are other, simpler memorials here in the church, for some of the people scratched their names on the glass of the windows and on some of the walls, before they trudged wearily away: 'Glen Calvie people was in the churchyard here, 24 May 1845. Glen Calvie people, the wicked generation.' There is even a sad note in the church visitors' book, where Martyn Wilson from Maine in the USA wrote on 8 May 1994: 'My great-great-grandfather and mother were married in this church'. Four generations on and the heart is still Highland.

There was an ironic sequel to all this. During the Crimean War it became necessary to recruit men to replenish the Scots regiments mauled in the fighting, and there was then no conscription to swell the ranks ravaged by warfare, cholera or the Russian winter. The Queen at Windsor and the Government in London suddenly remembered those useful Highland soldiers and sent to the Highlands for willing recruits. The Highlanders would not come.

The Queen and her Ministers were shocked and surprised, for they had taken the loyalty of the Highlanders for granted. One reason for this refusal to enlist was given in a Highland newspaper, which reported the views of many Highlanders. 'We have no country left to fight for. You took away our country and gave it to the sheep. Very well, since you have preferred sheep to men, let sheep defend you.'

That was telling them, and soon there was more. The Government tried blandishments and the factors and lairds tried threats, but the Highlanders still would not budge. Then the 'Great Improver' himself, the Duke of Sutherland, a man whose factors had driven thousands of men and women from their homes and turned Sutherland into one great sheep run, decided to take a hand in this matter. The Duke, who must have been arrogant, ignorant or just plain stupid, seems to have thought that a personal appeal from him would bring the young Highlanders flocking to the Colours. He may even have thought that he enjoyed the love and respect of the people, but if he thought that he was soon to learn otherwise.

The Duke emerged from the ducal seat at Dunrobin Castle and went about the country, calling all the men to public meetings. There he explained the situation as to a group of yokels, asked for volunteers, offered a bounty from his own sporran, and sat down to await the rush. Nobody moved. After a pause the Duke got up again and asked why the people were not responding to his request and coming forward to fight the Czar. One of the audience told him:

> If the Czar of Russia should take possession of Dunrobin Castle next term we could not expect worse treatment at his hands than we have had at the hands of your family for the last fifty years. How can you expect to find men, among the ruins of this country? The few which have been found have more sense than to go to a field of slaughter. But Your Grace may take comfort from the fact that although you cannot find fighting men you can sell plenty of mutton to those who are now serving in the armies.

That was plain talking and the Duke did not like it. The young men of Ross and Sutherland then sent an address to the newspapers saying that they were not afraid to fight, but that this was not their quarrel. They had been ordered to leave their land and would not leave it to fight for the people who were so willing to dispossess them.

The Highland Clearances went on until the end of the last century, until the Crofting Act gave the people some security of tenure, but by then it was too late for most of the Highland people. Today the glens are empty and the race has gone and no amount of tartan-wearing and bagpipe-playing will bring the old ways back.

Croick Church was built by that man of many parts, Thomas Telford, on land donated by the Rosses and completed in 1827. The first minister, Robert Williamson, remained in the parish until he emigrated to Nova Scotia in the 1840s, taking a lot of the congregation with him.

That is where many of the Highlanders went, to the Maritime Provinces of Canada; when I rode my bike across Prince Edward Island a year or so ago, I stopped at many of the neat graveyards and found them full of Scottish names – Murray, Ross, Macdonald, Maclean – and when I stopped a man on a tractor to ask the way to the MacLeods' Bed-and-Breakfast he scratched his head and said, 'Well, we are all called MacLeod around here . . . but you can stay at my place if you like.'

That old sadness apart, Keith and I had another day of glorious walking, along the strath from Croick and over the hill to Glen Oykel where Geoff and Ginger were to park and walk to meet us. The strath is wide and open with a few pine plantations and a single croft to fix our position as we walked along, the burn rushing by our side to provide some refreshment.

I had long since decided that walking through Scotland was much more enjoyable than walking through Ireland.

Though I bow to none in my love of that country, Ireland is rather more suited to cyclists. The drove roads and tracks that seam these glens of the Scottish Highlands are perfect walking routes on which you can make good time while enjoying splendid scenery. We made rapid progress up the track until we reached the point where we must turn off and head up and over the hill to Glen Oykel. Then we ran into a snag: deer fences.

The Highland sheep boom of the last century did not last. It lasted long enough to destroy the Highland way of life, and there are plenty of sheep in the Highlands today, but the great days of the industry ended in the last century. Ironically enough, part of the decline was due to the Clearances. When those dispossessed clansmen finally arrived in Australia or New Zealand they discovered lands ideal for sheep. Those lands grew wealthy off the sheep's back, and every pound earned by Australian or New Zealand sheep farmers was a pound out of the pockets of the lairds. It is hard to feel sorry for them.

Unfortunately, the decline in sheep farming did very little for the common people of the Highlands. By the time their wool market fell away, the lairds had discovered a new source of income in grouse-shooting and deer-stalking, neither of which called for a large force of workers and both of which did well or better on empty hillsides. Most of the glens now support a shooting lodge or two to which rich people come from many countries, but especially from Arabia, America and Germany, to shoot the grouse and stalk the stag.

Those who hunt and shoot are probably correct and quite sincere when they say that their activities are a part of conservation, because if the animals were not kept for shooting they would not be kept at all. The red deer have increased so much that they are becoming a menace to the land, cropping it bare in places, and therefore have to be culled. In an attempt to keep them on the hill and out of the fertile glens, the landowners have erected deer fences, which can prove a sore trial to the cross-country walker.

Deer fences are not to be stepped across or taken lightly. The red deer can leap any normal fence, and these were about 12 feet high and strongly staked, a formidable obstacle even if we had been inclined to climb them. I preferred to go along the edge of the fence, and we went plugging up the hill and through the bogs, being pushed ever further off the route dictated by my compass until we came to yet another fence, completely barring our route up the hill. There was clearly nothing for it but to climb it, which we did by clambering up the supporting poles and heaving ourselves over the top, dropping down into the muddy heather on the far side.

That left us feeling rather done in, so we stopped in a sheltered hollow to eat a bit of chocolate and take a nip of whisky, but the wind was too sharp to permit any long delay. We therefore had to move on fairly soon, picking our way up the hill, across the heather.

On we went, puffing up over a series of false crests, until quite suddenly the Oykel glen lay before us and a wonderful, totally unexpected, mountain panorama opened up to the north. Away to our left now lay a great series of glorious snow-topped peaks we had yet to identify, and we sat in the heather with the map, trying to decide on which was Ben More Assynt, which was Canisp, which one, surely that one, was the sugarloaf of Suilven.

I have rarely seen such splendid country. Even better, we had the right weather to enjoy it, clear and cold, with not a scrap of cloud or mist to screen the glory from our eyes. The glen below us was a moving brown carpet, a great herd of red deer drifting away from us down into the shelter of the woods. There was the Oykel Bridge and that building must be the Oykel Bridge Hotel, a popular shooting and fishing hotel where people in boots would surely be welcome and the kettle was on the hob.

Here now, coming up towards us, were Geoff and Ginger, puffing well and leaning heavily on their walking sticks. Since a little suffering is good for the soul, Keith and I sat down and waited until they reached us at the top of the hill. We studied the map and gloried in the scenery, and then it was suggested that we went down to the hotel and got together with one of those great big Highland teas, with jam and scones and Dundee cake. Then we might have another pot of tea before we set off down the glen and did a few more miles to our stop that night.

Thus are traditions established. After that we finished every day with tea, scones and cake and with that much decided, we lumbered back onto our feet and with our eyes on those splendid mountains to the north, went down together to Glen Oykel.

14

Crossing Sutherland

> It is a fine thing to be out in the hills alone. A man
> can hardly be a beast or a fool, alone on a great
> mountain.
>
> Rev. Francis Kilvert, 1840–79

The Reverend Francis Kilvert was a travelling man, but I
would not accept his advice about travelling in the mountains and certainly not in these Scottish mountains beyond
Glen Oykel, where the great bulk of Ben More Assynt
looms up to the north.

As we forged steadily north and west up here, a score of
splendid peaks, many still tipped with snow at the sunny
end of May, hinted at just how bleak these hills can become
when the weather turns foul, and how wise I was to travel
there with a group of good companions.

On the other hand, I was thinking of killing Keith. Every
night I lay biting the pillow while he trumpeted away on
the far side of the room, and after a few days of sleepless
nights I had murder on my mind. Unable to sleep, I recalled
those many times in my youth when my grandmother, her
eyesight failing, would have me sit and read to her from the
newspapers. Her favourite accounts came from the latest

murder trials, recounting the crimes of ghastly people like Haigh, Heath and Christie, the serial killers. In those pre-television days the newspapers gave a blow-by-blow, spare-the-reader-nothing account of the murderer's activities and that day's doings at the Old Bailey, leading up to the guilty verdict, the black cap and the inevitable appointment with Mr Albert Pierrepoint, the public hangman.

I would sit by her bed, reading about strangulation, throat-cutting, axe murders, arsenic poisoning, dismemberment, bodies disposed in acid baths, bodies hidden in cupboards or bodies buried under the floorboards – God knows what this did to my youthful psyche – while my grannie sat up there in her bonnet like something out of Little Red Riding Hood, nodding away at the juicy bits. 'Ah weel,' she would say, as the jury retired to consider their verdict, 'Ah canna' tell if the man is guilty or no.... but he sounds like the kind of man who would be none the worse for a hanging.'

After several sleepless nights I was beginning to feel the same way about my old mate Keith. My only consolation was that Geoff was having similar problems with Ginger. We would emerge from our rooms or cabins every morning, our eyes black-ringed like pandas, crazed with lack of sleep, wondering how much time we would get for murder on account of snoring.

On the other hand the walking hereabouts, from Glen Oykel up to Lochinver and beyond was simply superb, the mountains marvellous, the views sublime. I have never seen such splendid country as that we walked through north of Glen Oykel, under the loom of Ben More Assynt, between sharp-peaked Suilven and the great surge of Canisp, our path winding beside deep blue lochs and rippling burns, with red deer drifting away on the hills and sheep scattering before us like apple blossom in the breeze. It was, in a word, glorious.

By now we had established a certain routine. Geoff and Ginger would take Keith and I to the start of the day's walk. They would them go off to find accommodation on the far side of the mountain before walking back from the finishing point to join us. Sometimes we would take one car ahead in the evening, and in that case the four of us would go along together all day in one cheerfully argumentative party.

After a day or two of this, Geoff took me on one side and told me that Ginger was a bit concerned at our constant bickering. I was amazed. Geoff and I have been bickering, wrangling and arguing for the best part of thirty years with never a real cross word. We share one of those curious English habits, one which confuses all foreigners but especially Americans, by which the more you like someone the more you insult and abuse them. Geoff and I have been insulting each other for nearly three decades and we look forward to many more arguments in the years ahead. After I told Ginger that, he felt better and got down to some abuse himself. We all got along famously, but a bit of arguing always helps to pass away the day.

Mostly we argued about my map-reading. The others thought my methods very hit-and-miss, though since the weather stayed fine and we walked on well-marked tracks the amount of map-reading required was minimal. I enjoy cross-country navigation but I have no objection to taking the easy way, if it happens to be going in the right direction and, in spite of my initial objections, having two cars proved both a bonus and a danger.

The bonus was lighter loads to carry each day and the chance to see more of this wonderful country after the day's walk had been done. The danger was that Geoff, obsessed with the scenery, would insist on driving to or from our rendezvous at great speed with his head over his shoulder. There were perfectly good views ahead but he seemed to prefer the ones behind:

'Coo ... er ... will you (screech of tyres) take a look at *that* ... that is (violent swerve) bloody *marvellous* ... get out of the way, sheep.... What a stunning (scream of brakes) place for a photo.' Every evening he put years on me, driving like that, but he was quite right about the landscape.

Sutherland is our kind of country. It covers an area of 2,200 square miles and has only 13,000 people, which makes it the least populated area in Europe. More to Geoff's purpose, there are no traffic lights and no round-abouts. The only distractions are the mountains, the lochs, the stunning views and vistas.

I'm not usually a man for mountains. I prefer ridges and the plains but these mountains of Sutherland are curious because although they are real mountains, great imposing hunks of rock and heather, very beautiful and well ar-ranged, they are not particularly high. Canisp is only 846 metres, twin-peaked Suilven can forge no higher than 731 metres on her northern crest and 723 metres on the southern one while Cul Mor in the Inverpolly Nature Reserve is only 849 metres. Mighty Ben More Assynt is just 998 metres, and though that makes it a Munro it is hardly a giant. They may not be high but they certainly look high.

In fact, they look huge. They dominate this rippling, folded, loch-dotted and burn-threaded landscape; they are mirrored in the waters and they give this land an imposing grandeur. The views are so wonderful that they brought us out every evening, even after a full day on the trail, to see more of it and soak in a natural glory that was even more glorious for being so unexpected. I have been lucky enough to see a great many beautiful places but few can match and none can surpass these hills of Sutherland beyond Glen Oykel.

*

We came down the hill to Oykel Bridge and fell into the Oykel Bridge Hotel crying out for tea. This hotel, and most of the others hereabouts are fishing and shooting hotels, catering for those people who enjoy sitting all day in a boat on the loch or wading about rushing rivers, chest-deep and wearing waders. Since I am not a sporting type I had never met such people before, but they were unfailingly courteous, full of love for the surrounding countryside and very interested in wildlife. The salmon fishing, I gathered, was not what it was, as the East Europeans were long-lining the salmon out in the Atlantic, and fewer and fewer wild fish were getting back to spawn. Catches were down and the future looked bleak.

The shooting revenue was also down, partly from the current depression, partly because the collapse of the Soviet Union and the opening-up of Eastern Europe had provided their wealthy German clientele with new and cheaper places to go and hunt the deer. Apart from the fishermen and stalkers, the bulk of the visitors to Oykel were hillwalkers and Munro-baggers who swarm into the hills every weekend. Ben More Assynt, the main Munro hereabouts, is proving a nice little source of income for the local hotels, while other sources are in decline.

Our hotel that night, the motel at Altnacealgach, stands just across the road from the Borralan loch, below Ben More Assynt. We got there in the sudden still of the late evening, that time when the winds drop and the midges flourish, our arrival delayed by pots of tea and pints of beer at Oykel Bridge. Those consumed, we took a fine, wide track through the woods, east of the road that runs right through Glen Oykel. This track leads to Loch Ailsh where we struck another road leading up to another sporting lodge and this brought us down to the main road again, and up to the motel in good time for dinner. The English are here too, for this motel is run by a cheerful, hospitable couple from Essex – the Scots still being remarkably thin on the ground – and they gave us a very good evening over dinner and around the bar.

The motel caters for fishermen and walkers, and the owners were even then holding a parcel of food and maps for a long distance walker who was going to stage through there some time soon, on his way from Land's End to John o'Groats, a walk of some 900 miles, even without diversions. That evening we also awaited the arrival of a walker who was coming in the opposite direction from the one we were due to take on the morrow, south from Lochinver. He had still not arrived by the time we went to bed and was not about by the time we left in the morning.

Morning was freezing. I went out, felt the air whip around my ears and went back to recommend hats, scarves and windproofs. The walk that day was a long one and we were going as a party, leaving one car here, Geoff and Ginger having already taken the other one on towards Lochinver. With a stiff day ahead, we began with breakfast and a good bicker before trudging down the road towards Elphin and picking up the path north, beside the bridge over the Ledmore river that links Borralan with the Cam Loch.

From here the track leads up the eastern side of the loch and then veers over the hills to Lochan Fada and then on, between the heights of Canisp and Suilven to the eastern edge of Loch na Gainimh. This path is a splendid route with these two peaks soaring up on either hand. By mid-morning we could already see figures on the peaks, small moving dots against the sky, and were wondering whether to scramble up to one or the other summit and join them when we saw another walker, a speck on the trail ahead but coming steadily towards us. This turned out to be a solitary walker from Leipzig in what had been East Germany; and an offer of chocolate brought him to a halt for a chat.

This was his third walk in Western Europe since the reunification of Germany; he had spent the previous night in Lochinver and now had to forge on to Bonar Bridge and get a train for London and the flight home. He had only had a week in Scotland but he was enjoying every minute of it. We offered some more biscuits to send him on his way, and he was soon just a dot on the trail behind. . . . 'But isn't it something,' said Ginger 'that a kid from a former Communist state, kept in for years, can now go where he likes and enjoy the freedom we have always taken for granted.'

We made good time that day but the country was really too beautiful to rush. We took photos and inspected wild flowers, watched a cuckoo skulking about in the copses and scanned the sky for the golden eagle, ambling along up to the road by Little Assynt, where the footpath ran out. Here we picked up the car left the night before and took the road back round Loch Assynt to Altnacealgach to pick up the other one. This gave Geoff yet another chance to scare me half to death again and all of us a chance to recce the next day's route from Tumore. We also stopped to take a look at the romantic ruins of Ardvreck Castle on the western shore of Loch Assynt, the place where the Marquis of Montrose was finally betrayed, captured, kept imprisoned and sent to his hanging in Edinburgh.

'What did they hang him for?' asked Keith, as we got out of the car for a look. 'Snoring,' said Geoff and I together.

The problem with James Graham, the Marquis of Montrose, was that he trusted Charles Stuart, King of England. Montrose believed that any man who was King of two Kingdoms, England and Scotland, must be a man of his word. Oliver Cromwell was another leading figure of the time who made the same mistake, but when he discovered his error Cromwell cut off the King's head. Montrose found out far too late, and went to the gallows for it.

It is a fact that nothing brings an event or a period to life as much as the words of a person who was there, or some form of physical evidence, especially on the ground. Battlefields, they say, are scars on the face of history, and the same holds good for ruined castles. They hanged James Graham by the Mercat Cross in Edinburgh, on a gallows 30 feet high, but the gallows have long gone and many people were put to death in that little spot above Canongate. The place that brings James Graham back to life is here in the wild Highlands, where he spent his last days of freedom before he was cooped up in the castle of the Macleods at Ardvreck.

It was a beautiful evening, the Assynt loch as still as any millpond, a deep, smooth blue, reflecting the outlines of the surrounding hills. As ever, there was not a soul about and as an evening it was just about perfect, but there was that grim, ruined keep on a point of land jutting into the lake, and a sad tale to hang about it.

The first requirement of the story is to understand the difference between the 'National Covenant', the one signed on a slab at Greyfriars Church in Edinburgh and the 'Solemn League and Covenant' signed later between the Covenanter Scots and the Parliamentary English. The National Covenant was designed to protect the civil rights and religous freedoms of the Scots against interference from the king; Montrose supported the National Covenant and believed that Charles I would abide by its terms, but there was a snag in it.

It will be recalled that the overall aims of the National Covenant were to restrict the powers of the king and ensure that the land was ruled by law and the will of the people as expressed through Parliament, not by the king's will and whim. So far, so reasonable, but one of the clauses in the National Covenant was a requirement to support the king in his majesty ... and what if the king in his majesty decided to ignore the clauses of the Covenant?

The Solemn League and Covenant went a good deal further than the National Covenant. The basic problem now was that while the English quarrel with the king was political, the Scots really fell out with him over the matter of religion. The Covenanters required the English to get rid of their bishops and aimed to assimilate *all* the reformed churches into one Puritan faith, with dire penalties for any who stood out against it.

In return for their support in this ambition, the Covenanters made common cause with the English Parliament against King Charles I and sent troops to aid the Parliamentary Army in England. For Montrose this was one Covenant too far, for apart from treason it must involve oppressing dissenters and persecuting those who preferred their own version of the Christian doctrine. In 1643 Montrose therefore broke with the Covenanters and offered his sword to the King.

This at once made Montrose a traitor both to the Covenanters and their leader, Archibald Campbell, the Earl of Argyll, but there could be no half measures in this civil and religious war. The King did not make Montrose very welcome either, though he made him a Marquis. Montrose then raised a Highland Army, largely from the Macdonalds, who would join anyone offering a fight against the Campbells, and at Tippermuir near Perth, on 1 September 1643, his force of Scots clansmen and Irish kerns met a much larger Covenanter Army. After one volley, which exhausted their slender supply of ammunition, the Highlanders charged in with their swords and drove the Covenanters from the field. The killing was considerable and the booty was immense.

After such a victory, the Irish and the Highlanders would normally have gone home with their loot, but by sheer leadership and willpower Montrose kept them in the field, rewarding them with the bloody sack of Aberdeen.

By now all the Campbells were in the field and marching north to give battle. Montrose harassed them as they advanced, while avoiding a general engagement. In November the Earl of Argyll was obliged to give up the hunt for Montrose and withdrew to winter quarters at Inveraray. Montrose, however, kept the field. With reinforcements from all the anti-Campbell clans he made a winter march over the Grampians to fall on the Campbells, first at Inveraray at Christmas time, and again in February 1644 at Inverlochy.

Montrose took the Campbells completely by surprise at Inverlochy, leading his army in a night march through deep snow and a blizzard, around the shoulder of Ben Nevis to fall on the dismayed Campbells just after dawn. Such was the slaughter at Inverlochy – over 1,500 men were killed in the fight – that it was a generation before the Campbell clans were again at full strength.

Montrose was doing wonders for the King's cause in the Highlands, but the King's cause was on the wane everywhere else. After Naseby, the writing was on the wall and the Cavalier doom was plain for everyone to see. Montrose's supporters then began to fall away. In 1645 the remnants of his Royalist Army was destroyed at Philiphaugh and, although Montrose was dragged away from the rout by his Captains, the Covenanters hanged and shot and drowned their prisoners, especially the Irish, until Royalist hopes in the Highlands were totally extinguished.

Montrose then vanished for a while, perhaps to France. While he was gone, the King's struggle was finally brought to an end and King Charles himself made prisoner by the Scots. The Scots then handed Charles over to the English, who took him south to a prison on the Isle of Wight. Then, inevitably, the Scots and the English fell out. On his promise to accept the Covenant, the Scots promised the King an army of 20,000 men with which to crush Parliament and regain his Kingdom. It did not work out like that.

In 1648 Cromwell's New Model Army crushed the Scots at Preston. After that defeat, the Protestants under Argyll held sway in Scotland. Argyll welcomed Cromwell into Edinburgh as a liberator and greeted him as a prince. With his northern frontier secured and the Scots quiescent, Cromwell put Charles I on trial in London and, in January 1649, he cut off the King's head.

This was a mistake. The Scots were perfectly capable of executing their own monarch and were shocked when the English did it for them. In February 1649, within a week of the old King's execution, the Scots declared his son, Charles II, as King of Scotland.

All this is baffling stuff for it involves two kingdoms, various wars, a dictator and at least two different interpretations of the Protestant faith. Only a skilled Puritan divine could really make sense of it, but the simple fact is that both sides, English and Scots, were trying to impose their version of the Puritan faith over the whole island, and political settlements tended to disintegrate on the rock of religion. Politics, however, are universal, and the Scots wanted it both ways: they wanted to retain the monarchy but they wanted the monarchy bound by the Covenant.

On condition that he swore to accept the Covenant, King Charles II was invited to Scotland for his coronation. Not surprisingly, Charles was willing to swear to anything, but he was reluctant to come to the country that had handed his father over to Parliament, without first testing the waters. The man he chose to take the risk was the gallant Marquis of Montrose, who might, just, gain Scotland for the King without the King needing to swear to the Covenant.

Montrose landed at Duncansby Head with a small force

in the spring of 1650. Two weeks later his army was smashed and scattered by a Covenanter force at Carbisdale in Sutherland. Montrose fled away, into the hills of Assynt, to the wild country we were now traversing. After a few weeks, ragged and starving, he asked for help from the local Macleods who, knowing a bargain when they had it to hand, kept him prisoner here at Ardvrek and then sold him to Argyll for £25,000, accepting half of the payment in oatmeal and sending Montrose under guard to Edinburgh.

With his last captain defeated, Charles II capitulated. On 7 May 1650 he agreed to the Covenant and took ship for Scotland. His surrender was not quick enough to save Montrose from the vengeance of the Campbells, and there is no evidence that the new King requested the release of his loyal Captain. Montrose was sacrificed and given to his enemies. On 21 May, dressed in his best and with ribbons in his hat, the gallant Marquis was brought to his death in Edinburgh. His old enemy the Earl of Argyll lurked behind a curtain to watch the hangman turn him off the ladder. It is worth adding that when King Charles II sat on the English throne, he totally ignored his oath to the Covenant.

This castle by Loch Assynt stands in a beautiful spot, and somehow the beauty of the setting makes the story of Montrose even sadder. The point is that the castle makes the story of Montrose seem true, and not just another old legend. This was a place in the story that still endures, a milestone on the march of time. Montrose will have looked on these hills at this time of year, maybe on an evening much like this one. He must have known what his fate would be, for the Campbells would not be forgiving once they had him in their power.

We poked about the stones and clambered on the ruined walls, but the walls of the dungeon in which Montrose would have been kept have long since fallen away. After a while we gave up looking and went back to Lochinver, my thoughts with that little armed band that headed out from here, 300 years ago, with a man in the middle lashed firmly in his saddle.

It is a lovely spot though, this castle by Loch Assynt, and one well worth seeing.

Lochinver is a pin-bright little town. This tiny fishing port is situated at the head of Loch Inver, which is actually more of a bay, an inlet on the rugged west coast and very beautiful, framing the blue waters of the Atlantic with rocky walls. We spent the night there in a very good B&B, warmly recommended by the Tourist Office. The Tourist Office was always our first port-of-call in any West Highland village, for these offices are full of information, sell books and postcards and run a reservation service, a service most useful for the wandering Sassenach.

Lochinver also possesses an excellent fish shop by the quay, one with a restaurant at the back looking out onto the loch. We checked in there for dinner and an argument, the arguing mostly over whether I could or could not dowse for water. My dowsing ability had gone downhill somewhat in the last few days, though none of the others would try it. Then my dowsing rods vanished, probably hurled into the nearest bog by one of the others, and that was another bone of contention gone. The main port-of-call next morning was Achins Bookshop and Coffee Shop at nearby Inverkirkaig. This is one of the most remote of Britain's bookshops, but a good place to buy books and drink coffee and, best of all, run by a Scot. We browsed about, had a chat with the owner, urging him to stock this book when it eventually appeared, and stocked up with shortbread. By half past ten we had exhausted the immediate possibilities of Lochinver and had set out again, forging over the hills towards Cape Wrath.

Over the next few days we enjoyed great walking, in country that seemed to become more beautiful by the mile. Keith and I walked the daily hill sections, each day hooking our path closer to the north-west, while Geoff or Ginger drove round to meet us at the far end and walked back in to meet us. It worked well and we revelled in it. We went on like this from Tumore, on a splendid path round the great Y-shaped mass of Quinag, a mountain which has various peaks and rises to 808 metres on the Sail Gharbh. We passed by the glen down to Loch an Leothaid, where Keith and I met a couple of birdwatchers who had just seen two golden eagles soaring at head height down the glen ahead. This couple came from Worthing in Sussex, which is about as far away as you can get on mainland Britain, and they had been coming up here for the last 25 years, undeterred by distance or the midge clouds of summer.

That night we arrived at Kylesku, another little fishing port, on the headland between Loch a Chairn Bhain which opens out to the sea, and the inland finger-lochs leading up to Glen Coul and Gleann Dubh. While Keith and I fell into the pub screaming for tea, Geoff and Ginger were still full of energy, and took off for a boat cruise up Loch Glencoul, to see the seals and the waterfalls of Coul. The Falls of Coul are the highest waterfalls in Great Britain, and had there been any recent rain they might have been spectacular. As it was, Geoff and Ginger saw a trickle of water and a few seals, but they returned to spend the evening telling us of all we had missed.

Kylesku is a pretty spot, surrounded by good walking trails, some of which we could see that evening through Geoff's field glasses, attractive footpaths that you might ache to get the boots on, running above the lochs and along the empty hillsides. However, you have to be strong-minded when walking across a country, and stick to the designated plan, or you will never get anywhere. The next day, therefore, we pressed on past Duartmore.

I squashed the suggestion of a day walk hereabouts over breakfast and we took up another trail which took us up through the Duartmore Forest on the road to Scourie. There Keith and I cut off north again, past the fishery by Duartmore Bridge and then across wonderfully empty country, dappled with countless lochs and lochans. Our path weaved through a watery maze, round the bogs and burns under the hump of Ben Stack, following a clear track to Laxford Bridge.

Apart from a few places, like Lochinver and Laxford Bridge, fishing ports on the coast or by the lochs, Sutherland is terribly empty. The 'Improvers' of the Clearances did their work all too well up here, but they left this a wonderful country for hillwalkers. Next day we went on again up the new road and round the coast to Kinlochbervie, our last stop before the final push up the coast for Cape Wrath. The end was almost in sight; I had come a long way from Kirk Yetholm and was already sorry that the walk was almost over.

Decisions, decisions ... this country is really too much for one visit or one walk, however long and well directed. It is too wild, too beautiful, too well provided with trails, too empty of people, too much entirely. Granted, we had the rare advantage of good weather, those long chilly days of hard winds tempered by lots of sunshine, which can make even a grimy industrial city look acceptable. Up here the sun turned this stunning landscape into a northern paradise and the effect was overwhelming. Those who fancy I exaggerate about this country of Ross and Sutherland must come up in May and October and see it for themselves. Words alone are not sufficient.

We spent our last but one evening in Sutherland at the Old School House Restaurant in Kinlochbervie which, like many of these hospitable places, is run by an English family and has guest rooms at the back. This little hotel-restaurant is set in the old village school house and the dining room is designed to recall one's schooldays, a gimmick that seems to work better with adults than schoolchildren. 'Best Vegetarian Food ever,' says one adult notice in the Visitor's Book while 'Will come in my gymslip and suspenders next time,' indicates that at least one guest has got into the spirit of the place. On the other hand, another comment, in a childish scrawl says simply, 'The children's portions are not big enough.'

Having an eye for the curious, I liked a claim chalked on the menu blackboard: 'All puddings served with fresh cream. Chips available on request.' My all-time favourite in hotel claims-that-might-have-been-better-phrased, remains the one I ran into on a reception desk in Canada: 'For one month only at just $125 a night: our Honeymoon Suite, with four-poster bed, lake view and private bathroom. Accommodates up to three.'

We dined well that night at the Old School House. We sent Keith to the corner for demanding more pudding, and spent the rest of the evening – and evenings now lasted until nearly eleven – looking over the surrounding sea and landscapes, trying to marry up the features on the map with the features on the ground. This proved a potent source of argument even without Keith croodling over Tess, the in-house golden retriever, and Geoff, eyes clamped to his binoculars, uttering moans of joy as he scanned the mountains.

I have to avoid hyperbole but it's hard. Inland now lay another great mountain mass, hunched shoulders of grey rock and jutting peaks, which turned out to be Arkle, to the south, and Foinaven to the north, just two gems in a wonderful jumble of hills and mountains filling the sky away to the east, their glory matched by the splendid seascapes to the north and south.

It needed Keith to bring us down to earth. While Geoff and I were slavering over Arkle and Foinaven, Keith was poring over the map. 'Fancy that,' he said, tapping it with his finger. 'Someone has named those mountains after a couple of racehorses.' It is hard to tell when he is joking sometimes.

Reading the map is a great distraction in Sutherland, at least for a walker. Looking over the map we could see many fine walks around this tumbled country, especially a good, long, circular walk out towards those particular peaks, on a track leading from Lochstack Lodge towards Arkle and then round the north-west face of that mountain to the walls of Foinaven. With a day or two in hand we could have done that one, coming out to the north after a cross-country tramp beside the Loch a Garbh-bhaid Mor, a very tempting one-day journey through more of this marvellous country.

However, we really had to get on. The final objective of the journey from the Border was almost in sight and our time was running out. Tramping up to Laxford Bridge we had walked onto the last map, and when we spread it out on a table at the School House, there was Cape Wrath, a rocky shoulder to the north, jutting into the Atlantic. Looking at the map, Cape Wrath still seemed a very long way away, but when I got there and slapped the wall of that lighthouse that would be the end of this journey. No more walking after that. Finish! And this time I mean it.

I always hate the end of anything, but with the end almost in sight I wanted to get it over with. Besides, we had to arrive at the Cape Wrath lighthouse soon, before David Elliot finished cutting the peat in his bothy by the Kyle of Durness and returned to Billericay. Otherwise we faced an 11-mile road walk from the lighthouse to the Durness Ferry after a long day's haul up the coast to the lighthouse from Kinlochbervie. Otherwise we had to get the ferry and find somewhere to stay, or we could camp.

'We are not camping,' said Geoff. Geoff had been saying that with increasing conviction for the last nine days. With that much settled I went to phone David and arrange our final rendezvous.

This proved difficult. I got on to the bothy but David was out. The man who answered replied to my query, 'Is that you, David?' by saying 'No, it's Stan,' and to 'Are you the shepherd?' by saying, 'No, I'm a nuclear physicist.' This was not quite what I expected in the wilds of Sutherland.

It took a few more calls before I got through to David. He had to leave for London in two days' time and could not join us for the final stage. He would, however, pick us up at the lighthouse on the following day and drive us down to the Kyle 'Just ask the lighthouse keeper to give me a ring,' he said. Stan, his shepherd, would drive us down to the ferry on the following morning, and that would be that.

'Would Stan be the nuclear physicist?' I asked.

'That's right,' said David, 'Stan actually is a nuclear physicist but he prefers to be a shepherd.'

I see.

Before I got too confused, I hung up and tackled the other problem: how would we get back to Kinlochbervie if we all walked up to Cape Wrath? Geoff and Ginger had got mulish about taking one car up to the Kyle that evening and we all wanted to do the bash up to the lighthouse tomorrow. That was right and proper, for we must all do the last bit together. The problem was to get back again.

A glance at the map will explain the dilemma. From the lighthouse to the ferry at Durness was about 11 miles. David and Stan would help us on that section, so no problem. Then we had to cross the ferry and make our way back 20 miles or more to Kinlochbervie. We needed a lift, but four men with rucksacks is a lot to lift. Our hosts at the

School House suggested we ring the ferryman at Durness but he was out, probably ferrying. Finally we tracked down Iris. Iris runs the Durness school bus. In her delightful West Highland accent, Iris said she would pick us up in two days' time on the Durness side of the ferry and bring us back from Cape Wrath. That settled the last bit; all we had to do now was get up to Cape Wrath and finish this walk.

15

Reaching Cape Wrath

I like a definite form in what my eyes are to rest
upon; and if landscapes were sold by the sheet,
penny plain and twopence coloured, I should go
the length of twopence every day of my life.
Robert Louis Stevenson, 1879

I now had just 24 hours to reach the two objectives of this
journey: the lighthouse at Cape Wrath and my conclusions
about Scotland. On one level the latter was quite easy: I
was very taken with the place. In fact, I was totally
knocked out by it. Scotland is a wonderfully beautiful
country, especially if you see it on foot.

With the possible exception of the coast just around
Dunbar, Scotland had revealed itself as one of the most
beautiful places on earth. Can there be another place on
earth which boasts such a variety of attractions? The
Borders, the wilds of Rannoch, the Braes of Balquhidder,
the West Highland Way, Glen Coe, the lochs of the Great
Glen, Eriska and Arisaig, Castle Stalker, Culloden, Strath
Rusdale ... all this and more, and all of it had been
beautiful.

As for the last week, walking north from Croik and Glen

Oykel, over the hills of Ross and Sutherland, had un-doubtedly been one of the most wonderful experiences of my travelling life. A man would have to have the sensitivity of a stone not to be awed by the sheer physical beauty of the Western Highlands, and like the rest of the party I was completely in love with the Scottish landscape, especially north of the Highland Line.

As for the other part, my self-discovery as a Scot, that was harder. I have never felt a stranger in Scotland. When you have spent the greater part of your life travelling, you don't feel a stranger anywhere, or, indeed, at home anywhere. The problem was that I had not met many Scots. Indeed, apart from one or two individual encounters and the *ceilidh* at Evanton, I had hardly met any Scots at all. This was not for want of trying, but the Highlanders are especially hard to find. Most of the people I had met on this journey – residents, hoteliers, farmers or visitors – had been English; Scotland-loving English perhaps, but English nevertheless.

What had surprised me, and had filled the notebooks that would provide the basis for this book, was not how much I had learned, but how much I had remembered. I now knew about the whisky and the poetry, about Burns and Scott and the rest, about Bannockburn and Sheriffmuir and why Bonnie Prince Charlie got thrashed at Culloden. I had investigated the Loch Ness Monster and tried for the definitive answer on what to wear under a kilt. It all helps.

On the memory front, many things had come flooding back. Until I made this journey I had not realised what fun I had had in Scotland over the years and what good friends I had shared it with all those years ago. I phoned a few of the Old and Bold to remind them of the good old days and it was like opening a great vault of memory, jammed with wild days and wild deeds. Fun, though, remembering.

On the last day there was a feeling that had not been

there before: a sense that I had found something once familiar, though as we got into our hard-hitting gear I could not put my finger on it. Well, no matter. The way to pull something from the back of your mind is to think of something else; it will eventually appear as a fully fledged thought. If you can hang onto it then and set it down quickly, it will be exactly what you are looking for. I put that in my mind, forgot about the rest, heaved on the pack for the last time and we set off down the road for Cape Wrath.

The first leg of our journey was not very long. We went no further than the nearest shop, where we stocked up with bottles of wine for the final celebration at David's bothy. If David was going to push out the fatted sheep then the least we could do was provide the grog to go with it. The bottles added very little to the weight of the packs and gave us something to look forward to as we pushed out towards the North.

As with some of the other sections on this Odyssey, no one we had asked in Kinlochbervie seemed to know exactly how far it was to Cape Wrath, only that it was a fair step. I had calculated that it would be the best part of 20 miles from the Old School House to the lighthouse, and a lot of that would be along the coastal path close to the edge of the cliffs, with gulls and puffins and seals in sight all along the way. Terrific.

Fortunately, I kept that opinion to myself. In the event it took a full day of relentless slogging, so this estimate is probably about right, but otherwise we were starved of distractions, so be aware that the path to Cape Wrath is simply a beautiful slog.

The route begins along the edge of a loch or two by Kinlochbervie with the sea on the other side of the hill. We walked on a good road, up past the main hotel in Kinlochbervie and then along an up-and-down path to

Blairmore. Here another track turns off north, clearly waymarked for Sandwood Bay. This track is driveable, but driving is not encouraged and we saw no cars that morning apart from a camper-van or two parked by Loch na Gainimh. This part of the north-west coast up to Sandwood Bay is about to be purchased by the John Muir Trust to add to the land they already hold near North Berwick. I think they had better be quick about it.

It was yet another of those bitter days, the air as clear as crystal but too cold for comfort. It took us a little over two hours to reach Sandwood Bay and we met a few other walkers on the way, most of them heading north for a day on the sands and a walk back in the evening. On the crest of the pass that leads over and down to Sandwood Bay I peeled off left to the cliffs, while the others went down to the bay. I cut up across the heather to the headland, hoping for a close look and a photo of the sharp spike of rock set in the sea just offshore here, known as Am Buachaille. This feature looks like the far more famous Old Man of Hoy, but when I got to the headland I could not see it.

In fact, the headland was a trap. There was a series of crumbling rocky shelves which concealed the view beyond and were tricky to get down. Below me to the north I could see tiny figures walking along the golden shore, some of which would be Geoff, Ginger and Keith, leaving tracks across the sea-smoothed sands of the bay, but of the Am Buachaille rock I could see no sign whatsoever.

What I could see, apparently at no great distance to the North, was a slim white building. Shading my eyes and staring hard, this revealed itself as the tower and lantern of a lighthouse. Back to the map again to check, for it seemed too clear and close but there could be no doubt. That was the lighthouse at Cape Wrath and it could be no other; the end of this walk was quite literally in sight, and for a moment I felt quite elated.

Trying to avoid retracing my steps to the path, I then managed to get myself to a crumbling, rocky ledge that felt too exposed, with a sheer drop to the rocks below. After that, I gave up the attempt to find the cliff edge and turned back, trudging over the hill again onto the track and down to the bay.

Sandwood Bay is a beauty spot but a lonely one. Only hillwalkers can get there and so it remains pristine, untouched, wildly beautiful. Sandwood was a gold and blue haven on this sharp spring day, framed by the mountains that lie above the Strath Shinary, the river that feeds Sandwood Loch. This lies at the back of the beach, behind a wall of sand and sea-washed gravel, with just one exit route letting the water of the loch pour out into the sea. Geoff was standing at the edge of the beach on a flat rock, half-covered with the incoming tide, taking pictures, and when I splashed through the last ripples of the waves to join him, I saw Am Buachaille, just to the south, standing up against the blue sky like a dark pencil.

'I could see the lighthouse at Cape Wrath from up there,' I told Geoff, 'and with any luck we will be there in a couple of hours.'

I could not have been more wrong.

Before we left the beach we met a couple of backpackers, English ones inevitably, who had just walked south from the lighthouse. They estimated it would take about four hours to get there and advised us to stay as close as we could to the cliff edge, where the path was more obvious and the views sublime. This seemed a sound suggestion. The Atlantic today was a smooth, unruffled blue, in spite of the biting wind, and we could see the loom of distant islands to the west, which must be Harris and the Outer Hebrides. A walk along the cliffs should be delightful.

I don't want to discourage anyone from making the walk

from Sandwood Bay to Cape Wrath. It is a great walk, but, if our experience that afternoon is anything to go by, this classic route can be something of an endurance test. We saw no sign of the hermit who is supposed to live hereabouts, and no sign of the mermaid who is said to haunt Sandwood Bay. In fact, after we left the bay we did not see a soul.

This was a good thing as the wind and terrain soon gave us more than enough to cope with. Before long I began to realise that my companions, who had not had weeks on the trail to get used to this sort of effort, were finding this steep, up-and-down terrain and the piercing headwind something of a struggle. It has to be added that no one complained.

On we went then, butting into the wind as we struggled up steep and sometimes very steep gullies, or turned off our direct route for the umpteenth time, to find a way across a stream or around a lochan or picked our way up to the head of a small waterfall to edge across the top. The terrain north of Sandwood Bay is all tilted and jumbled, and a piece of level ground is hard to find and does not last long. We found a river, Strath Chailleach, and tried to find a crossing place. Giving up after half a mile we splashed across as best we could and I think Keith fell in. Then we found another burn equipped with stepping stones and Ginger fell in.

The path up to Cape Wrath looks easy enough on the map but is a lot harder on the ground. Staying as close as we could to the cliff edge simply meant that we had steeper hillsides to negotiate. Gullies run into the cliff edge and have to be descended into for a couple of hundred feet or more, and then climbed out of once again. All this meant hard work and slow going. The lighthouse was still there, a white fingerpost against the blue sky, coming into sight now and again to beckon us on, but walk as we would, it seemed to get no nearer. How the young Robert Louis

Stevenson ever got to this wild spot hardly bears thinking about. Young Louis was not very fit, but get here he did and he enjoyed it.

'Life,' he wrote, 'is very liveable under the open sky; it is in houses mostly that the blue devils consort.' The blue devils were alive and well on that blustery day by Cape Wrath. Stevenson is one of my favourite writers, which is why this journey has been full of him and to take my mind off the terrain, I switched on the 'Skull Cinema' and thought about Stevenson.

Robert Louis Stevenson was born in Edinburgh on 13 November 1850, the only son of Thomas Stevenson, a famous man in the city. Young Louis' grandfather was a great civil engineer, another Robert, a man who had made his name building lighthouses, and in 1850 was the head of that marvellously named company, The Board of Northern Lights, a company charged with building and maintaining lighthouses all around the dangerous coast of Scotland.

Robert Stevenson the elder came to fame in Scotland by building the Bell Rock Lighthouse, a task that took all his ingenuity and four years to complete, but many of these Scottish lighthouses were put up by the Stevenson family and I never see one but I think of RLS.

Son Thomas had followed his father into the business and by the time Louis was born – he was never called Robert – the family reputation was well established; they were building lighthouses as far away as India, New Zealand and Japan. The Stevensons were also Inspectors of Lighthouses in Scotland, and the young Stevenson, who often accompanied his father on these tours of inspection, once recorded visiting 17 lighthouses in a single day, which must have worn the little lad out.

Young Louis was not a strong child. He had a chronic bronchial condition which later led to tuberculosis, and was often obliged to stay in bed or spend his holidays in the

South of France or England, where private tutors continued his education. Louis always wanted to be a writer but family loyalty sent him to study engineering. When he showed no interest in that subject and failed to attend lectures, he was diverted into the study of law. This was a little more successful and he was called to the Bar in 1875 but still cared for nothing but literature.

Today, just 100 years after his death in 1894, Stevenson is best remembered in Britain as the author of children's stories and poems, *Treasure Island, Kidnapped, Catriona, A Child's Garden of Verses* and the rest. That is not how Stevenson was seen in his lifetime or in the years after his death in Samoa. When the news reached London, the literary establishment went into mourning, and Arthur Quiller-Couch found no dissenting views to his obituary: 'Stevenson is dead,' he wrote, 'and now there is no one left to write for.

> Our children and grandchildren will rejoice in his books but we of the living generation possessed in the living man something they can never know. So long as he lived – though he were far from us, though we had never spoken to him and he had never heard our names – we always wrote our best for Stevenson.

Stevenson was at once the simplest and best of writers; he was a storyteller, a master of the plain tale, plainly told, a creator of unforgettable characters and places: Long John Silver, Alan Breck Stewart, Dr Jekyll and Mr Hyde, the Land of Counterpane, all these and more came to life under his pen. How much more he might have achieved had he lived beyond the age of 44 can only be wondered at. He never made a fortune and he lived long before the time when honours and titles and vast amounts of cash are given to the producers of meretricious trash. The title he was given by the Samoans after he died was the best of epitaphs: they called him *Tusitala*, the 'Teller of Tales', and he would have been happy with that.

Even thoughts of Stevenson could not distract me for long for this was a tough day. At about five in the evening we struggled up to the lighthouse Stevenson's family built in 1828, arriving at least three hours after our intended time. We reached the road from the ferry to the lighthouse some distance to the east of the Cape and crawled round the last hill of Dunan More to see the lighthouse before us at last, apparently deserted.

'Bugger-all chance of a cream tea there,' said Geoff. 'Just wait till I get my hands on Reggie. Come on, Rob, lead us in and we can all take your picture.'

The lighthouse at Cape Wrath throws a beam for more than 27 miles across the surrounding sea and stands inside a walled compound. Once inside, Geoff and the rest collapsed on the grass, sheltered at last from the relentless wind, while I went to find a keeper. At first I did not notice that Geoff was feeling poorly. I left him sprawled on the grass, his head cradled in his arms, and went for a prowl. First I went through the gate at the back of the lighthouse and out to the edge of the cliffs at a point where they fall sheer away for hundreds of feet into the sea. The waves were rolling in from the west to crash at the base of the cliffs and I could see the flat outline of the Orkney Islands quite clearly just to the north. It was a splendid, breezy, somewhat vertiginous spot, but I was very weary now and the others were no better. I slapped the base of the lighthouse to prove my point and, that done, it was time to call David. I tracked down one of the lighthouse-keepers in the engine shed and it appeared we were expected.

'Here ye are at last,' he said. 'Ye're verra' late ... but I'll away phone David.'

He did, but no need. Suddenly there came a terrible noise from the track and a very battered car pulled into the courtyard, its exhaust pipe trailing on the rocks. It stopped in a cloud of blue smoke to disgorge a young man in breeches and a well-darned sweater, a man much younger than I had expected from his voice on the telephone, and not looking a bit like a plastic surgeon.

'I'm David Elliot,' he said, shaking my hand, 'and it looks as if you could all use a drink.'

Being a doctor requires a gift for diagnosis. Some of us, and certainly Geoff, were suffering from a touch of exposure. A very long day, hard walking in a freezing wind, in clothes wet with sweat which chilled whenever we stopped, can do that to you. Geoff was now grey and shivering and not looking too clever, apart from being very subdued and quite unable to bicker. I had an attack of the shivers that did not go away for hours. Ginger said several times that this was the hardest thing he had done, which was gratifying. Even Keith was temporarily subdued though that did not last long. One sniff of the whisky bottle that evening and Keith became very lively indeed.

However, we had done it. We had also had a good time doing it, which is the main thing. This walk won't make the record books, but it will provide a tale or two and a few laughs for the years ahead, and there is a certain pleasure in that. That might have been part of our elation at the time, but there was also the happy thought that now we did not have to walk another yard and could get out of the wind and into the whisky. We piled into David's car, filling it with bodies, walking sticks, boots and rucksacks, and set off down the road to the Kyle of Durness.

Getting there took longer than expected. This was partly because David's car was very old and not used to carrying five people and partly because bits kept falling off. Every hundred yards or so there would be a loud explosion from the engine and frantic revving and the car would stall. Otherwise David had to get out and drag free a piece of metal trapped underneath, which he would then hurl into the back.

'I really must get this brute serviced one of these days,' he said vaguely. 'I come up here as often as I can ... two or three times a year, to cut peat or stalk the hinds – I'm up here every October for the stalking – and any other time when I can't stand the south anymore. This time, apart from cutting some peat, we brought in the sheep. They will have to be sheared though it is hardly worth it, the price of wool being what it is. The wool up here is pretty coarse, the kind they use for making carpets. With the housing market the way it is, there is no profit in it. However, shearing makes the sheep more comfortable. They need to be done before it gets too hot, and we have to do it now before the sun gets too strong or the sheep will get sunburned.'

I was surprised to hear that sheep can get sunburned. Apparently, when the shepherds take the fleece off, the sheep are pink and tender underneath, so it can happen. You learn something new every day on a trip like this.

Apart from supporting sheep and deer, Cape Wrath is a firing and bombing range for the Army, Navy and Air Force, and from time to time the Cape has to be closed and the sheep driven to shelter while the military take over. Historically, this was the Viking part of Scotland, a place that belonged to the Kings of Norway for much of history. The name 'Wrath' which sounds both dramatic and very suitable for such a high, wild spot, is actually a corruption of the Norse word '*Hvarf*' which means a 'turning point', the place where the turbulent Pentland Firth gives way to the equally dangerous waters of the wide Atlantic. On this day, squashed into David's car, it simply looked beautiful, the Kyle of Durness as blue and gold as any Pacific atoll.

We arrived at Daill where David's bothy, which is

actually a croft, was now surrounded by a huge flock of sheep. All of them were bleating away for dear life, filling the evening air with that far-from-harmonious cacophony. Here, too, was Stan, a small, cheery figure, straight out of Tolkien, who had indeed been a lecturer in nuclear physics but now preferred to be a shepherd, odd-job man and, at the moment, cook: starving as we were, a very good cook.

A vast pot of potatoes and a huge pan of sausages were already on the stove, four mattresses and a pile of blankets awaited our pleasure in an upstairs room and the teapot was full. We produced our thank-offering of wine to general applause and David countered with a bottle of whisky which quickly vanished. The evening then went with a swing and it got pretty noisy with everyone talking at once.

We told David and Stan about the walk and they told us about life in this remote corner of the British Islands where life, if never easy, is never dull.

'Take suits,' said David.

'Suits?' we asked.

'Suits,' said David. 'Down south, I have to wear a suit every day . . . the patients expect it. Up here, you only have to wear a suit for funerals, so most people only have one suit, and since they hardly get used they last a lifetime. Come to a funeral up here – and if somebody dies up here, everyone goes to the funeral – and you will see a parade of British Men's Fashion over the last 50 years. The Al Capone, the Demob, the Flares, the Peg-top Trouser and the Shawl Lapel. It's a living museum of fashion history up here.'

Not many people know that.

We also heard of lively nights in the pub and summer days picnicking with the children on the sandy shores of the Kyle of Durness, of fishing for salmon and stalking the deer . . . it all sounded idyllic.

Some time later, probably around midnight, the booze ran out and we all went to bed. How we got up the stairs, Heaven alone knows. We then fell asleep, out cold on our mattresses, so worn out with walking and revelry that even a thunderous duet from Keith and Ginger did not awaken us until morning. When we awoke we were all very poorly.

Sometime around dawn I recall hearing the sound of a motorbike as David set off to ride round the Kyle on his way back to Billericay. More than that I cannot recall until Stan appeared with big mugs of tea and said we ought to leave for the ferry.

It all worked. The arrangements went as planned, beginning with a car ride to the ferry along the bumpety track above the Kyle, high above a glorious vista of golden sand spits, white-tipped waves and blue water. Looking down from the track we could see where a dozen fat Atlantic seals had hauled themselves up onto the sand to bask in the sun on this clear, sharp morning. The ferry soon arrived from across the water, a small boat with the outboard puttering, loaded with walkers heading for the lighthouse, aiming to catch the bus that runs up and down between the Kyle and the Cape in summer.

We said our thanks and goodbyes to Stan and crossed to the far side. Iris came along with the school bus right on time, and half an hour later we were back at Kinlochbervie, sorting out our gear for the long drive home.

The moment of decision had arrived. Was I a Scot or was I not, and whatever I was, did it matter? Let us consider the evidence. I was born in Scotland of Scots parents, so that was a start. On the other hand I had lived out of Scotland all my life, except for periodic forays and drunken excursions, most of them years ago. Until this trip, and the background work that went into it, I had known very little of Scotland and nothing at all of Scots history. Since history is the love of my life, that is shameful, but I had now made amends on that score.

So, what of Scotland? If I am a Scot with a toe-hold in the country and a foot-hold in the world, what message can I pass on after this walk from the Border to Cape Wrath? What had I learned, and was it worth the effort?

To the last point the answer is yes, well worth it, and why did I wait so long? I have found Scotland and I will come back to it, not from any sense of national obligation, or some jingoistic fervour, but because this is a country that deserves to be loved and has to be visited. Trust me.

At least these words of praise should help me avoid the fate foretold by Sir Walter Scott for those who spurned their native land:

> Despite those titles, power and pelf,
> The wretch, concentred all in self,
> Living, shall forfeit fair renown,
> And, doubly dying, shall go down
> To the vile earth from which he sprung,
> Unwept, unhonour'd and unsung.

Well, there was an unpleasant forecast, but since I would by then be dead and out of it, it holds fewer fears than Sir Walter might have supposed.

This question of country is no light matter, but a love of country depends on the people more than the place. You cannot love stones or hills, however beautiful, without thinking of the people who live there. Well, I can't, and most of the people I know and love live in England.

I have found my own country again and found it wonderful, and when I go there in future I shall go there as a Scot and my accent has nothing to do with it. As the doctor said to Tony Hancock, 'We are not all Rob Roys.'

There was, of course, a postscript. Geoff started it all as

we left Kinlochbervie by jerking a thumb at me and saying, 'Any moment now he will start his "That's it. Never again. I'm hanging up my boots. No more walking for me," speech. If I had a quid for every time I've heard it, I could buy a new car. Come on, Rob, say it.'

Well, you have to indulge old friends.

'I'm hanging up my boots,' I said. 'This was it; never again . . . no more walking for me . . . honest!'

One of these days I might mean it.

Appendix: Kit List

The amount of kit you take on a cross-country walk depends on whether or not you intend to camp. This is not as simple a decision as you might suppose, for the available accommodation may not be in the right place or even open, and some allowance must be made for things going wrong. On the other hand less weight means more distance and I have always taken far more kit than I actually used or needed.

However, and as a basis to work on, herewith the list for Scotland:

Clothing worn: Daisy Roots' DR VETTA boots
loopstitched socks
Rohan 'Bags'
gaiters
wool shirt
Pampas jacket
neckerchief.

Clothing carried: six pairs loopstitched socks
1 pair Rohan 'Bags'
1 pullover
2 shirts, one cotton, one wool

underwear, 2 sets
handkerchiefs
1 set Sprayway rain and windproofs
1 pair trainers
1 hat (balaclava)
1 scarf.

All the above in a Karrimor Jaguar V1 rucksack together with

Equipment: 1 tent
1 sleeping bag
2 Silva compasses (one carried)
2 notebooks, pens, pencils
6 rolls colour film ASA 100
1 Buck knife
OS maps of Scotland, from the Border to Cape Wrath
1 mug, knife, fork, spoon, plate and food container
first aid kit
washing kit and hand towel
money
credit cards
sunglasses
spare reading glasses.

Select Bibliography

Robert Aitkin, *The West Highland Way*, HMSO, 1984.

James Boswell, *The Journal of A Tour to The Hebrides*, Penguin, 1984.

John Buchan, *The Thirty-Nine Steps*, Wordsworth Classics, 1993.

Samuel Johnson, *A Journey to the Western Isles*, Penguin, 1984.

Eric Linklater, *The Prince in the Heather*, Hodder, 1966.

Alastair Alpin MacGregor, *The Highlands of Scotland in Pictures*, Odhams, 1950.

H.V. Morton, *In Search of Scotland*, Methuen, 1929.

W. Murray, *The Companion Guide to The West Highlands of Scotland*, Collins, 1968.

W. Notstine, *The Scot in History*, Cape, 1946.

John Prebble, *Glencoe*, Holt Rinehart, 1966.

John Prebble, *Culloden*, Penguin, 1967.

John Prebble, *The Highland Clearances*, Penguin, 1969.

John Prebble, *The Lion in the North*, Penguin, 1973.

Scotland: The Rough Guide (various authors), Rough Guides, 1994.

W. Douglas Simpson, *The Highlands of Scotland*, Hale, 1976.

Robert Louis Stevenson, *Travels with a Donkey in the Cevennes*, Chatto, 1986.

Robert Louis Stevenson, *Kidnapped*, Wordsworth Classics, 1993.

Robert Louis Stevenson, *Catriona*, Canongate, 1989.

Robert Louis Stevenson, *Essays and Poems*, Everyman, 1992.

Gilbert Summers, *Exploring Rural Scotland*, Christopher Helm, 1990.

Touring Scotland, Scottish Tourist Board, 1993.

Index

Note: Individual battles, lochs, rivers, and mountains appear under the generic headings: 'battles and battlefields', 'lochs', etc.

Warner Books now offers an exciting range of quality titles by both established and new authors. All of the books in this series are available from:

Little, Brown and Company (UK),
P.O. Box 11,
Falmouth,
Cornwall TR10 9EN.

Alternatively you may fax your order to the above address. Fax No. 01326 317444.

Payments can be made as follows: cheque, postal order (payable to Little, Brown and Company) or by credit cards, Visa/Access. Do not send cash or currency. UK customers and B.F.P.O.: please send a cheque or postal order (no currency) and allow £1.00 for postage and packing for the first book, plus 50p for the second book, plus 30p for each additional book up to a maximum charge of £3.00 (7 books plus).

Overseas customers including Ireland please allow £2.00 for postage and packing for the first book, plus £1.00 for the second book, plus 50p for each additional book.

NAME (Block Letters) ....

....

ADDRESS ....

....

....

☐ I enclose my remittance for ....

☐ I wish to pay by Access/Visa Card

Number ☐☐☐☐☐☐☐☐☐☐☐☐☐☐☐☐

Card Expiry Date ☐☐☐☐